Guru Nanak's
ASA DI VAR

A ballad composed in musical measure Asa

Books by the same author

All books are in English; Guru-bani text, where relevant, is both in Punjabi and English.

Year of publication/book list

2003
1. Guru Granth Sahib – An Advance Study, Volume 2 (January 2003)

2002
1. Guru Granth Sahib – An Advance Study, Volume 1
2. Sikh Religion and the Sikh People (3rd revised edition)
3. Sikhism – An Introduction (2nd revised and enlarged edition)
4. Japji – A Way to God Realisation (3rd edition) (Sterling Publishers)

2001
1. Sikhism – 1000 questions answered
2. Guru Granth Sahib, An Introductory Study (enlarged edition).
3. Sikh Philosophy, Facts and Fundamentals of Sikh Religion (2nd edition)
4. Japjee – The Sikh Morning Prayer (Illustrated deluxe edition) (English Book Depot)

2000
1. Bhagat Bani
2. Sikh Religion and the Sikh People (2nd edition) *'Adjudged best book of the year'*

1999
1. Sikhism – An Introduction
2. Saint Soldier (The Khalsa Brotherhood)
3. Comparative Studies of World Religions
4. The Creation of Khalsa (Edited)
5. Japji, "Á Way to God Realisation". (2nd edition) *'Adjudged one of the best available translations in English'*

1998/97
1. Guru Angad Dev, Life, History and Teachings
2. Nitnem (The Daily Sikh Prayers) (Translation in both easy Punjabi and English)
3. Khushi de Hanju – (KuSI dy hMJU) Punjabi poetry

1996
1. The Sikh Marriage ceremony (*Anand Karaj*)
2. Baramah (The twelve months)

1995
1. Kirtan Sohila and Ardas
2. Gurbani – God's word
3. Jap Sahib, Swayas and Ardas, Master compositions of Guru Gobind Singh Ji (Translation followed by relevant Sakhis {life stories}) (Sterling Publishers, New Delhi))
4. Janoon – (jnUn) Punjabi poetry

1994/93
1. Rehras & Kirtan Sohila – "The torch to pass through the darkness of death, and the lyric that speaks of lacerations and pangs of separation." (Translation followed by relevant Sakhis (life stories) (Sterling)
2. Sikh Philosophy, Facts and Fundamentals of Sikhism (1st edition)
3. Puniya da chand – (puinAw dw cMn) Punjabi poetry

1992/91
1. Japji (1st edition)
2. Sikh Religion and the Sikh People (1st edition)

1990
1. Being a Sikh

1989/88
1. Ideal Man, Guru Gobind Singh's Concept of a Saint Soldier. (Khalsa College, London)

1984
1. Invasion of Golden Temple (Khalsa College, London Press)

1983
1. Sikh Festivals (London)

1982
1. Sikhs & Sikhism (London)

All books except where indicated are published by Hemkunt Press, New Delhi.

GURU NANAK'S

ASA DI VAR

A ballad composed in musical measure *Asa*

A divine composition – the listening of which fulfils all human desires

Dr. Sukhbir Singh Kapoor
Vice Chancellor World Sikh University London

Mrs. Mohinder Kaur Kapoor

STERLING PUBLISHERS PRIVATE LIMITED

MUSICAL NOTATION OF RAGA ASA

राग आसा

वादी—म	ठाठ —बिलावल	समां रात चौठा पहिर
संवादी—स	जात —ऊडव संपूरन	

र
पकड़ स,र म प ध, प म, ग र स र ग. स ।

आरोह स र म प ध सं ।

अवरोह सं न ध प म ग र स ।

सुर-विसथार

    ग न   न   स र
स—नध, स—र, स, पप—पधस—सरग—रस, पप—म, पपस—गरग, स

        ग र   र
स—म—ग, र, स—सरम, गर, रग स—म—पध, पम, गास, रग, गास—सरमगाध—

        ग र   गध   र
पनधपम—गार रग स—रमपधप—धपनधपम—म प—मगारसरग, सं

        र   न   ग
स—सरम—प, धप, धपम—प, मगारस र, स—प, धस—रमपधसंनधप—धपनधपम

       र
ग, सरग स—र—सनधपधपस—गारग स—रमपधसं—रसं—नध—पम—पधसं—नसरं

       र
संनध—पनधपम—गारसरग, स

              प
स—रमपध. पनधपम—पधसं—रसं—म, पधसं—गां, सं—संरसंनध—मप—
धपनधसंनधपमगर—सरगरसनधपधपस—रमपधसं—न धपम—पध, पनधपमगर सरग,
र   रनप प ग र र
स—म—पधसं — पधसंरंगंसं गांरगं, सं—ध, म—ध, म, रगाग, स—

                    सं
स—मगपमधपनधसंनरसं—पधसंरंगं—रंगं—सरसंनध, पम—प,नध—प—धपनधपम—

               र   गं रं
पधसं नध, पम, गर, सरग, स—म, पधसं—नसंनधपधसं पधसंरंसं—रंगं सं—रंसंनध,

        न   ग र   न
पधनसं—नध, प धपम—पमगर; स रग स—मगर, धनुपधम—सं ध,पम—संरंसंनध,

             र   र
पम—पधसंरंगं सं नध, पम—पध, नधसंनधपमगर, सरगरग, स—म—पधसंरंगं, गांरंसंरंगं.

       रं   रं
सं—मं, पंमंगंरंगंसं पधनधपधसं, नध, पम, ग्रपसंनधपमगर, सरगरगास

STERLING PUBLISHERS PRIVATE LIMITED
A-59 Okhla Industrial Area, Phase-II, New Delhi-110020.
Tel: 26387070, 26386209;   Fax: 91-11-26383788
E-mail: ghai@nde.vsnl.net.in; www.sterlingpublishers.com

Guru Nanak's Asa di Var
© 2004, Sukhbir Singh Kapoor
ISBN 81 207 2653 7

PRINTED IN INDIA

Published by Sterling Publishers Pvt. Ltd., New Delhi-110 020.
Typeset by Vikas Compographics, New Delhi-110020.
Printed at Sai Early Learners (P) Ltd, New Delhi-110 020.

Dedicated

to

Waheguru

for

choosing us to spread

His message

Editorial Note

To understand the English translation of footnotes read the following:

1. Almost every important word in the Punjabi text has been given an individual footnote number and the English meaning of the word is recorded in the relevant footnote.

2. At other places a group of words have been underlined and a joint footnote number is given to that group. The English meaning of the group is given in the relevant footnote e.g. ਤਪ ਉਪਰਿ ਤੀਰਥਾਂ (page 71), here three words 'tap' 'upar' and 'teerthaa' have been grouped together and one line meaning of the group appears in the footnote.

3. For the key to transliteration use the following table:

KEY TO TRANSLITERATION

Gurmukhi	Roman	Gurmukhi	Roman	Gurmukhi	Roman
ਕ	ka	ਤ	ta	ਅ	a
ਖ	kha	ਥ	tha	ਆ	a
ਗ	ga	ਦ	da	ਇ	i/y/e
ਘ	gha	ਧ	dha	ਈ	i
ਙ	n	ਨ	na	ਉ	u/o
ਚ	cha/c	ਪ	pa	ਊ	u
ਛ	chha	ਫ	pha	ਏ	e
ਜ	ja	ਬ	ba	ਐ	ai/ae
ਝ	jha	ਭ	bha	ਓ	0
	n	ਮ	ma	ਔ	au
ਟ	t	ਯ	ya	੦	m/n
ਠ	tha	ਰ	ra	:	n
ਡ	da	ਲ਼	la	ਸ	s
ਢ	dha	ਵ	va	ਸ਼	s
ਣ	n	ੜ	ra	ਹ	ha

CONTENTS

Introduction   1

Pauri 1 with 3 sloaks (Guru Nanak 2, Guru Angad 1)   8

Pauri 2 with 3 sloaks (Guru Nanak 2, Guru Angad 1)   12

Pauri 3 with 2 sloaks (Guru Nanak 2)   18

Pauri 4 with 2 sloaks (Guru Nanak 2)   24

Pauri 5 with 2 sloaks (Guru Nanak 2)   29

Pauri 6 with 2 sloaks (Guru Nanak 2)   36

Pauri 7 with 2 sloaks (Guru Nanak 1, Guru Angad 1)   42

Pauri 8 with 2 sloaks (Guru Nanak 2)   47

Pauri 9 with 2 sloaks (Guru Nanak 2)   52

Pauri 10 with 2 sloaks (Guru Nanak 2)   58

Pauri 11 with 3 sloaks (Guru Nanak 3)   64

Pauri 12 with 4 sloaks (Guru Nanak 2, Guru Angad 2)   71

Pauri 13 with 2 sloaks (Guru Nanak 2)   78

Pauri 14 with 2 sloaks (Guru Nanak 2)   83

Pauri 15 with 4 sloaks (Guru Nanak 4)   88

Pauri 16 with 2 sloaks (Guru Nanak 2)   95

Pauri 17 with 2 sloaks (Guru Nanak 2)   101

Pauri 18 with 3 sloaks (Guru Nanak 3)   105

Pauri 19 with 2 sloaks (Guru Nanak 2)   110

Pauri 20 with 2 sloaks (Guru Nanak 2)   115

Pauri 21 with 2 sloaks (Guru Angad 2)   120

Pauri 22 with 5 sloaks (Guru Angad 5)   124

Pauri 23 with 2 sloaks (Guru Angad 2)   130

Pauri 24 with 2 sloaks (Guru Nanak 1, Guru Angad 1)   133

INTRODUCTION

The ballad in musical mode Asa, popularly called *Asa Di Var* is sung at the places of Sikh worship in the early hours of the morning. In Harimandir Sahib (The Golden Temple), Amritsar, it starts at 4.00 a.m.

It is a master composition of Guru Nanak. In its present form, as recorded in *Guru Granth Sahib*, it contains 24 stanzas called *pauris* and 59 (60) couplets called *sloaks*. All the pauris are composed by Guru Nanak whereas, out of 59 sloaks, 44 are composed by Guru Nanak and 15 by Guru Angad Dev.

In the *Puratan Janamsakhi*, an authentic life account of Guru Nanak, this composition is attributed to two possible occasions. In *sakhi* (story) number 32 there is a reference of first nine stanzas of the composition, which according to a tradition, were recited by Guru Nanak when he met Sheikh Kamal, an heir of Sheikh Farid of Pak Pattan. In these stanzas there is a description of a dual between two rival forces of good and evil and Waheguru presiding and watching it.

In *sakhi* number 37 there is a reference of other fifteen stanzas being addressed to Duni Chand of Lahore. In these stanzas the Guru has highlighted the futility of hoarding wealth instead of sharing it with needy people.

The construction of the ballad is as follows:
1. Three sloaks, two of Guru Nanak and one of Guru Angad precede the 1st and 2nd pauris.
2. Two sloaks, both of Guru Nanak precede pauris: 3rd, 4th, 5th, 6th, 8th, 9th, 10th, 13th, 14th, 16th, 17th, 19th and 20th.
3. Two sloaks, one of Guru Nanak and one of Guru Angad precede 7th, 24th pauris
4. Three sloaks of Guru Nanak precede the 11th pauri.
5. Four sloaks, two of Guru Nanak and two of Guru Angad precede the 12th pauri.
6. Four sloaks of Guru Nanak precede the 15th pauri.
7. Three sloaks of Guru Nanak precede the 18th pauri.
8. Two sloaks of Guru Angad precede 21st and 23rd pauris.
9. Five sloaks of Guru Angad precede the 22nd pauri.

The counting of the total sloaks is summarised as follows:
1. Pauris 1, 2, 11 and 18 are preceded by three sloaks each = 12 sloaks.
2. Pauris 12 and 15 are preceded by four sloaks each= 8 sloaks
3. Pauri 22 is preceded by five sloaks= 5 sloaks
4. Other 17 pauris are preceded by two sloaks each=34 sloaks

Grand total of all sloaks = 59

1

However, at times, many people count sloak "Dukh Daru…" which precedes pauri twelve, as two sloaks and thus counting the total number of sloaks as 60 rather than 59.

Regarding the construction of *vars* in *Guru Granth Sahib*, two different schools of thought exist. The first school affirms that the original vars consisted only of pauris and the sloaks were added by Guru Arjan, when he compiled *Guru Granth Sahib*. According to this school, Guru Arjan had collected and collated sloaks separately from the other banis and distributed them amongst, *vars*, *chhants* (chhants of Guru Arjan) and special compositions (e.g., Jap Ji, Sukhmani, Bawan Akhri and Thithe, etc). wherever appropriate. The sloaks which could not be so distributed and fitted were then assembled and put in the concluding section of *Guru Granth Sahib* under the caption of *'Sloak varan te vadheek'*.

The second school affirms that both pauris and sloaks formed the structure of the *vars* from the times of Guru Nanak.

The description of the *vars* in *Guru Granth Sahib* can be described as following:

In total there are 22 vars in Guru Granth Sahib, of which 21 are composed by the Sikh Gurus and one jointly by minstrels Satta & Balwand.

Where 20 vars have a format of sloaks and pauris, one var of Guru Arjan, in raga Basant, and a var of Satta & Balwand, in raga Ramkali, have no sloaks, and stanzas are also without any caption of 'pauris'.

The composers of the Guru-vars in the ascending order are:
Guru Nanak = 3, Guru Amardas = 4, Guru Arjan = 6, Guru Ramdas = 8

Only 17 raga-chapters have vars in them.

Four ragas (Gauri, Gujri, Ramkali and Maru) have 2 vars each.

16 vars have a comment 'Shud' at the end.
1 var has a comment of 'Shud kechay' at the end.
4 vars have no comment - Shud/Shud Keechay- at the end.

Guru Arjan's vars have only his own sloaks in them.

There are also banis which have a format of sloaks and pauris but which are not titled as vars, e.g. Bawan Akhri and Thithe in raga Gauri.

Seven vars where the composer of the var and of the sloaks, inserted therein, is the same	Raga		
Five vars of Guru Arjan	Gauri, Gujri, Ramkali, Maru, Jaitsiri	Sixth var of Guru Arjan in raga Basant has only three pauris and has no sloaks. The title of 'pauri' on the stanzas is also missing	
One var of Guru Amardas	Raga Gurji		
One var of Guru Ramdas	Raga Kanra		
Four Ragas with two vars	**First var**	**Second var**	**Remarks**
Raga Gauri Raga Gujri Raga Ramkali Raga Maru	Guru Ramdas Guru Amardas Guru Amardas Guru Amardas	Guru Arjan Guru Arjan Guru Arjan Guru Arjan	Sudh, Sudh keechey Sudh, Sudh Sudh, Sudh Sudh, no remakrs
Three Vars where Guru Arjan's pauris appear with the pauris of the main composer			
Raga Gauri	Var Guru Ramdas	Pauris 27-31, pages 315-317	Pauri 31 titled as 'Pauri M: 5' is similar to pauri 12 composed by Guru Ramdas page 306. There is a remark 'Sudhi at the end'
Raga Sarang	Var Guru Ramdas	Pauri 35 (page 1251)	Sudh
Raga Malhar	Var Guru Nanak	Pauri 27 (page 1291)	Pauri is titled as 'Pauri navin (new) M:5. There is a remark 'Shud' at the end.
The spelling of the word Pauri Generally the heading is 'Pauri'	Exceptionally it is headed as 'Pavri'	See pages: 139 (pauri 4), pages 142, 143, 1097	Page 250, 251, 253, 255, 259 (in Bawan Akhri)
Longest and shortest Guru-vars Longest var is of Guru Ramdas in raga Sarang. It has 36 pauris and 72 sloaks	Shortest var(in addition to var in raga Basant which has only 3 pauris), is also of Guru Ramdas in raga Bilawal. It has 13 pauris with 27 sloaks		

One explanation of the comment 'shud' is that Guru-bani recorded in this raga, selected at random, was found to be correct in the first proofreading.

At another place the comment 'shud keechey' has been used. It means that there were some errors in the first proofreading and were corrected in the subsequent proofreading.

The ragas where there is a recording of such comments were probably chosen at random. Thus ragas which have no comments were not so chosen.

The other point of view regarding the above remarks is that the comments 'Shud' and 'Shud keechey' relate only to the proofreading of the 'Vars' and not to the whole Guru-bani of that raga.

The overall theme of the Asa di Var can be summarised as:

Number of Pauris	Theme
1	Waheguru is witnessing the great play after creating the universe
2	Human beings are sent in this world to meditate on the name of God and to live a truthful life
3	Those who love only material things, they waste their lives
4	Those who are blessed, they are freed from transmigration and come in the union of Waheguru
5	Waheguru's name is the greatest liberator
6	God is all bountiful
7	Only those people can meditate on God who are meek and are devoid of vices
8	Those who are blessed, Waheguru dwells in their hearts
9	Waheguru's saints are humble and God-fearing.
10	The dust of saints' feet be put on the devotees' foreheads.
11	Human efforts are important, but God's intervention and blessings are far more important
12	The people are judged according to their karmas
13	The world is compared with a vast ocean, where the tides of vices are rising all the time. The teacher-Guru helps devotees to cross that ocean
14	The facial beauty is transitory. Only good karmas accompany one into the next world

15	God's blessings are required for His ultimate acceptance
16	God is the only sustainer of the universe
17	Always remember that the ultimate goal of all of us is union with God
18	The real honours of a person are his good and noble deeds
19	The people are slave of their desires
20	The life of a person is very short. One must live an honest life and should remain engrossed in the meditation of God.
21	A person harvests whatever he sows
22	Those who live within God's laws, they are honoured by him.
23	God himself is the creator, sustainer and the destroyer.
24	God is the real support of all of us.

The gist of the above is that God had created this world in his own image and had sent human beings to meditate on His name and live an honest life. The majority of them, on the other hand, have indulged themselves in vices and have forgotten the Commands of Waheguru.

The goal of all human beings was liberation from transmigration and people had to change their lives to achieve that goal. People needed to meditate on the name of God and to perform noble deeds to attain *Mukti*. The blessings of God were required for liberation from worldly tangles. But alas the man had forgotten all laws of morality, ethics and religion.

Since the times of Guru Arjan Dev, a tradition had started to recite chhants, 8-13 of Guru Ramdas (pages 448-451 of *Guru Granth Sahib*), composed in raga Asa, along with the Asa Di Var. The six chhants so chosen have in total 24 padas. One pada is sung before every pauri, thus each of the 24 pauris of Asa Di Var is preceded by a pada of Guru Ramdas's chhants. I have followed the same tradition to arrange the bani in that order in this book.

I am very grateful to Mrs. Poonam Kapoor, my erstwhile support, for her guidance, continuous conselling and help to complete this challenging work. My thanks are also due to Sukhdip Kaur Khaira for designing and arranging the manuscript in its present form.

Dr. Sukhbir Singh Kapoor

London

8th November 2003

ੴ ਸਤਿ ਨਾਮੁ ਕਰਤਾ ਪੁਰਖੁ ਨਿਰਭਉ ਨਿਰਵੈਰੁ ਅਕਾਲ ਮੂਰਤਿ ਅਜੂਨੀ ਸੈਭੰ ਗੁਰ ਪ੍ਰਸਾਦਿ

There is one God of the whole universe
(Unity of God)

He is the Truth
(The only reality, one who remains forever)

He is the Omnipresent-creator

He is beyond all fears

He is beyond all enmity

He is beyond death
(His form is beyond destruction)

He is not born

He is self-illuminated

He is realised with His own Grace
(To qualify for His Grace, one must graduate in performing meditation and living a truthful life {noble deeds})

॥ ਆਸਾ ਮਹਲਾ ੧ ॥
Musical measure raga Asa, composer Guru Nanak

ਵਾਰ ਸਲੋਕਾ ਨਾਲਿ ਸਲੋਕ ਭੀ ਮਹਲੇ ਪਹਿਲੇ ਕੇ ਲਿਖੇ
Var and *Sloaks* composed by Guru Nanak

ਟੁੰਡੇ ਅਸ ਰਾਜੈ ਕੀ ਧੁਨੀ ॥**

Asraj was the son of King Sarang. Asraj's stepbrothers, Sardul Rai and Sultan Khan once wounded him by deceit and threw him into a well. He was rescued by peddlers. They took him to a different country. The king of that country had died the previous night. He was childless. The ministers decided that whosoever would enter first in the morning, would be coronated as the new king. By God's will, Asraj was first to enter that city and was made the king of that kingdom. He then fought with his stepbrothers, defeated them and became the king of his father's empire. This episode was composed as a var and sung in a specific tune. Guru Hargobind recommended *Asa Di Var* to be sung in this tune.

◆ ◆ ◆

ਆਸਾ ਮਹਲਾ ੪ ਛੰਤ ਘਰੁ ੪ ॥

आसा महला ੪ छंत घरु ੪ ॥

Asa Mehla 4 chhant ghar 4.

Asa Mehla 4, chhant ghar 4.

ਹਰਿ ਅੰਮ੍ਰਿਤ ਭਿੰਨੇ ਲੋਇਆ ਮਨੁ ਪ੍ਰੇਮਿ ਰਤੰਨਾ ਰਾਮ ਰਾਜੇ ॥

हरि अंम्रित भिंने लोइणा मनु प्रेमि रतंना राम राजे ॥

har amrit bhinnay lo-inaa man paraym ratannaa raam raajay.

My eyes are wet with the nectar of the Waheguru,
and my mind is imbued with His love, O King of Kings.

ਮਨੁ ਰਾਮਿ ਕਸਵਟੀ ਲਾਇਆ ਕੰਚਨ ਸੋਵਿੰਨਾ ॥

मनु रामि कसवटी लाइआ कंचनु सोविंना ॥

man raam kasvatee laa-i-aa kanchan sovinnaa.

Waheguru applied His touch-stone to my mind,
and turned it into pure solid gold.

ਗੁਰਮੁਖਿ ਰੰਗਿ ਚਲੂਲਿਆ ਮੇਰਾ ਮਨੁ ਤਨੋ ਭਿੰਨਾ ॥

गुरमुखि रंगि चलूलिआ मेरा मनु तनो भिंना ॥

gurmukh rang chalooli-aa mayraa man tano bhinnaa.

As a true believer, I am dyed in the deep red colour of the poppy,
and my mind and body are soaked with Waheguru's love.

ਜਨੁ ਨਾਨਕੁ ਮੁਸਕਿ ਝਕੋਲਿਆ ਸਭੁ ਜਨਮੁ ਧਨੁ ਧੰਨਾ ॥੧॥

जनु नानकु मुसकि झकोलिआ सभु जनमु धनु धंना ॥ ੧ ॥

jan naanak musak jhakoli-aa sabh janam Dhan Dhannaa. ||1||

I am drenched with Waheguru's fragrance; and my life has
become worth living. (1)

Pauri 1 with 3 sloaks
(Guru Nanak 2, Guru Angad 1)

ਸਲੋਕੁ ਮਃ ੧ ॥

1. ਬਲਿਹਾਰੀ ਗੁਰ ਆਪਣੇ ਦਿਉਹਾੜੀ੍ਰ ਸਦ ਵਾਰ੍ਰ ॥
2. ਜਿਨਿ ਮਾਨਸ ਤੇ ਦੇਵਤੇ ਕੀਏ ਕਰਤ ਨ ਲਾਗੀ ਵਾਰ੍ਰ ॥ ੧ ॥

ਮਹਲਾ ੨ ॥

1. ਜੇ ਸਉ੍ਰ ਚੰਦਾ ਉਗਵਹਿ੍ਰ ਸੂਰਜ ਚੜਹਿ ਹਜਾਰ ॥
2. ਏਤੇ੍ਰ ਚਾਨਣ ਹੋਦਿਆਂ ਗੁਰ ਬਿਨ ਘੋਰ੍ਰ ਅੰਧਾਰ੍ਰ ॥ ੨ ॥

ਮਃ ੧ ॥

੧. ਨਾਨਕ ਗੁਰੂ ਨ ਚੇਤਨੀ੍ਰ ਮਨਿ ਆਪਣੈ ਸੁਚੇਤ੍ਰ ॥
੨. ਛੁਟੇ੍ਰ ਤਿਲ੍ਰ ਬੂਆੜ੍ਰ ਜਿਉ ਸੁੰਵੇ੍ਰ ਅੰਦਰਿ ਖੇਤ॥
੩. ਖੇਤੈ ਅੰਦਰਿ ਛੁਟਿਆ ਕਹੁ ਨਾਨਕ ਸਉ੍ਰ ਨਾਹ੍ਰ ॥
੪. ਫਲੀਅਹਿ ਫੁਲੀਅਹਿ੍ਰ ਬਪੁੜੇ੍ਰ ਭੀ ਤਨ ਵਿਚਿ੍ਰ ਸੁਆਹ੍ਰ ॥ ੩ ॥

सलोकु मः १ ॥

1. बलिहारीं गुर आपणे दिउहाड़ी सद वारं ॥
2. जिनि माणस ते देवते कीइे करत न लागी वारं ॥ १ ॥

महला २ ॥

1. जे सतुं चंदा उगवहि सूरज चड़हि हजार ॥
2. इेते चानण होदिआँ गुर बिनु घोरं अंधारं ॥ २ ॥

मः १ ॥

१. नानक गुरू न चेतनीं मनि आपणै सुचेतं ॥
२. छुटे तिलं बूआड़ं जिउ सुंञे अंदरि खेत ॥
३. खेतै अंदरि छुटिआ कहु नानक सतुं नाहं ॥
४. फलीअहि फुलीअहिं बपुड़े भी तन विचिं सुआहं ॥ ३ ॥

Sloak Mehla 1.

1. balihaaree[1] gur aapnay[2] di-uhaarhee[3] sad vaar[4].
2. jin maanas tay dayvtay kee-ay karat na laagee vaar.[5] ||1||

Mehla 2.

1. jay sa-o[6] chandaa ugvahi[7] sooraj charheh hajaar.
2. aytay[8] chaanan hidi-aaN gur bin ghor[9] anDhaar.[10] ||2||

Mehla 1.

1. naanak guroo na chaytnee[11] man aapnai suchayt[12].
2. chhutay[13] til[14] boo-aarh[15] ji-o sunjay[16] andar khayt.
3. khaytai andar chhuti-aa kaho naanak sa-o[17] naah[18].
4. falee-ah fulee-ah[19] bapurhay[20] bhee tan vich[21] su-aah[22]. ||3||

---

1 I am a sacrifice to
2 My Waheguru
3 In a day
4 A thousand times
5 Time
6 Hundred
7 Rise
8 So much
9 Dense
10 Darkness
11 Remember
12 Thinking oneself as clever in one's own mind
13 To be left
14 Sesame
15 One which is not genuine
16 Deserted
17 Hundred
18 Owners
19 Fruit and flower
20 Unfortunate
21 And in their body
22 Ash

Theme

Sloak Mehla 1

Waheguru can do and undo things in a moment

Mehla 2

There is solid darkness all around if there is no faith in Waheguru

Mehla 1

Without meditation life is a heap of ashes

Literal Meaning

Sloak Mehla 1

1. In a course of a day I sacrifice myself a thousand times on my Waheguru,
2. Who has transformed human to gods in a moment.

Mehla 2

1. If hundred moons shine and thousand suns rise.
2. Still without true faith in Waheguru, the total shine is overshadowed by the dense darkness of ignorance.

Mehla 1

1. Those who do not meditate on the name of Waheguru, and think themselves to be too clever,
2. They are deserted even in the ripe fields like burnt sesame.
3. They are left on the farms as if they have no real master (hundred common owners).
4. Those unfortunate think they have blossomed, but within them there is no fruit or flower, but only ash.

ਪਉੜੀ ॥

1. ਆਪੀਨੈ ਆਪੁ ਸਾਜਿਓ²³ ਆਪੀਨੈ ਰਚਿਓ ਨਾਉ ²⁴ ॥
2. ਦੂਜੀ ਕੁਦਰਤਿ ²⁵ ਸਾਜੀਐ²⁶ **ਕਰਿ ਆਸਣੁ** ²⁷ **ਡਿਠੋ ਚਾਉ**²⁸ ॥
3. ਦਾਤਾ ਕਰਤਾ ਆਪਿ ਤੂੰ ਤੁਸਿ²⁹ ਦੇਵਹਿ³⁰ ਕਰਹਿ ਪਸਾਉ³¹॥
4. ਤੂੰ ਜਾਣੋਈ ਸਭਸੈ³² ਦੇ³³ ਲੈਸਹਿ³⁴ ਜਿੰਦੁ ਕਵਾਉ³⁵ ॥
5. ਕਰਿ ਆਸਣੁ ਡਿਠੋ ਚਾਉ ॥ ੧ ॥

पउड़ी ॥

1. आपीनै आपु साजिए²³ आपीनै रचिए नाउ ²⁴ ॥
2. दूयी कुदरति ²⁵ साजीऐ²⁶ करि आसणु ²⁷डिठो चाउ²⁸ ॥
3. दाता करता आपि तूं तुसि²⁹ देवहि³⁰ करहि पसाउ³¹॥
4. तूं जाणोई सभसै³² दे³³ लैसहि³⁴ जिंदु कवाउ³⁵ ॥
5. करि आसणु डिठो चाउ ॥ १ ॥

Pauri.

1. aapeen^{H}ai aap saaji-o^{23} aapeen^{H}ai rachi-o naa-o^{24} .
2. d̲uyee kud̲rat̲^{25} saajee-ai^{26} kar aasan̲^{27} d̲it̲ho chaa-o^{28} .
3. d̲aat̲aa kart̲aa aap too^N tusi^{29} d̲ayveh^{30} karahi pasaa-o^{31} .
4. too^N jaan̲o-ee sab̲hsai^{32} d̲ay^{33} laisahi^{34} jind̲ kavaa-o^{35} .
5. kar aasan̲ d̲it̲ho chaa-o. ||1||

Theme
Pauri 1
Waheguru watches his creation with great excitement

Literal Meaning
Pauri 1
1. Waheguru created himself and created his Word (*shabad*).
2. He then created the universe and watched it with great excitement.
3. O! The giver of the bounties, you are the creator, you are the giver and in your pleasure you shower mercy.
4. You know the inner thoughts of all and with your one word you give and take away life.
5. You watch your creation with great excitement.

---

[23] Waheguru is self-illuminated
[24] Waheguru himself uttered the Shabad (Nam)
[25] Manifested world
[26] He has created

[27] Sitting on His throne
[28] To watch with excitement
[29] To be pleased, to be happy
[30] To give
[31] To show mercy

[32] You are the creator of everything
[33] To give life
[34] To take away life
[35] With the pronouncement of a single word

ਹਰਿ ਪ੍ਰੇਮ ਬਾਣੀ ਮਨੁ ਮਾਰਿਆ ਅਣੀਆਲੇ ਅਣੀਆ ਰਾਮ ਰਾਜੇ ॥

हरि प्रेम बाणी मनु मारिआ अणीआले अणीआ राम राजे ॥

har paraym baanee man maari-aa anee-aalay anee-aa raam raajay.

The Shabad of Waheguru's love is a pointed arrow,
which has pierced my mind, O King of Kings.

ਜਿਸੁ ਲਾਗੀ ਪੀਰ ਪਿਰੰਮ ਕੀ ਸੋ ਜਾਨੈ ਜਰੀਆ ॥

जिसु लागी पीर पिरंम की सो जाणै जरीआ ॥

jis laagee peer piramm kee so jaanai jaree-aa.

Only those who feel the pain of this eternal love,
know how to endure it.

ਜੀਵਨ ਮੁਕਤਿ ਸੋ ਆਖੀਐ ਮਰਿ ਜੀਵੈ ਮਰੀਆ ॥

जीवन मुकति सो आखीऐ मरि जीवै मरीआ ॥

jeevan mukat so aakhee-ai mar jeevai maree-aa.

Those who detach themselves, and remain detached while yet alive,
are said to be Jivan Mukta, liberated while yet alive.

ਜਨ ਨਾਨਕ ਸਤਿਗੁਰੁ ਮੇਲਿ ਹਰਿ ਜਗੁ ਦੁਤਰੁ ਤਰੀਆ ॥੨॥

जन नानक सतिगुरु मेलि हरि जगु दुतरु तरीआ ॥ २ ॥

jan naanak satgur mayl har jag dutar taree-aa. ||2||

O Waheguru, unite us with the True Guru,
that he may ferry us over the terrifying world-ocean. ||2||

Pauri 2 with 3 sloaks
(Guru Nanak 2, Guru Angad 1)

ਸਲੋਕੁ ਮਃ ੧ ॥

1. ਸਚੇ ਤੇਰੇ ਖੰਡੳੈ ਸਚੇ ਬ੍ਰਹਮੰਡੳ੭ ॥
2. ਸਚੇ ਤੇਰੇ ਲੋਅੳ੪ ਸਚੇ ਆਕਾਰੳ੮ ॥
3. ਸਚੇ ਤੇਰੇ ਕਰਣੇ ੪੦ਸਰਬ ਬੀਚਾਰੳ੧ ॥
4. ਸਚਾ ਤੇਰਾ ਅਮਰੁ੪੨ ਸਚਾ ਦੀਬਾਣੁ੪੩ ॥
5. ਸਚਾ ਤੇਰਾ ਹੁਕਮੁ੪੪ ਸਚਾ ਫੁਰਮਾਣੁ੪੫ ॥
6. ਸਚਾ ਤੇਰਾ ਕਰਮੁ੪੬ ਸਚਾ ਨੀਸਾਣੁ੪੭ ॥
7. ਸਚੇ ਤੁਧੁ ਆਖਹਿ ਲਖ ਕਰੋੜਿ ॥
8. ਸਚੈ ਸਭਿ ਤਾਣਿ੪੮ ਸਚੈ ਸਭਿ ਜੋਰਿ੪੯ ॥
9. ਸਚੀ ਤੇਰੀ ਸਿਫਤਿ ਸਚੀ ਸਾਲਾਹ੫੦ ॥
10. ਸਚੀ ਤੇਰੀ ਕੁਦਰਤਿ ਸਚੇ ਪਾਤਿਸਾਹ ॥
11. ਨਾਨਕ ਸਚੁ ਧਿਆਇਨਿ ਸਚੁ ॥
12. ਜੋ ਮਰਿ ਜੰਮੇ ਸੁ ਕਚੁ ਨਿਕਚੁ੫੧ ॥ ੧ ॥

सलोकु मः १ ॥

1. सचे तेरे खंडॳै सचे ब्रहमंडॳ੭ ॥
2. सचे तेरे लोअॳ੪ सचे आकारॳ੮ ॥
3. सचे तेरे करणे ੪੦सरब बीचारॳ੧ ॥
4. सचा तेरा अमरु੪੨ सचा दीबाणु੪੩ ॥
5. सचा तेरा हुकमु੪੪ सचा फुरमाणु੪੫ ॥
6. सचा तेरा करमु੪੬ सचा नीसाणु੪੭ ॥
7. सचे तुधु आखहि लख करोड़ि ॥
8. सचै सभि ताणि੪੮ सचै सभि जोरि੪੯ ॥
9. सची तेरी सिफति सची सालाह੫੦ ॥
10. सची तेरी कुदरति सचे पातिसाह ॥
11. नानक सचु धिआइनि सचु ॥
12. जो मरि जंमे सु कचु निकचु੫੧ ॥ १ ॥

Sloak Mehla 1.

1. sachay tayray khand[36] sachay brahmand[37].
2. sachay tayray lo-a[38] sachay aakaar[39].
3. sachay tayray karnay[40] sarab beechaar[41].
4. sachaa tayraa amar[42] sachaa deebaan[43].
5. sachaa tayraa hukam[44] sachaa furmaan[45].
6. sachaa tayraa karam[46] sachaa neesaan[47].
7. sachay tuDh aakhahi lakh karorh.
8. sachai sabh taan[48] sachai sabh jor[49].
9. sachee tayree sifat sachee saalaah[50].
10. sachee tayree kudrat sachay paatisaah.
11. naanak sach Dhi-aa-in sach.
12. jo mar jammay so kach nikach[51]. ||1||

---

[36] Cosmic regions
[37] Celestial spheres
[38] Domains
[39] Creation, shapes
[40] Plans
[41] Concepts

[42] Dispensation
[43] Rules
[44] Order
[45] Pronouncement
[46] Grace
[47] Stamp, mark, recognition

[48] Might, power
[49] Operations
[50] Adoration
[51] Rawest of raw, fragile

ਮਃ ੧ ॥

1. ਵਡੀ ਵਡਿਆਈ ਜਾ ਵਡਾ ਨਾਉ ॥
2. ਵਡੀ ਵਡਿਆਈ ਜਾ ਸਚੁ ਨਿਆਉ^{੫੨} ॥
3. ਵਡੀ ਵਡਿਆਈ ਜਾ ਨਿਹਚਲ ਥਾਉ^{੫੩} ॥
4. ਵਡੀ ਵਡਿਆਈ ਜਾਣੈ ਆਲਾਉ^{੫੪} ॥
5. ਵਡੀ ਵਡਿਆਈ ਬੁਝੈ ਸਭਿ ਭਾਉ^{੫੫} ॥
6. ਵਡੀ ਵਡਿਆਈ ਜਾ ਪੁਛਿ ਨ ਦਾਤਿ ॥
7. ਵਡੀ ਵਡਿਆਈ ਜਾ ਆਪੇ ਆਪਿ ॥
8. ਨਾਨਕ ਕਾਰ^{੫੬} ਨ ਕਥਨੀ ਜਾਇ ॥
9. ਕੀਤਾ ਕਰਣਾ ਸਰਬ ਰਜਾਇ^{੫੭} ॥ ੨ ॥

ਮਹਲਾ ੨ ॥

1. ਇਹੁ ਜਗੁ ਸਚੈ ਕੀ ਹੈ ਕੋਠੜੀ ਸਚੇ ਕਾ ਵਿਚਿ ਵਾਸੁ ॥
2. ਇਕਨ੍ਾਹੁਕਮਿ ਸਮਾਇ^{੫੮} ਲਏ ਇਕਨਾ ਹੁਕਮੇ ਕਰੇ ਵਿਣਾਸੁ^{੫੯} ॥
3. ਇਕਨਾ ਭਾਣੈ^{੬੦} ਕਢਿ ਲਏ ਇਕਨਾ ਮਾਇਆ ਵਿਚਿ ਨਿਵਾਸੁ ॥
4. ਏਵ ਭਿ ਆਖਿ ਨ ਜਾਪਈ ਜਿ ਕਿਸੈ ਆਣੇ ਰਾਸਿ^{੬੧} ॥
5. ਨਾਨਕ ਗੁਰਮੁਖਿ ਜਾਣੀਐ ਜਾ ਕਉ ਆਪਿ ਕਰੇ ਪਰਗਾਸੁ^{੬੨} ॥ ੩ ॥

---

⁵² Justice
⁵³ Eternal seat
⁵⁴ Our utterances
⁵⁵ Innermost urges, affection

मः १ ॥

1. वडी वडिआई जा वडा नाउ ॥
2. वडी वडिआई जा सचु निआउ^{५२} ॥
3. वडी वडिआई जा निहचल थाउ^{५३} ॥
4. वडी वडिआई जाणै आलाउ^{५४} ॥
5. वडी वडिआई बुझै सभि भाउ^{५५} ॥
6. वडी वडिआई जा पुछि न दाति ॥
7. वडी वडिआई जा आपे आपि ॥
8. नानक कार^{५६} न कथनी जाइ ॥
9. कीता करणा सरब रजाइ^{५७} ॥ २ ॥

महला २ ॥

1. इहु जगु सचै की है कोठड़ी सचे का विचि वासु ॥
2. इकना्हुकमि समाइ^{५८} लए इकना हुकमे करे विणासु^{५९} ॥
3. इकना भाणै^{६०} कढि लए इकना माइआ विचि निवासु ॥
4. एव भि आखि न जापई जि किसै आणे रासि^{६१} ॥
5. नानक गुरमुखि जाणीऐ जा कउ आपि करे परगासु^{६२} ॥ ३ ॥

---

⁵⁶ God's workings
⁵⁷ Under God's rules
⁵⁸ To merge in
⁵⁹ Destroy

Mehla 1.

1. vadee vadi-aa-ee jaa vadaa naa-o.
2. vadee vadi-aa-ee jaa sach ni-aa-o^{52}.
3. vadee vadi-aa-ee jaa nihchal thaa-o^{53}.
4. vadee vadi-aa-ee jaanai aalaa-o^{54}.
5. vadee vadi-aa-ee bujhai sabh bhaa-o^{55}.
6. vadee vadi-aa-ee jaa puchh na daat.
7. vadee vadi-aa-ee jaa aapay aap.
8. naanak kaar^{56} na kathnee jaa-ay.
9. keetaa karnaa sarab rajaa-ay^{57}. ||2||

Mehla 2.

1. ih jag sachai kee hai koth-rhee sachay kaa vich vaas.
2. iknHaa hukam samaa-ay^{58} la-ay iknHaa hukmay karay vinaas^{59}.
3. iknHaa bhaanai^{60} kadh la-ay iknHaa maa-i-aa vich nivaas.
4. ayv bhe aakh na jaap-ee je kisai aanay raas^{61}.
5. naanak gurmukh jaanee-ai jaa ka-o aap karay pargaas^{62}. ||3||

---

⁶⁰ Redemption
⁶¹ To whom Waheguru's grace may bless
⁶² To radiate with divine light

Theme

Sloak Mehla 1 (Guru Nanak)

Waheguru's creation is a reality and not an illusion.

Mehla 2 (Guru Nanak)

Waheguru is all-powerful. He is unquestionable and beyond description.

Literal Meaning

Sloak Mehla 1

O! Waheguru

1. Real (true) are your cosmic regions and real are your celestial spheres.
2. Real are all your domains and real are shapes and forms of your creation.
3. Real are your plans and real are your concepts.
4. Real is your dispensation and real are your rules.
5. Real are your orders and real are your laws.
6. Real are your bounties and real are your plans.
7. Millions and trillions believe in you and in your creation.
8. Real are your powers and real are your operations.
9. Real are your qualities and real are your adorations.
10. Real are your protective forces O! My true Master.
11. Those who believe in Waheguru are the perfect human beings,
12. And the non-believers are fragile and subject to transmigration.

Mehla 2

1. Great is his (Waheguru's) glory! Sublime is his name.
2. Great is his glory! Virtuous is his justice.
3. Great is his glory! And eternal is his abode.
4. Great is his glory! He values our utterances.
5. Great is his glory! He knows our inner thoughts.
6. Great is his glory! He showers his bounties without discrimination.
7. Great is his glory! He is the greatest of all.
8. His doings and actions are beyond expression.
9. Everything happens at his will and according to his commandments.

Theme

Mehla 3 (Guru Angad)

This world is an abode of Waheguru. He distributes his bounties according to his own will.

Literal Meaning

Mehla 3

1. This world is one of the abodes of Waheguru, and in here he dwells at his will.
2. According to his wish, a few blessed ones (virtuous) merge in him, and others (sinners) he lets go astray.
3. In his will, a few blessed one (virtuous) are redeemed and others (deluded in maya) are forsaken to decay.
4. No one could say, whom Waheguru may bless
5. And it is only the God-blessed souls to whom Waheguru radiates his light.

ਪਉੜੀ ॥

1. ਨਾਨਕ ਜੀਅ ਉਪਾਇ [63] ਕੈ ਲਿਖਿ ਨਾਵੈ [64] ਧਰਮੁ ਬਹਾਲਿਆ [65] ॥
2. ਓਥੈ ਸਚੇ ਹੀ ਸਚਿ ਨਿਬੜੈ [66] ਚੁਣਿ ਵਖਿ ਕਢੇ ਜਜਮਾਲਿਆ [67] ॥
3. ਥਾਉ ਨ ਪਾਇਨਿ [68] ਕੂੜਿਆਰ [69] ਮੁਹ ਕਾਲੈ ਦੋਜਕਿ ਚਲਿਆ ॥
4. ਤੇਰੈ ਨਾਇ ਰਤੇ ਸੇ ਜਿਣਿ [70] ਗਏ ਹਾਰਿ ਗਏ ਸਿ ਠਗਣ ਵਾਲਿਆ ॥
5. ਲਿਖਿ ਨਾਵੈ ਧਰਮੁ ਬਹਾਲਿਆ ॥ ੨ ॥

पउुड़ी ॥

1. नानक जीअ उपाइ [63] कै लिखि नावै [64] धरमु बहालिआ [65] ॥
2. ऊथै सचे ही सचि निबड़ै [66] चुणि वखि कढे जजमालिआ [67] ॥
3. थाउ न पाइनि [68] कूड़िआर [69] मुह कालै दोजकि चलिआ ॥
4. तेरै नाइ रते से जिणि [70] गए हारि गए सि ठगण वालिआ ॥
5. लिखि नावै धरमु बहालिआ ॥ २ ॥

Pauri.

1. naanak jee-a upaa-ay [63] kai li<u>kh</u> naavai [64] <u>Dh</u>aram bahaali-aa [65].
2. othai sachay hee sach nib<u>rh</u>ai [66] chun vak<u>h</u> kadhay jajmaali-aa [67].
3. thao na paini [68] kuriar [69] muh kalai dozak chalia.
4. tayrai naa-ay ratay say jin [70] ga-ay haar ga-ay se <u>thagan</u> vaali-aa.
5. li<u>kh</u> naavai <u>Dh</u>aram bahaali-aa. ||2||

Literal Meaning
Pauri

1. Waheguru created the world, assigned to everyone his/her tasks and appointed a Justice to judge their actions.
2. In the court of the Judge, only truth prevails and sinners are punished.
3. The liars find no place therein, their faces being blackened with sins, they are pushed into hell to suffer therein.
4. Those imbued in your divine name finally depart, vindicated with glory and rogues are damned.
5. This is how the deeds of human beings are judged, the virtuous rewarded and the sinner punished.

Theme
Pauri

Waheguru watches his wondrous creation from his abode with great excitement

---

[63] After making the universe
[64] To assign
[65] Righteous tasks

[66] In the God's realm, only truth prevails
[67] Sinners
[68] To find a place in heavens

[69] Liars
[70] Winners

ਹਮ ਮੂਰਖ ਮੁਗਧ ਸਰਣਾਗਤੀ ਮਿਲੁ ਗੋਵਿੰਦ ਰੰਗਾ ਰਾਮ ਰਾਜੇ ॥

हम मूरख मुगध सरणागती मिलु गोविंद रंगा राम राजे ॥

ham moorakh mugaDh sarnaagatee mil govind rangaa raam raajay.

I am foolish and ignorant, but I have taken to Waheguru's sanctuary,
bless me to merge with the love of the Master of the Universe,
O King of Kings.

ਗੁਰਿ ਪੂਰੈ ਹਰਿ ਪਾਇਆ ਹਰਿ ਭਗਤਿ ਇਕ ਮੰਗਾ ॥

गुरि पूरै हरि पाइआ हरि भगति इक मंगा ॥

gur poorai har paa-i-aa har bhagat ik mangaa.

Through the perfect Guru, I have obtained Waheguru,
and I beg for His blessing of devotion.

ਮੇਰਾ ਮਨੁ ਤਨੁ ਸਬਦਿ ਵਿਗਾਸਿਆ ਜਪਿ ਅਨਤ ਤਰੰਗਾ ॥

मेरा मनु तनु सबदि विगासिआ जपि अनत तरंगा ॥

mayraa man tan sabad vigaasi-aa jap anat tarangaa.

My mind and body blossom forth through the word of the Shabad;
I meditate on Waheguru of infinite waves.

ਮਿਲਿ ਸੰਤ ਜਨਾ ਹਰਿ ਪਾਇਆ ਨਾਨਕ ਸਤਸੰਗਾ ॥੩॥

मिलि संत जना हरि पाइआ नानक सतसंगा ॥ ३ ॥

mil sant janaa har paa-i-aa naanak satsangaa. ||3||

Meeting with the humbl saints helps us
find Waheguru in the satsangaa. ||3||

Pauri 3 with 2 sloaks
(Guru Nanak 2)

ਸਲੋਕ ਮਃ ੧ ॥

1. ਵਿਸਮਾਦੁ[71] ਨਾਦ[72] ਵਿਸਮਾਦੁ ਵੇਦ[73] ॥
2. ਵਿਸਮਾਦੁ ਜੀਆ[74] ਵਿਸਮਾਦੁ ਭੇਦ[75] ॥
3. ਵਿਸਮਾਦੁ ਰੂਪ ਵਿਸਮਾਦੁ ਰੰਗ ॥
4. ਵਿਸਮਾਦੁ ਨਾਗੇ ਫਿਰਹਿ ਜੰਤ[76] ॥
5. ਵਿਸਮਾਦੁ ਪਉਣੁ ਵਿਸਮਾਦੁ ਪਾਣੀ ॥
6. ਵਿਸਮਾਦੁ ਅਗਨੀ ਖੇਡਹਿ ਵਿਡਾਣੀ[77] ॥
7. ਵਿਸਮਾਦੁ ਧਰਤੀ ਵਿਸਮਾਦੁ ਖਾਣੀ[78] ॥
8. ਵਿਸਮਾਦੁ ਸਾਦਿ[79] ਲਗਹਿ ਪਰਾਣੀ [80] ॥
9. ਵਿਸਮਾਦੁ ਸੰਜੋਗੁ[81] ਵਿਸਮਾਦੁ ਵਿਜੋਗੁ[82] ॥
10. ਵਿਸਮਾਦੁ ਭੁਖ[83] ਵਿਸਮਾਦੁ ਭੋਗੁ[84] ॥
11. ਵਿਸਮਾਦੁ ਸਿਫਤਿ ਵਿਸਮਾਦੁ ਸਾਲਾਹ[85] ॥
12. ਵਿਸਮਾਦੁ ਉਝੜ[86] ਵਿਸਮਾਦੁ ਰਾਹ[87] ॥
13. ਵਿਸਮਾਦੁ ਨੇੜੈ ਵਿਸਮਾਦੁ ਦੂਰਿ ॥
14. ਵਿਸਮਾਦੁ ਦੇਖੈ ਹਾਜਰਾ ਹਜੂਰਿ [88] ॥
15. ਵੇਖਿ ਵਿਡਾਣੁ[89] ਰਹਿਆ ਵਿਸਮਾਦੁ ॥
16. ਨਾਨਕ ਬੁਝਣੁ ਪੂਰੈ ਭਾਗਿ [90] ॥ ੧ ॥

सलोक मः १ ॥

1. विसमादु[71] नाद[72] विसमादु वेद[73] ॥
2. विसमादु जीअ[74] विसमादु भेद[75] ॥
3. विसमादु रूप विसमादु रंग ॥
4. विसमादु नागे फिरहि जंत[76] ॥
5. विसमादु पउणु विसमादु पाणी ॥
6. विसमादु अगनी खेडहि विडाणी[77] ॥
7. विसमादु धरती विसमादु खाणी[78] ॥
8. विसमादु सादि[79] लगहि पराणी [80] ॥
9. विसमादु संजोगु[81] विसमादु विजोगु[82] ॥
10. विसमादु भुख[83] विसमादु भोगु[84] ॥
11. विसमादु सिफति विसमादु सालाह[85] ॥
12. विसमादु उझड़[86] विसमादु राह[87] ॥
13. विसमादु नेड़ै विसमादु दूरि ॥
14. विसमादु देखै हाजरा हजूरि [88] ॥
15. वेखि विडाणु[89] रहिआ विसमादु ॥
16. नानक बुझणु पूरै भागि [90] ॥ १ ॥

Sloak Mehla 1.

1. vismaad[71] naad[72] vismaad vayd[73].
2. vismaad jee-a[74] vismaad bhayd[75].
3. vismaad roop vismaad rang.
4. vismaad naagay fireh jant[76].
5. vismaad pa-un vismaad paanee.
6. vismaad agnee khaydeh vidaanee[77].
7. vismaad Dhartee vismaad khaanee[78].
8. vismaad saad[79] lageh paraanee[80].
9. vismaad sanjog[81] vismaad vijog[82].
10. vismaad bhukh[83] vismaad bhog[84].
11. vismaad sifat vismaad saalaah[85].
12. vismaad oujharh[86] vismaad raah[87].
13. vismaad nayrhai vismaad door.
14. vismaad daykhai haajraa hajoor[88].
15. vaykh vidaan[89] rahi-aa vismaad.
16. naanak bujhan poorai bhaag.[90] ||1||

---

[71] Wondrous, wonderful, marvellous, full of suspense, all praise
[72] Melodies of the Cosmic Order, the sound
[73] The knowledge radiated by world scriptures
[74] Creatures
[75] Kinds, varieties
[76] Creatures who wander around naked (the whole creation, except humans)
[77] One which works wonders
[78] Different modes of reproduction (by egg, semen, water and sweat)
[79] Tastes
[80] People are attached with
[81] Union, to be together
[82] Seperation
[83] Hunger
[84] Consumption
[85] Eulogy, praises
[86] Wilderness, deviation
[87] The right path, the true path
[88] Watching Waheguru face to face
[89] Wondrous creation, wondrous objects
[90] The perfect one, perfectly fortunate

ਮਃ ੧ ॥

1. ਕੁਦਰਤਿ[91] ਦਿਸੈ[92] ਕੁਦਰਤਿ ਸੁਣੀਐ ਕੁਦਰਤਿ ਭਉ[93] ਸੁਖ[94] ਸਾਰੁ[95] ॥

2. ਕੁਦਰਤਿ ਪਾਤਾਲੀ ਆਕਾਸੀ ਕੁਦਰਤਿ ਸਰਬ ਆਕਾਰੁ[96] ॥

3. ਕੁਦਰਤਿ ਵੇਦ ਪੁਰਾਣ ਕਤੇਬਾ[97] ਕੁਦਰਤਿ ਸਰਬ ਵੀਚਾਰੁ[98] ॥

4. ਕੁਦਰਤਿ ਖਾਣਾ ਪੀਣਾ ਪੈਨਣੁ ਕੁਦਰਤਿ ਸਰਬ ਪਿਆਰੁ ॥

5. ਕੁਦਰਤਿ ਜਾਤੀ[99] ਜਿਨਸੀ[100] ਰੰਗੀ ਕੁਦਰਤਿ ਜੀਅ ਜਹਾਨ ॥

6. ਕੁਦਰਤਿ ਨੇਕੀਆ ਕੁਦਰਤਿ ਬਦੀਆ ਕੁਦਰਤਿ ਮਾਨੁ ਅਭਿਮਾਨ ॥

7. ਕੁਦਰਤਿ ਪਉਣੁ ਪਾਣੀ ਬੈਸੰਤਰੁ ਕੁਦਰਤਿ ਧਰਤੀ ਖਾਕੁ ॥

8. ਸਭ ਤੇਰੀ ਕੁਦਰਤਿ ਤੂੰ ਕਾਦਿਰੁ[101] ਕਰਤਾ[102] ਪਾਕੀ ਨਾਈ ਪਾਕੁ[103] ॥

9. ਨਾਨਕ ਹੁਕਮੈ ਅੰਦਰਿ ਵੇਖੈ[104] ਵਰਤੈ ਤਾਕੋ ਤਾਕੁ[105] ॥ ੨ ॥

Mehla 1.

1. kudrat[91] disai[92] kudrat sunee-ai kudrat bha-o[93] sukh[94] saar[95].

2. kudrat paataalee aakaasee kudrat sarab aakaar[96].

3. kudrat vayd puraan kataybaa[97] kudrat sarab veechaar[98].

4. kudrat khaanaa peenaa painHan kudrat sarab pi-aar.

5. kudrat jaatee[99] jinsee[100] rangee kudrat jee-a jahaan.

6. kudrat naykee-aa kudrat badee-aa kudrat maan abhimaan.

7. kudrat pa-un paanee baisantar kudrat Dhartee khaak.

8. sabh tayree kudrat tooN kaadir[101] kartaa[102] paakee naa-ee paak[103].

9. naanak hukmai andar vaykhai[104] vartai taako taak.[105] ||2||

---

[91] The working of Waheguru; rules and laws of regulating this world, God's will
[92] We see according to God's rules.
[93] Fear (of death, of falling ill, of loosing money, etc.)
[94] Happiness
[95] The source or root (cause of fear, happiness and grief, etc.)
[96] All *patals* (life beneath the earth, – neatherlands skies and creatures on earth move according to God's rules
[97] Semitic religions' scriptures
[98] Mechanism of thinking
[99] Various kinds of shapes and forms (e.g., big and small dogs)
[100] Species
[101] All powerful, omnipotent
[102] Creator
[103] Holiest of the holy
[104] Knowing inner thoughts of each and every one

Theme

Sloak Mehla 1

Every type of creation, its features, its qualities and aspects are a suspense for the humankind. The world is full with wondrous objects.

Literal Meaning

Sloak Mehla 1

The wondrous universe:

1. Wondrous are the sounds, which have been travelling in the atmosphere since the beginning of time and the melodies they have spread in the Cosmic Order. Wondrous are also the scriptures, which explain the suspense of your drama.
2. Wondrous are your creation and the varieties of life and objects you have created.
3. Wondrous are the numerous forms within each variety and wonderful are the colours you have put in there.
4. Wondrous and uncountable are creatures, which roam about naked unlike humans.
5. Wondrous are the scientific properties of both air and water.
6. Wondrous is fire (energy) which steers life.
7. Wondrous is the earth and wondrous are the modes of reproduction.
8. Wondrous are the tastes, habits and sentiments of the creation.
9. Wondrous are feelings of union and separation.
10. Wondrous is the hunger and modes of its satisfaction.
11. Wondrous are the reactions of praises and eulogies.
12. Wondrous are the perceptions of destruction and construction.
13. Wondrous is the sensation of closeness and distance.
14. Wondrous is the notion of meeting Waheguru face to face.
15. Wondrous, wonderful and strange are his ways.
16. Only fortunate can unfold God's mystery.

Mehla 2

Everything in this planet and all other planets moves under the laws of Waheguru

Mehla 2

Kudrat – The Rules

1. The power of seeing and listening, the feeling of fear and happiness are all rooted in the divine laws.
2. The working of all lives under, over and on the earth is regulated by God's rules.
3. All world scriptures, Vedas, Puranas and Semitic books are authored by God.
4. The vegetation, the waters, the coverings and the attachment to them are all controlled by God's laws.
5. Waheguru designs all the form and shapes of species, the colour and contours of creation.
6. Vices, virtues, honour and slander all work within God's commands.
7. Waheguru commands winds, waters, fires and earth.
8. You are omnipotent, the creator and holiest of the holy.
9. Everything works under your laws and there is none above you. You are self-illuminated.

ਪਉੜੀ ॥

1. ਆਪੀਨੈ[106] ਭੋਗ ਭੋਗਿ[107] ਕੈ ਹੋਇ ਭਸਮੜਿ[108] ਭਉਰੁ[109] ਸਿਧਾਇਆ[110] ॥

2. ਵਡਾ ਹੋਆ[111] ਦੁਨੀਦਾਰੁ[112] ਗਲਿ[113] ਸੰਗਲੁ[114] ਘਤਿ ਚਲਾਇਆ[115] ॥

3. ਅਗੈ[116] ਕਰਣੀ ਕੀਰਤਿ ਵਾਚੀਐ ਬਹਿ ਲੇਖਾ ਕਰਿ ਸਮਝਾਇਆ ॥

4. ਥਾਉ ਨ ਹੋਵੀ[117] ਪਉਦੀਈ[118] ਹੁਣਿ ਸੁਣੀਐ ਕਿਆ ਰੂਆਇਆ[119] ॥

5. ਮਨਿ ਅੰਧੈ[120] ਜਨਮੁ ਗਵਾਇਆ ॥ ੩ ॥

पउड़ी ॥

1. आपीनै[106] भोग भोगि[107] कै होइ भसमड़ि[108] भउरु[109] सिधाइआ[110] ॥

2. वडा होआ[111] दुनीदारु[112] गलि[113] संगलु[114] घति चलाइआ[115] ॥

3. अगै[116] करणी कीरति वाचीऐ बहि लेखा करि समझाइआ ॥

4. थाउ न होवी[117] पउदीई[118] हुणि सुणीऐ किआ रूआइआ[119] ॥

5. मनि अंधै[120] जनमु गवाइआ ॥ ३ ॥

Pauri.

1. aapeen[H]ai[106] bhog bhog[107] kai ho-ay bhasmarh[108] bha-ur[109] siDhaa-i-aa[110].

2. vadaa ho-aa[111] duneedaar[112] gal[113] sangal[114] ghat chalaa-i-aa[115].

3. agai[116] karnee keerat vaachee-ai bahi laykhaa kar samjhaa-i-aa.

4. thaa-o na hovee[117] pa-udee-ee[118] hun sunee-ai ki-aa roo-aa-i-aa[119].

5. man anDhai[120] janam gavaa-i-aa. ||3||

Theme

Pauri

The world is an action ground. We perform our deeds (karmas) and are then rewarded or punished accordingly. Waheguru is the sole judge of our karmas.

Literal Meaning

Pauri

1. Humans are given life, some waste it in self-indulgence and luxuries, and forget that at the end of day their bodies will be reduced into a heap of ashes.
2. The noose of death will forcibly take them away
3. In the life thereafter, the account of karmas will be opened.
4. The offenders will find no place of refuge when the punishment will be announced.
5. Why do you have to waste your life by indulging in harmful activities.

[106] All humans are given freedom to perform their acts
[107] After enjoying all amenities of life
[108] A heap of ashes
[109] Soul
[110] Leaving body

[111] Death, to die
[112] Worldly man
[113] Around the neck
[114] Chain
[115] Forcibly

[116] In the court of Waheguru
[117] No place of refuge is found
[118] When the soul is punished, punishment
[119] No one would listen to his/her cries
[120] O! blind person, entangled person

ਦੀਨ ਦਇਆਲ ਸੁਨਿ ਬੇਨਤੀ ਹਰਿ ਪ੍ਰਭ ਹਰਿ ਰਾਇਆ ਰਾਮ ਰਾਜੇ ॥

ਦੀਨ ਦਇਆਲ ਸੁਣਿ ਬੇਨਤੀ ਹਰਿ ਪ੍ਰਭ ਹਰਿ ਰਾਇਆ ਰਾਮ ਰਾਜੇ ॥

deen da-i-aal sun bayntee har parabh har raa-i-aa raam raajay.

O Merciful to the meek, hear my prayer my Waheguru;
You are my Master, O King of Kings.

ਹਉ ਮਾਗਉ ਸਰਨਿ ਹਰਿ ਨਾਮ ਕੀ ਹਰਿ ਹਰਿ ਮੁਖਿ ਪਾਇਆ ॥

ਹਤੁ ਮਾਗਤੁ ਸਰਣਿ ਹਰਿ ਨਾਮ ਕੀ ਹਰਿ ਹਰਿ ਮੁਖਿ ਪਾਇਆ ॥

ha-o maaga-o saran har naam kee har har mukh paa-i-aa.

I beg for the refuge of Waheguru's Name;
I utter this prayer again and again.

ਭਗਤਿ ਵਛਲੁ ਹਰਿ ਬਿਰਦੁ ਹੈ ਹਰਿ ਲਾਜ ਰਖਾਇਆ ॥

ਭਗਤਿ ਵਛਲੁ ਹਰਿ ਬਿਰਦੁ ਹੈ ਹਰਿ ਲਾਜ ਰਖਾਇਆ ॥

bhagat vachhal har birad hai har laaj rakhaa-i-aa.

It is the Waheguru's natural way to love His devotees;
O Master, please preserve my honour!

ਜਨੁ ਨਾਨਕੁ ਸਰਣਾਗਤੀ ਹਰਿ ਨਾਮਿ ਤਰਾਇਆ ॥੪॥੮॥੧੫॥

ਜਨੁ ਨਾਨਕੁ ਸਰਣਾਗਤੀ ਹਰਿ ਨਾਮਿ ਤਰਾਇਆ ॥ ੪ ॥ ੮ ॥ ੧੫ ॥

jan naanak sarnaagatee har naam taraa-i-aa. ||4||8||15||

We have entered your sanctuary and have been saved by
Your Name ||4||8||15||

Pauri 4 with 2 sloaks

(Guru Nanak 2)

ਸਲੋਕ ਮਃ ੧ ॥

1. ਭੈ¹²¹ ਵਿਚਿ ਪਵਣੁ¹²² ਵਹੈ ਸਦਵਾਉ¹²³ ॥
2. ਭੈ ਵਿਚਿ ਚਲਹਿ ਲਖ ਦਰੀਆਉ ॥
3. ਭੈ ਵਿਚਿ ਅਗਨਿ ਕਢੈ ਵੇਗਾਰਿ¹²⁴ ॥
4. ਭੈ ਵਿਚਿ ਧਰਤੀ ਦਬੀ ਭਾਰਿ¹²⁵ ॥
5. ਭੈ ਵਿਚਿ ਇੰਦੁ¹²⁶ ਫਿਰੈ ਸਿਰ ਭਾਰਿ¹²⁷ ॥
6. ਭੈ ਵਿਚਿ ਰਾਜਾ ਧਰਮੁ¹²⁸ ਦੁਆਰੁ¹²⁹ ॥
7. ਭੈ ਵਿਚਿ ਸੂਰਜ ਭੈ ਵਿਚਿ ਚੰਦੁ ॥
8. ਕੋਹ ਕਰੋੜੀ¹³⁰ ਚਲਤ¹³¹ ਨ ਅੰਤੁ¹³² ॥
9. ਭੈ ਵਿਚਿ ਸਿਧ¹³³ ਬੁਧ ¹³⁴ ਸੁਰ¹³⁵ ਨਾਥ¹³⁶ ॥
10. ਭੈ ਵਿਚਿ ਆਡਾਣੇ¹³⁷ ਆਕਾਸ ॥
11. ਭੈ ਵਿਚਿ ਜੋਧ¹³⁸ ਮਹਾਬਲ¹³⁹ ਸੂਰ¹⁴⁰ ॥
12. ਭੈ ਵਿਚਿ ਆਵਹਿ ਜਾਵਹਿ ਪੂਰ¹⁴¹ ॥
13. ਸਗਲਿਆ¹⁴² ਭਉ¹⁴³ ਲਿਖਿਆ ਸਿਰਿ ਲੇਖੁ ॥
14. ਨਾਨਕ ਨਿਰਭਉ¹⁴⁴ ਨਿਰੰਕਾਰੁ¹⁴⁵ ਸਚੁ ਏਕੁ ॥ ੧ ॥

सलोक मः १ ॥

1. भै²¹ विचि पवणु²² वहै सदवाउ²³ ॥
2. भै विचि चलहि लख दरीआउ ॥
3. भै विचि अगनि कढै वेगारि²⁴ ॥
4. भै विचि धरती दबी भारि²⁵ ॥
5. भै विचि इंदु²⁶ फिरै सिर भारि²⁷ ॥
6. भै विचि राजा धरमु²⁸ दुआरु²⁹ ॥
7. भै विचि सूरजु भै विचि चंदु ॥
8. कोह करोड़ी³⁰ चलत³¹ न अंतु³² ॥
9. भै विचि सिध³³ बुध ³⁴ सुर³⁵ नाथ³⁶ ॥
10. भै विचि आडाणे³⁷ आकास ॥
11. भै विचि जोध³⁸ महाबल³⁹ सूर⁴⁰ ॥
12. भै विचि आवहि जावहि पूर⁴¹ ॥
13. सगलिआ⁴² भउ⁴³ लिखिआ सिरि लेखु ॥
14. नानक निरभउ⁴⁴ निरंकार⁴⁵ सचु एकु ॥ १ ॥

Sloak Mehla 1.

1. bhai[121] vich pavan[122] vahai sadvaa-o[123].
2. bhai vich chaleh lakh daree-aa-o.
3. bhai vich agan kadhai vaygaar[124].
4. bhai vich Dhartee dabee bhaar[125].
5. bhai vich ind[126] firai sir bhaar[127].
6. bhai vich raajaa Dharam[128] du-aar[129].
7. bhai vich sooraj bhai vich chand.
8. koh karorhee[130] chalat[131] na ant[132].
9. bhai vich siDh[133] buDh[134] sur naath[136].
10. bhai vich aadaanay[137] aakaas.
11. bhai vich joDh[138] mahaabal[139] soor[140].
12. bhai vich aavahia jaaveh poor[141].
13. sagli-aa[142] bha-o[143] likhi-aa sir laykh.
14. naanak nirbha-o[144] nirankaar[145] sach ayk. ||1||

---

[121] Under the command of Waheguru, under the fear of God
[122] Wind (strong breeze)
[123] Breeze (mild breeze)
[124] To perform defined jobs
[125] With all its weight
[126] Clouds
[127] Weight of water, inclination to pour
[128] Dharamraj (the Chief Justice, of the Central Court of *Karma*)
[129] The door of Waheguru's abode, Dharamraj is standing at Waheguru's gateway
[130] Crore (million) miles
[131] Moving on a specific orbit
[132] Have been moving for infinite number of years
[133] Holy people
[134] Learned people, scholars
[135] Gods, devtas
[136] Master of yogic sciences
[137] Being set at a fixed place
[138] Warriors
[139] Knights
[140] Valiant heroes
[141] Hordes, multitude numbers
[142] All of them, as described above
[143] Fear, destiny, command
[144] Fearless
[145] Formless

The stage of the worldly drama:

1. ਨਾਨਕ ਨਿਰਭਉ ਨਿਰੰਕਾਰੁ ਹੋਰਿ ਕੇਤੇ[146] ਰਾਮ[147] ਰਵਾਲ[148] ॥
2. ਕੇਤੀਆ ਕੰਨ੍[149] ਕਹਾਣੀਆ ਕੇਤੇ ਬੇਦ[150] ਬੀਚਾਰ[151] ॥
3. ਕੇਤੇ ਨਚਹਿ ਮੰਗਤੇ[152] ਗਿੜਿ ਮੁੜਿ ਪੂਰਹਿ ਤਾਲ[153] ॥
4. ਬਾਜਾਰੀ[154] ਬਾਜਾਰ ਮਹਿ ਆਇ ਕਢਹਿ[155] ਬਾਜਾਰ ॥
5. ਗਾਵਹਿ ਰਾਜੇ ਰਾਣੀਆ ਬੋਲਹਿ ਆਲ ਪਤਾਲ[156] ॥
6. ਲਖ ਟਕਿਆ[157] ਕੇ ਮੁੰਦੜੇ[158] ਲਖ ਟਕਿਆ ਕੇ ਹਾਰ[159] ॥
7. ਜਿਤੁ ਤਨਿ ਪਾਈਅਹਿ ਨਾਨਕਾ ਸੇ ਤਨ ਹੋਵਹਿ ਛਾਰ[160] ॥
8. ਗਿਆਨੁ ਨ ਗਲੀਈ[161] ਢੂਢੀਐ ਕਥਨਾ[162] ਕਰੜਾ[163] ਸਾਰੁ ॥
9. ਕਰਮਿ[164] ਮਿਲੈ ਤਾ ਪਾਈਐ ਹੋਰ ਹਿਕਮਤਿ[165] ਹੁਕਮੁ ਖੁਆਰੁ[166] ॥ ੨ ॥

---

1. नानक निरभउ निरंकारु होरि केते[146] राम[147] रवाल[148] ॥
2. केतीआ कंन[149] कहाणीआ केते बेद[150] बीचार[151] ॥
3. केते नचहि मंगते[152] गिड़ि मुड़ि पूरहि ताल[153] ॥
4. बाजारी[154] बाजार महि आइ कढहि[155] बाजार ॥
5. गावहि राजे राणीआ बोलहि आल पताल[156] ॥
6. लख टकिआ[157] के मुंदड़े[158] लख टकिआ के हार[159] ॥
7. जितु तनि पाईअहि नानका से तन होवहि छार[160] ॥
8. गिआनु न गलीई[161] ढूढीऐ कथना[162] करड़ा[163] सारु ॥
9. करमि[164] मिलै ता पाईऐ होर हिकमति[165] हुकमु खुआरु[166] ॥ २ ॥

Mehla 1.

1. naanak nir<u>bha</u>-o nirankaar hor kay<u>t</u>ay[146] raam[147] ravaal[148].
2. kay<u>t</u>ee-aa kan^H[149] kahaa<u>n</u>ee-aa kay<u>t</u>ay bay<u>d</u>[150] beechaar[151].
3. kay<u>t</u>ay nacheh mang<u>t</u>ay[152] gi<u>rh</u> mu<u>rh</u> pooreh <u>t</u>aal[153].
4. baajaaree[154] baajaar meh aa-ay ka<u>dh</u>eh[155] baajaar.
5. gavai raje rania bolai aal pa<u>t</u>al[156].
6. lakh takia[157] ke mundarare[158] lakh takia ke haar[159].
7. jit tan paiaih <u>n</u>anka se tan havaih chhar[160].
8. gianu <u>n</u>a galili[161] dhudhiai kathna[162] karara[163] saar.
9. karam[164] milai ta paiai hor hitmat[165] hukamu khuar[166].

---

[146] Numerous
[147] Rama, prophets
[148] Reduced to dust
[149] Krishna
[150] Vedas, scriptures
[151] Thoughts
[152] Beggars, in fact, we all are beggars in the court of Waheguru
[153] Keeping pace with rhythm (time)
[154] The guiser, false appearance
[155] To present a false show
[156] Irresponsible talk, words normally spoken by a drunkard
[157] Indian rupees
[158] Earrings
[159] Necklace
[160] Ashes, dust
[161] Talk (irrelevant)
[162] To describe
[163] Like munching of steel
[164] Grace of Waheguru
[165] Devices
[166] Ruinous, destructive

Theme

Sloak Mehla 1

Everything moves according to Waheguru's plans and rules

Mehla 2

Waheguru has sent many prophets into this world with his message. Prophets' words have become scriptures. Human beings have to work hard to understand these scriptures.

Literal Meaning

Sloak Mehla 1 (Waheguru's laws and his plans)

1. Under Waheguru's command blows strong wind and light breeze.
2. Under his control flows many thousand rivers.
3. Under his control fire performs its functions.
4. Under his control earth bears the burden of things.
5. Under his control clouds carry tonnes of water under their wings.
6. Under his command *Dharamraj* delivers his judgement.
7. Under his control sun and moon travel in their orbits, and
8. They have been moving in that orbit for countless years.
9. Under his command are, saints, scholars, gods and yogis.
10. Under his control the sky has been fixed in the space.
11. Under his control are all warriors, knights and valiant heroes.
12. Under his control everyone comes and goes from this world.
13. At the forehead of every one is written the writ of Waheguru, and
14. He himself is above all writs and commandments.

Mehla 2

1. Waheguru is fearless and formless and is the greatest; other gods like Ram are mere dust of his feet.
2. There are countless stories of Krishna and multifarious interpretations of scriptures.
3. Countless people beg at God's door and to please him they perform various acts and dance at various tunes.
4. Many enact dramas in public parks.
5. They disguise as kings and queens and utter nonsensical words.
6. Sometimes they wear expensive earrings and costly necklaces.
7. In these myriads they forget that one day all will reduce to ashes.
8. Knowledge cannot be gained with mere words and casual pranks, its acquisition is as hard as munching steel, but
9. It can be gained with Waheguru's Grace, other methods are futile trials.

ਪਉੜੀ ॥	ਪਉੜੀ ॥	## Pauri.
1. ਨਦਰਿ ਕਰਹਿ ਜੇ ਆਪਣੀ ਤਾ ਨਦਰੀ ਸਤਿਗੁਰੁ ਪਾਇਆ ॥	1. ਨਦਰਿ ਕਰਹਿ ਜੇ ਆਪਣੀ ਤਾ ਨਦਰੀ ਸਤਿਗੁਰ ਪਾਇਆ ॥	1. nadar karahi jay aapnee taa nadree satgur paa-i-aa.
2. ਏਹੁ ਜੀਉ ਬਹੁਤੇ ਜਨਮ ਭਰੰਮਿਆ[167] ਤਾ ਸਤਿਗੁਰਿ ਸਬਦੁ ਸੁਣਾਇਆ ॥	2. ਏਹੁ ਜੀਉ ਬਹੁਤੇ ਜਨਮ ਭਰੰਮਿਆ[167] ਤਾ ਸਤਿਗੁਰਿ ਸਬਦੁ ਸੁਣਾਇਆ ॥	2. ayhu jee-o bahutay janam bharammi-aa[167] taa satgur sabad sunaa-i-aa.
3. ਸਤਿਗੁਰ ਜੇਵਡੁ ਦਾਤਾ ਕੋ ਨਹੀ ਸਭਿ ਸੁਣਿਅਹੁ ਲੋਕ ਸਬਾਇਆ[168] ॥	3. ਸਤਿਗੁਰ ਜੇਵਡੁ ਦਾਤਾ ਕੋ ਨਹੀ ਸਭਿ ਸੁਣਿਅਹੁ ਲੋਕ ਸਬਾਇਆ[168] ॥	3. satgur jayvad daataa ko nahee sabh suni-ahu lok sabaa-i-aa.[168]
4. ਸਤਿਗੁਰਿ ਮਿਲਿਐ ਸਚੁ ਪਾਇਆ ਜਿਨੀ ਵਿਚਹੁ ਆਪੁ ਗਵਾਇਆ[169] ॥	4. ਸਤਿਗੁਰਿ ਮਿਲਿਐ ਸਚੁ ਪਾਇਆ ਜਿਨੀ ਵਿਚਹੁ ਆਪੁ ਗਵਾਇਆ[169] ॥	4. satgur mili-ai sach paa-i-aa jin^Hee vichahu aap gavaa-i-aa.[169]
5. ਜਿਨਿ ਸਚੋ ਸਚੁ ਬੁਝਾਇਆ[170] ॥ ੪ ॥	5. ਜਿਨਿ ਸਚੋ ਸਚੁ ਬੁਝਾਇਆ[170] ॥ ੪ ॥	5. jin sacho sach bujhaa-i-aa.[170] ||4||

Theme	**Literal Meaning**
Pauri	**Pauri**
It is the Grace and Name of God, which can release human beings from the cycle of transmigration.	1. With Waheguru's grace a true teacher can be found.
	2. With Waheguru's shabad, intricacies of transmigration are explored.
	3. Waheguru is the greatest, let everyone comprehend this truth.
	4. With Waheguru's realisation ego and pride vanishes.
	5. These are the facts of truth, the whole truth and nothing but the truth.

---

[167] To wander

[168] The whole universe

[169] Destroying self-conceit, getting rid of one's ego.

[170] To realise, to understand

ਆਸਾ ਮਹਲਾ ੪ ॥
आसा महला ४ ॥
Asa Mehla 4.
Asa Mehla 4

ਗੁਰਮੁਖਿ ਢੂੰਢਿ ਢੂਢੇਦਿਆ ਹਰਿ ਸਜਣੁ ਲਧਾ ਰਾਮ ਰਾਜੇ ॥
गुरमुखि ढूंढि ढूढेदिआ हरि सजणु लधा राम राजे ॥
gurmukh dhoondh dhoodhaydi-aa har sajan laDhaa raam raajay.
As a true devotee, I searched and searched, and at the
end found my true Friend, the King of Kings.

ਕੰਚਨ ਕਾਇਆ ਕੋਟ ਗੜ ਵਿਚਿ ਹਰਿ ਹਰਿ ਸਿਧਾ ॥
कंचन काइआ कोट गड़ विचि हरि हरि सिधा ॥
kanchan kaa-i-aa kot garh vich har har siDhaa.
Within the walled fortress of my golden body Waheguru
has been revealed.

ਹਰਿ ਹਰਿ ਹੀਰਾ ਰਤਨੁ ਹੈ ਮੇਰਾ ਮਨੁ ਤਨੁ ਵਿਧਾ ॥
हरि हरि हीरा रतनु है मेरा मनु तनु विधा ॥
har har heeraa ratan hai mayraa man tan viDhaa.
Waheguru is a jewel, a diamond;
my mind and body are pierced through.

ਧੁਰਿ ਭਾਗ ਵਡੇ ਹਰਿ ਪਾਇਆ ਨਾਨਕ ਰਸਿ ਗੁਧਾ ॥੧॥
धुरि भाग वडे हरि पाइआ नानक रसि गुधा ॥ १ ॥
Dhur bhaag vaday har paa-i-aa naanak ras guDhaa. ||1||
By the great good fortune of my karmas, I have found the
Master and am permeated with His sublime essence. ||1||

Pauri 5 with 2 sloaks
(Guru Nanak 2)

ਸਲੋਕ ਮਃ ੧ ॥

1. ਘੜੀਆ[171] ਸਭੇ ਗੋਪੀਆ[172] ਪਹਰ[173] ਕੰਨੁ[174] ਗੋਪਾਲੁ[175] ॥

2. ਗਹਣੇ ਪਉਣੁ ਪਾਣੀ ਬੈਸੰਤਰੁ ਚੰਦੁ ਸੂਰਜੁ ਅਵਤਾਰ ॥

3. ਸਗਲੀ ਧਰਤੀ ਮਾਲੁ ਧਨੁ ਵਰਤਣਿ ਸਰਬ ਜੰਜਾਲ[176] ॥

4. ਨਾਨਕ ਮੁਸੈ[177] ਗਿਆਨ ਵਿਹੂਣੀ[178] ਖਾਇ ਗਇਆ[179] ਜਮਕਾਲੁ[180] ॥ ੧ ॥

सलोक मः १ ॥

1. घड़ीआ[171] सभे गोपीआ[172] पहर[173] कंनु[174] गोपाल[175] ॥

2. गहणे पउणु पाणी बैसंतरु चंदु सूरजु अवतार ॥

3. सगली धरती मालु धनु वरतणि सरब जंजाल[176] ॥

4. नानक मुसै[177] गिआन विहूणी[178] खाइ गइआ[179] जमकालु[180] ॥ १ ॥

Sloak Mehla 1.

1. gharhee-aa[171] sabhay gopee-aa[172] pehr[173] kan[H174] gopaal[175].

2. gahnay pa-un paanee baisantar chand sooraj avtaar.

3. saglee Dhartee maal Dhan vartan sarab janjaal[176].

4. naanak musai[177] gi-aan. vihoonee[178] khaa-ay ga-i-aa [179]jamkaal.[180] ||1||

---

[171] 60 time divisions of a day and night; a *ghari* is equivalent to 24 minutes

[172] Female cowherds

[173] 8 time divisions of a day; a *pehr is* equivalent to 3 hours.

[174] Krishna (here the word is used in plural sense i.e., many Krishnas)

[175] Herdsmen, those who look after and milk the cows; Gopal is also the name of Krishna

[176] Those are all maya (entanglements)

[177] Plundered, robbed

[178] Without

[179] Eaten up

[180] Messenger of death

ਮਃ ੧ ॥

1. ਵਾਇਨਿ[181] ਚੇਲੇ ਨਚਨਿ ਗੁਰ ॥
2. ਪੈਰ ਹਲਾਇਨਿ ਫੇਰਨਿ ਸਿਰ ॥
3. ਉਡਿ ਉਡਿ ਰਾਵਾ[182] ਝਾਟੈ ਪਾਇ ॥
4. ਵੇਖੈ ਲੋਕੁ ਹਸੈ ਘਰਿ ਜਾਇ ॥
5. ਰੋਟੀਆ ਕਾਰਨਿ ਪੂਰਹਿ ਤਾਲ [183] ॥
6. ਆਪੁ ਪਛਾੜਹਿ[184] ਧਰਤੀ ਨਾਲਿ ॥
7. ਗਾਵਨਿ[185] ਗੋਪੀਆ ਗਾਵਨਿ ਕਾਨੁ ॥
8. ਗਾਵਨਿ ਸੀਤਾ ਰਾਜੇ ਰਾਮ ॥
9. ਨਿਰਭਉ ਨਿਰੰਕਾਰੁ ਸਚੁ ਨਾਮੁ ॥
10. ਜਾ ਕਾ ਕੀਆ[186] ਸਗਲ ਜਹਾਨੁ ॥
11. ਸੇਵਕ ਸੇਵਹਿ [187]ਕਰਮਿ[188] ਚੜਾਉ[189] ॥
12. ਭਿੰਨੀ ਰੈਣਿ[190] ਜਿਨਾ ਮਨਿ ਚਾਉ[191] ॥
13. ਸਿਖੀ[192] ਸਿਖਿਆ[193] ਗੁਰ ਵੀਚਾਰਿ [194] ॥
14. ਨਦਰੀ ਕਰਮਿ ਲਘਾਏ ਪਾਰਿ [195] ॥
15. ਕੋਲੂ[196] ਚਰਖਾ[197] ਚਕੀ[198] ਚਕੁ[199] ॥
16. ਥਲ[200] ਵਾਰੋਲੇ[201] ਬਹੁਤੁ ਅਨੰਤ ॥

[181] Playing music
[182] Dust
[183] To dance on correct tune
[184] To dash against
[185] To sing like, to sing imitating Krishna and Rama (e.g., Ramlila)
[186] Created
[187] Devotee who earnestly serves

ਮਃ ੧ ॥

1. ਵਾਇਨਿ[181] ਚੇਲੇ ਨਚਨਿ ਗੁਰ ॥
2. ਪੈਰ ਹਲਾਇਨਿ ਫੇਰਨਿ ਸਿਰ ॥
3. ਤੁਡਿ ਤੁਡਿ ਰਾਵਾ[182] ਝਾਟੈ ਪਾਇ ॥
4. ਵੇਖੈ ਲੋਕੁ ਹਸੈ ਘਰਿ ਜਾਇ ॥
5. ਰੋਟੀਆ ਕਾਰਣਿ ਪੂਰਹਿ ਤਾਲ [183] ॥
6. ਆਪੁ ਪਛਾੜਹਿ[184] ਧਰਤੀ ਨਾਲਿ ॥
7. ਗਾਵਨਿ[185] ਗੋਪੀਆ ਗਾਵਨਿ ਕਾਨੁ ॥
8. ਗਾਵਨਿ ਸੀਤਾ ਰਾਜੇ ਰਾਮ ॥
9. ਨਿਰਭਤੁ ਨਿਰੰਕਾਰੁ ਸਚੁ ਨਾਮੁ ॥
10. ਜਾ ਕਾ ਕੀਆ[186] ਸਗਲ ਜਹਾਨੁ ॥
11. ਸੇਵਕ ਸੇਵਹਿ [187]ਕਰਮਿ[188] ਚੜਾਉ[189] ॥
12. ਭਿੰਨੀ ਰੈਣਿ[190] ਜਿਨਾ ਮਨਿ ਚਾਉ[191] ॥
13. ਸਿਖੀ[192] ਸਿਖਿਆ[193] ਗੁਰ ਵੀਚਾਰਿ [194] ॥
14. ਨਦਰੀ ਕਰਮਿ ਲਘਾਏ ਪਾਰਿ [195] ॥
15. ਕੋਲੂ[196] ਚਰਖਾ[197] ਚਕੀ[198] ਚਕੁ[199] ॥
16. ਥਲ[200] ਵਾਰੋਲੇ[201] ਬਹੁਤੁ ਅਗਤ ॥

[188] The Grace of Waheguru
[189] Optimism
[190] Cool night
[191] Those who are drenched with Waheguru's name
[192] Teachings (noun)
[193] Learnt (verb)
[194] Discussing God's name

Mehla 1.

1. vaa-in[181] chaylay nachan gur.
2. pair halaa-in fayrni[H] sir.
3. ·ud ud raavaa[182] jhaatai paa-ay.
4. vaykhai lok hasai ghar jaa-ay.
5. rotee-aa kaaran pooreh taal[183].
6. aap pachhaarheh[184] Dhartee naal.
7. gaavan[185] gopee-aa gaavan kaan[H].
8. gaavan seetaa raajay raam.
9. nirbha-o nirankaar sach naam.
10. jaa kaa kee-aa[186] sagal jahaan.
11. sayvak sayveh [187]karam[188] charhaa-o[189].
12. bhinnee rain[190] jinHaa man chaa-o[191].
13. sikhee[192] sikhi-aa[193] gur veechaar[194].
14. nadree karam laghaa-ay paar[195].
15. koloo[196] charkhaa[197] chakee[198] chak[199].
16. thal[200] vaarolay[201] bahut anant.

[195] To sail through the ocean of world
[196] Oil-press
[197] Spinning wheel
[198] Hand-mill, quern
[199] Potter's wheel
[200] Desert
[201] Whirlwind

17. ਲਾਟੂ²⁰² ਮਾਧਾਨੀਆ²⁰³ ਅਨਗਾਹ²⁰⁴ ॥
18. ਪੰਖੀ ਭਉਦੀਆ²⁰⁵ ਲੈਨਿ ਨ ਸਾਹ ॥
19. ਸੂਐ²⁰⁶ ਚਾੜਿ ਭਵਾਈਅਹਿ ਜੰਤ²⁰⁷ ॥
20. ਨਾਨਕ ਭਉਦਿਆ ਗਨਤ ਨ ਅੰਤ ॥
21. ਬੰਧਨ ²⁰⁸ ਬੰਧਿ²⁰⁹ ਭਵਾਏ ਸੋਇ ²¹⁰ ॥
22. ਪਇਐ ਕਿਰਤਿ²¹¹ ਨਚੈ ਸਭੁ ਕੋਇ ॥
23. ਨਚਿ ਨਚਿ ਹਸਹਿ ਚਲਹਿ ਸੇ ਰੋਇ ॥
24. ਉਡਿ ਨ ਜਾਹੀ ਸਿਧ²¹² ਨ ਹੋਹਿ ॥
25. ਨਚਣੁ ਕੁਦਣੁ ਮਨ ਕਾ ਚਾਉ ॥
26. ਨਾਨਕ ਜਿਨ ਮਨਿ ਭਉ²¹³ ਤਿਨਾ ਮਨਿ ਭਾਉ²¹⁴ ॥ ੨ ॥

17. लाटू²⁰² माधाणीआ²⁰³ अनगाह²⁰⁴ ॥
18. पंखी भउदीआ²⁰⁵ लैनि न साह ॥
19. सूऐ²⁰⁶ चाड़ि भवाईअहि जंत²⁰⁷ ॥
20. नानक भउदिआ गणत न अंत ॥
21. बंधन ²⁰⁸ बंधि²⁰⁹ भवाइ सोइ ²¹⁰ ॥
22. पइऐ किरति²¹¹ नचै सभु कोइ ॥
23. नचि नचि हसहि चलहि से रोइ ॥
24. उडि न जाही सिध²¹² न होहि ॥
25. नचणु कुदणु मन का चाउ ॥
26. नानक जिन मनि भउ²¹³ तिना मनि भाउ²¹⁴ ॥ २ ॥

17. laatoo[202] maaDhaanee-aa[203] angaah[204].
18. pankhee bha-udee-aa[205] lain na saah.
19. soo-ai[206] chaarh bhavaa-ee-ah jant[207].
20. naanak bha-udi-aa ganat na ant.
21. banDhan [208]banDh[209] bhavaa-ay so-ay[210].
22. pa-i-ai kirat[211] nachai sabh ko-ay.
23. nach nach haseh chaleh say ro-ay.
24. ud na jaahee siDh[212] na hohi.
25. nachan kudan man kaa chaa-o.
26. naanak jin[H] man bha-o[213] tin[H]aa man bhaa-o.[214] ||2||

---

[202] Tops
[203] Churning staves
[204] Threshers (machines which separate grain from the husks)
[205] Somersaulting

[206] Iron rods
[207] Beings, jugglers
[208] Bonds, entanglement
[209] Bound
[210] Those who are swung around

[211] According to one's karma
[212] Ideal man
[213] Fear
[214] Love

Theme	Literal Meaning

Sloak Mehla 1

The sloak depicts the scene of divine drama (based on Krishna's *ras lila*)

The space is a vast stage where Sun and Moon are the leading actors, the time moments are their heroines, air, water and fire are heroines' ornaments, and mines and vegetation-mountains are their make-up material.

The central theme of the drama is that despite the exciting romance of the above actors, the stage is colourless without the presence of the Name of Waheguru in the delivery of their dialogues.

Mehla 2

The sloak depicts the scene of the worldly drama

The earth too is a vast stage where ordinary people are acting and dancing under the direction of their fake teachers (directors). Their acts and dialogues are absolutely colourless and boring for they are missing the Name of Waheguru in their dialogue delivery.

Sloak Mehla 1

1. Hours are the dancing milkmaids, and quarters of the day represent Krishna and his herdsmen
2. The air, water and fire are their ornaments. Everyone is dancing to please their gods – Sun and Moon – the icons of changing time.
3. The vast earth with its wealth of mines and vegetation is a perfect snare for human beings.
4. A person who is devoid of true knowledge gets caught in the cobweb of time and is effectively doomed.

Mehla 2

1. The devotees play music and their guru's dance to their tunes.
2. Watching their steps, they jerk and move their heads.
3. These actors raise dust with their foot beat, which is settled on their hair.
4. Onlookers, amused by all this, laugh, taunt and go their way.
5. All this drama is performed to earn a few loaves of bread.
6. For these earnings they, sometimes, strike their heads against the ground.
7. The disguised milkmaids and Krishnas sing.
8. Disguised Sitas and Ramas sing as well (e.g., in Ram-lilas).
9. Eternally true play is of fearless and formless Waheguru.
10. Who is the sole creator of the Universe.
11. Devotees' pious actions are real offerings to the Creator.
12. The nights, which the true devotees spend in meditation are really cool and sweet.

13. The spiritual awakening comes with the light of Waheguru.
14. Yet all this is gifted to humans only by Waheguru's grace.
15. Oil-presses, spinning wheels, grinding stones and potters' wheels,
16. Endless strong winds and hurricanes of deserts,
17. The spinning-tops, the churning staves, the threshing frames,
18. Birds roving non-stop in the sky,
19. All beings made to spin on stakes
20. All these ceaselessly spin.
21. The bonds in which are bound, make them rove and whirl.
22. Bound to the chains of their karma all people swing around.
23. Those who selfishly make fun here – in acute agony shall they depart from this world.
24. These pranks (tricks) will give them no spiritual merit.
25. Dancing and frolicking (jumping around) give only temporary pleasure. They have no food for the soul.
26. Waheguru's love is nurtured only in those who abide in his fear.

ਪਉੜੀ ॥

1. ਨਾਉ ਤੇਰਾ ਨਿਰੰਕਾਰੁ ਹੈ ਨਾਇ ਲਇਐ ਨਰਕਿ ਨ ਜਾਈਐ ॥
2. ਜੀਉ²¹⁵ ਪਿੰਡੁ²¹⁶ ਸਭੁ ਤਿਸ ਦਾ ਦੇ²¹⁷ ਖਾਜੈ²¹⁸ ਆਖਿ ਗਵਾਈਐ ॥
3. ਜੇ ਲੋੜਹਿ ਚੰਗਾ ਆਪਣਾ ਕਰਿ ਪੁੰਨਹੁ²¹⁹ ਨੀਚੁ ਸਦਾਈਐ ²²⁰ ॥
4. ਜੇ ਜਰਵਾਣਾ²²¹ ਪਰਹਰੈ²²² ਜਰੁ²²³ ਵੇਸ²²⁴ ਕਰੇਦੀ ਆਈਐ ॥
5. ਕੋ ਰਹੈ ਨ²²⁵ ਭਰੀਐ ਪਾਈਐ²²⁶ ॥ ੫ ॥

Theme

Pauri

To be an ideal person, one must possess the qualities of humility, philanthropy and holiness.

---

²¹⁵ Soul
²¹⁶ Body
²¹⁷ What is given
²¹⁸ To eat
²¹⁹ Donation, to donate

ਪਉੜੀ ॥

1. ਨਾਉ ਤੇਰਾ ਨਿਰੰਕਾਰੁ ਹੈ ਨਾਇ ਲਇਐ ਨਰਕਿ ਨ ਜਾਈਐ ॥
2. ਜੀਉ²¹⁵ ਪਿੰਡੁ ²¹⁶ਸਭੁ ਤਿਸ ਦਾ ਦੇ²¹⁷ ਖਾਜੈ²¹⁸ ਆਖਿ ਗਵਾਈਐ ॥
3. ਜੇ ਲੋੜਹਿ ਚੰਗਾ ਆਪਣਾ ਕਰਿ ਪੁੰਨਹੁ²¹⁹ ਨੀਚੁ ਸਦਾਈਐ ²²⁰ ॥
4. ਜੇ ਜਰਵਾਣਾ²²¹ ਪਰਹਰੈ²²² ਜਰੁ²²³ ਵੇਸ²²⁴ ਕਰੇਦੀ ਆਈਐ ॥
5. ਕੋ ਰਹੈ ਨ²²⁵ ਭਰੀਐ ਪਾਈਐ²²⁶ ॥ ੫ ॥

Literal Meaning

Pauri

1. Waheguru is formless and dwelling on his name, saves one from the punishment of hell.
2. Both our soul and body belong to him. Whatever he bestows, we all do live on it. It is senseless to count his countless bounties.
3. If one seeks good for oneself, one should do good to others, give financial assistance to the poor and live in humility.
4. However hard one may plan to put off the inexorable (unavoidable) death, it shall still come disguised, if nothing else, at least through the wide open door of old age.
5. Indeed, no one lives here after he/she has lived the total count of breaths allotted to them.

Pauri.

1. naa-o ṯayraa nirankaar hai naa-ay la-i-ai narak na jaa-ee-ai.
2. jee-o²¹⁵ pind ²¹⁶sabh ṯis daa ḏay²¹⁷ khaajai²¹⁸ aakh gavaa-ee-ai.
3. jay loṛheh changa aapnaa kar punnhu²¹⁹ neech saḏaa-ee-ai²²⁰.
4. jay jarvaanaa²²¹ parharai²²² jar²²³ vays²²⁴ karaydee aa-ee-ai.
5. ko rahai na²²⁵ bharee-ai paa-ee-ai.²²⁶ ||5||

---

²²⁰ Humility
²²¹ Signs of old age, (wrinkles, weak eyesight, bent body, etc.)
²²² A try to get rid off
²²³ Old age

²²⁴ Disguise (disguise as death)
²²⁵ No one lives here forever
²²⁶ When one completes his/her breath

ਪੰਥੁ ਦਸਾਵਾ ਨਿਤ ਖੜੀ ਮੁੰਧ ਜੋਬਨਿ ਬਾਲੀ ਰਾਮ ਰਾਜੇ ॥

ਪੰਥੁ ਦਸਾਵਾ ਨਿਤ ਖੜੀ ਮੁੰਧ ਜੋਬਨਿ ਬਾਲੀ ਰਾਮ ਰਾਜੇ ॥

panth dasaavaa nit kharhee munDh joban baalee raam raajay.

I stand by the roadside, and ask the way; I am just a youthful bride
of my Master, the King of Kings.

ਹਰਿ ਹਰਿ ਨਾਮੁ ਚੇਤਾਇ ਗੁਰ ਹਰਿ ਮਾਰਗਿ ਚਾਲੀ ॥

ਹਰਿ ਹਰਿ ਨਾਮੁ ਚੇਤਾਇ ਗੁਰ ਹਰਿ ਮਾਰਗਿ ਚਾਲੀ ॥

har har naam chaytaa-ay gur har maarag chaalee.

The teacher-Guru has caused me to remember the
Name of Waheguru; I follow the true path which leads to Him.

ਮੇਰੈ ਮਨਿ ਤਨਿ ਨਾਮੁ ਆਧਾਰੁ ਹੈ ਹਉਮੈ ਬਿਖੁ ਜਾਲੀ ॥

ਮੇਰੈ ਮਨਿ ਤਨਿ ਨਾਮੁ ਆਧਾਰੁ ਹੈ ਹਉਮੈ ਬਿਖੁ ਜਾਲੀ ॥

mayrai man tan naam aaDhaar hai ha-umai bikh jaalee.

The name of Waheguru, is the support of my mind and body;
I have burnt away the poison of ego.

ਜਨ ਨਾਨਕ ਸਤਿਗੁਰ ਮੇਲਿ ਹਰਿ ਹਰਿ ਮਿਲਿਆ ਬਨਵਾਲੀ ॥੨॥

ਜਨ ਨਾਨਕ ਸਤਿਗੁਰ ਮੇਲਿ ਹਰਿ ਹਰਿ ਮਿਲਿਆ ਬਨਵਾਲੀ ॥ ੨ ॥

jan naanak satgur mayl har har mili-aa banvaalee. ||2||

O true teacher-Guru, unite me with Waheguru, unite me with
Him, who is ever adorned with garlands of flowers. ||2||

Pauri 6 with 2 sloaks
(Guru Nanak 2)

ਸਲੋਕ ਮਃ ੧ ॥

1. ਮੁਸਲਮਾਨਾ ਸਿਫਤਿ ਸਰੀਅਤਿ²²⁷ ਪੜਿ ਪੜਿ ਕਰਹਿ ਬੀਚਾਰੁ ॥

2. ਬੰਦੇ ਸੇ ਜਿ²²⁸ ਪਵਹਿ ਵਿਚਿ ਬੰਦੀ²²⁹ ਵੇਖਣ ਕਉ ਦੀਦਾਰੁ²³⁰ ॥

3. ਹਿੰਦੂ ਸਾਲਾਹੀ²³¹ ਸਾਲਾਹਨਿ²³² ਦਰਸਨਿ ਰੂਪਿ ਅਪਾਰੁ²³³ ॥

4. ਤੀਰਥਿ ਨਾਵਹਿ ਅਰਚਾ²³⁴ ਪੂਜਾ ਅਗਰ²³⁵ ਵਾਸੁ²³⁶ ਬਹਕਾਰੁ²³⁷ ॥

5. ਜੋਗੀ ਸੁੰਨਿ²³⁸ ਧਿਆਵਨਿ ਜੇਤੇ²³⁹ ਅਲਖ²⁴⁰ ਨਾਮੁ ਕਰਤਾਰੁ ॥

6. ਸੂਖਮ ਮੂਰਤਿ²⁴¹ ਨਾਮੁ ਨਿਰੰਜਨ²⁴² ਕਾਇਆ ਕਾ ਆਕਾਰੁ²⁴³ ॥

7. ਸਤੀਆ²⁴⁴ ਮਨਿ ਸੰਤੋਖੁ ਉਪਜੈ²⁴⁵ ਦੇਣੈ ਕੈ ਵੀਚਾਰਿ²⁴⁶ ॥

8. ਦੇ ਦੇ ਮੰਗਹਿ²⁴⁷ ਸਹਸਾ ਗੂਨਾ²⁴⁸ ਸੋਭ ਕਰੇ ਸੰਸਾਰੁ²⁴⁹ ॥

9. ਚੋਰਾ ਜਾਰਾ²⁵⁰ ਤੈ ਕੂੜਿਆਰਾ²⁵¹ ਖਾਰਾਬਾ ਵੇਕਾਰੁ²⁵² ॥

सलोक मः १ ॥

1. मुसलमाना सिफति सरीअति²²⁹ पड़ि पड़ि करहि बीचारु ॥

2. बंदे से जि²²⁶ पवहि विचि बंदी²²⁶ वेखण कउ दीदारु²³⁰ ॥

3. हिंदू सालाही²³¹ सालाहनि²³² दरसनि रूपि अपारु²³³ ॥

4. तीरथि नावहि अरचा²³⁴ पूजा अगर²³⁵ वासु²³⁶ बहकारु²³⁷ ॥

5. जोगी मुनि²³⁶ धिआवनि जेते²³⁶ अलख²⁴⁰ नामु करतारु ॥

6. सूखम मूरति²⁴¹ नामु निरंजन²⁴² काइआ का आकारु²⁴³ ॥

7. सतीआ²⁴⁴ मनि संतोखु उपजै²⁴⁵ देणै कै वीचारि²⁴⁶ ॥

8. दे दे मंगहि²⁴⁷ सहसा गुणा²⁴⁸ सोभ करे संसारु²⁴⁹ ॥

9. चोरा जारा²⁵⁰ तै कूड़िआरा²⁵¹ खाराबा वेकारु²⁵² ॥

Sloak Mehla 1.

1. musalmaanaa sifat saree-at[227] parh parh karahi beechaar.

2. banday say je[228] paveh vich bandee[229] vaykhan ka-o deedaar[230].

3. hindoo saalaahee[231] saalaahan[232] darsan roop apaar[233].

4. tirath naaveh archaa[234] poojaa agar[235] vaas[236] behkaar[237].

5. jogee munn[238] Dhi-aavni[H] jaytay[239] alakh [240]naam kartaar.

6. sookham moorat[241] naam niranjan[242] kaa-i-aa kaa aakaar[243].

7. satee-aa[244] man santokh upjai[245] daynai kai veechaar[246].

8. day day mangeh[247] sahsaa goonaa[248] sobh karay sansaar[249].

9. choraa jaaraa[250] tai koorhi-aaraa[251] khaaraabaa vaykaar[252].

---

[227] Shariat, the Islamic law
[228] Those are the true devotees
[229] Fall in captivity of Islamic law
[230] Eager to have an audience with God
[231] Qualities (noun)
[232] To praise
[233] Many facets/many forms
[234] Flower-offering
[235] Eagle-wood

[236] Perfume
[237] To spread
[238] Void, meditation in a special state of mind
[239] Whose
[240] Unseen
[241] One who cannot be seen with our working faculties
[242] Immaculate
[243] To give a formal body form
[244] Generous

[245] Contentment is produced
[246] Thoughts to give in charity
[247] They give charity and then ask in return
[248] Thousand times more
[249] And also ask for worldly honour
[250] Adulterers
[251] Perjurer
[252] Evil-doers and sinners

10. ਇਕਿ[੨੫੩] ਹੋਦਾਂ[੨੫੪] ਖਾਇ ਚਲਹਿ ਐਥਾਊ ਤਿਨਾ ਭੀ ਕਾਈ[੨੫੫] ਕਾਰ[੨੫੬] ॥
11. ਜਲਿ ਥਲਿ ਜੀਆ ਪੁਰੀਆ [੨੫੭] ਲੋਆ[੨੫੮] ਆਕਾਰਾ[੨੫੯] ਆਕਾਰ[੨੬੦] ॥
12. ਓਇ[੨੬੧] ਜਿ ਆਖਹਿ ਸੁ ਤੂੰਹੈ ਜਾਣਹਿ ਤਿਨਾ ਭਿ ਤੇਰੀ ਸਾਰ[੨੬੨] ॥
13. ਨਾਨਕ ਭਗਤਾ ਭੁਖ ਸਾਲਾਹਣੁ[੨੬੩] ਸਚੁ ਨਾਮੁ ਆਧਾਰੁ ॥
14. ਸਦਾ ਅਨੰਦਿ ਰਹਹਿ ਦਿਨੁ ਰਾਤੀ ਗੁਣਵੰਤਿਆ ਪਾ ਛਾਰੁ [੨੬੪] ॥ ੧ ॥

ਮਃ ੧ ॥

1. ਮਿਟੀ ਮੁਸਲਮਾਨ ਕੀ ਪੇੜੈ[੨੬੫] ਪਈ ਕੁਮ੍ਹਿਆਰ [੨੬੬] ॥
2. ਘੜਿ ਭਾਂਡੇ[੨੬੭] ਇਟਾ ਕੀਆ ਜਲਦੀ ਕਰੇ ਪੁਕਾਰ ॥
3. ਜਲਿ ਜਲਿ ਰੋਵੈ ਬਪੁੜੀ[੨੬੮] ਝੜਿ ਝੜਿ[੨੬੯] ਪਵਹਿ ਅੰਗਿਆਰ[੨੭੦] ॥
4. ਨਾਨਕ ਜਿਨਿ ਕਰਤੈ ਕਾਰਣੁ ਕੀਆ[੨੭੧] ਸੋ ਜਾਣੈ ਕਰਤਾਰੁ ॥ ੨ ॥

[253] One mentioned above
[254] What one had
[255] Any
[256] Deeds (good deeds)
[257] Worlds
[258] Universe
[259] Tiniest of the tiny being

10. इकि[२५३] होदा[२५४] खाइ चलहि ऐथाऊ तिना भी काइी[२५५] कार[२५६] ॥
11. जलि थलि जीआ पुरीआ [२५७] लोआ[२५८] आकारा[२५९] आकार[२६०] ॥
12. एइि[२६१] जि आखहि सु तूंहै जाणहि तिना भि तेरी सार[२६२] ॥
13. नानक भगता भुख सालाहणु[२६३] सचु नामु आधारु ॥
14. सदा अनमदि रहहि दिनु राती गुणवंतिआ पा छारु [२६४] ॥ १ ॥

मः १ ॥

1. मिटी मुसलमान की पेड़ै[२६५] पड़ी कुम्हिआर [२६६] ॥
2. घड़ि भाँडे[२६७] इिटा कीआ जलदी करे पुकार ॥
3. जलि जलि रोवै बपुड़ी[२६८] झड़ि झड़ि[२६९] पवहि अंगिआर[२७०] ॥
4. नानक जिनि करतै कारणु कीआ[२७१] सो जाणै करतारु ॥ २ ॥

[260] Atoms
[261] The people
[262] Protection
[263] The hunger to sing Waheguru's glories
[264] The ash of the feet of virtuous
[265] Clod, knead
[266] Potter

10. ik[253] hodaa[254] khaa-ay chaleh aithaa-oo tinaa bhe kaa-ee[255] kaar[256].
11. jal thal jee-aa puree-aa [257]lo-aa[258] aakaaraa[259] aakaar[260].
12. o-ay[261] je aakhahi so too^{N}hai jaaneh tinaa bhe tayree saar[262].
13. naanak bhagtaa bhukh saalaahan[263] sach naam aaDhaar.
14. sadaa anand raheh din raatee gunvanti-aa paa chhaar.[264] ||1||

Mehla 1.

1. mitee musalmaan kee payrhai[265] pa-ee kum^{H}i-aar[266].
2. gharh bhaa^{N}day[267] itaa kee-aa jaldee karay pukaar.
3. jal jal rovai bapurhee[268] jharh jharh[269] paveh angi-aar[270].
4. naanak jin kartai kaaran kee-aa[271] so jaanai kartaar. ||2||

[267] Fashioning vessels
[268] Poor clay
[269] By ferocity
[270] Spark of fire
[271] The cause of creation

Theme	Literal Meaning

Sloak Mehla 1

The true devotees are always engrossed to meditate on the name of Waheguru and his Word is their saviour.

Sloak Mehla 1

1. The Muslim praise their religious law 'Shariat', over and over again; they read and reflect over it.
2. Those people are a chosen few who willingly embrace Waheguru's given bondage, to have an audience of him.
3. Hindus love God for his unsurpassed existence and unmatched beauty.
4. For obtaining his grace they bathe at holy places, make offerings to deities and burn incense before their images.
5. The yogis live in the void and try numerous yogic postures. They call him unknowable and unfathomable.
6. For satisfying their limited knowledge, they make God's images and worship him in that form.
7. The compassionate people are satisfied with offerings and alms.
8. They, normally, give a few unimportant objects in charity and in return they expect multifold returns, and further long for worldly honour as well.
9. There are, besides, thieves, enticers, liars and wicked sinners.
10. Then there are people who knowingly or unknowingly waste whatever little merit they may have earned.
11. What worth are then their lives?
12. Life exists in water, on land, in the three regions, in all spheres of the universe in multitude forms.
13. You are the only one who knows the numerous demands of all these creatures.
14. Your true devotees ever seek to meditate on your name; your name is, indeed, their support.
15. They live in everlasting happiness and always wish to be the dust at the feet of the blessed ones.

Theme	Literal Meaning

Mehla 2

When a person dies, the rituals of cremation or burial do not effect his/her karmas committed during his/her life time.

Mehla 2

1. When the clay of Muslims' graves is mounted on the potter's wheel,
2. And is shaped into pots and bricks, then, when baked in furnace, it cries in pain.
3. When this unlucky clay is baked sparks from it fly around, as if these were clay's own tears.
4. The Almighty Creator, is the only one who knows what is in store for human beings and why.

ਪਉੜੀ ॥

1. ਬਿਨੁ ਸਤਿਗੁਰ ਕਿਨੈ ਨ ਪਾਇਓ ਬਿਨੁ ਸਤਿਗੁਰ ਕਿਨੈ ਨ ਪਾਇਆ ॥

2. ਸਤਿਗੁਰ ਵਿਚਿ ਆਪੁ ਰਖਿਓਨੁ ਕਰਿ ਪਰਗਟੁ ਆਖਿ ਸੁਣਾਇਆ ੨੭੨ ॥

3. ਸਤਿਗੁਰ ਮਿਲਿਐ ਸਦਾ ਮੁਕਤੁ ਹੈ ਜਿਨਿ ਵਿਚਹੁ ਮੋਹੁ ਚੁਕਾਇਆ ੨੭੩ ॥

4. ਉਤਮੁ ਏਹੁ ਬੀਚਾਰੁ ਹੈ ਜਿਨਿ ਸਚੇ ਸਿਉ ਚਿਤੁ ਲਾਇਆ ॥

5. ਜਗਜੀਵਨੁ ੨੭੪ ਦਾਤਾ ਪਾਇਆ ॥ ੬ ॥

पउड़ी ॥

1. बिनु सतिगुर किनै न पाइउ बिनु सतिगुर किनै न पाइआ ॥

2. सतिगुर विचि आपु रखिएनु करि परगटु आखि सुणाइआ २९२ ॥

3. सतिगुर मिलिऐ सदा मुकतु है जिनि विचहु मोहु चुकाइआ २९३ ॥

4. उतमु इहु बीचारु है जिनि सचे सिउ चितु लाइआ ॥

5. जगजीवनु २९४ दाता पाइआ ॥ ६ ॥

Pauri.

1. bin sa<u>t</u>gur kinai na paa-i-o bin sa<u>t</u>gur kinai na paa-i-aa.

2. sa<u>t</u>gur vich aap ra<u>kh</u>i-on kar pargat aa<u>kh</u> sunaa-i-aa[272].

3. sa<u>t</u>gur mili-ai sa<u>d</u>aa muka<u>t</u> hai jin vichahu moh chukaa-i-aa[273].

4. u<u>t</u>am ayhu beechaar hai jin sachay si-o chi<u>t</u> laa-i-aa.

5. jagjeevan[274] <u>d</u>aa<u>t</u>aa paa-i-aa. ||6||

Theme

Pauri

People who remember Waheguru from their hearts have certainly realised him.

Literal Meaning

Pauri

1. Without the recourse of the true teacher-Guru, no one has ever got anywhere near Waheguru.

2. Waheguru himself resides in true teacher-gurus, and has made this truth known to the world through the *shabad*.

3. Teachings of the true-guru unveil modes of salvation; teachings also suggest the methods of getting rid of infatuations.

4. The highest ideal of humans should be to seek a communion with Waheguru, who is eternally true.

5. The communion enables one to realise the Almighty, who is the sole master of all the bounties.

---

[272] Open declaration

[273] The ego has vanished

[274] The life of the world

ਗੁਰਮੁਖਿ ਪਿਆਰੇ ਆਇ ਮਿਲੁ ਮੈ ਚਿਰੀ ਵਿਛੁੰਨੇ ਰਾਮ ਰਾਜੇ ॥

ਗੁਰਮੁਖਿ ਪਿਆਰੇ ਆਇ ਮਿਲੁ ਮੈ ਚਿਰੀ ਵਿਛੁੰਨੇ ਰਾਮ ਰਾਜੇ ॥

gurmukh pi-aaray aa-ay mil mai chiree vichhunay raam raajay.

O my Love, come and meet me; I have been separated from
You for so long, O my King of Kings.

ਮੇਰਾ ਮਨੁ ਤਨੁ ਬਹੁਤੁ ਬੈਰਾਗਿਆ ਹਰਿ ਨੈਣ ਰਸਿ ਭਿੰਨੇ ॥

ਮੇਰਾ ਮਨੁ ਤਨੁ ਬਹੁਤੁ ਬੈਰਾਗਿਆ ਹਰਿ ਨੈਣ ਰਸਿ ਭਿੰਨੇ ॥

mayraa man tan bahut bairaagi-aa har nain ras bhinnay.

My mind and body are sad; my eyes are wet with tears of separation.

ਮੈ ਹਰਿ ਪ੍ਰਭੁ ਪਿਆਰਾ ਦਸਿ ਗੁਰੁ ਮਿਲਿ ਹਰਿ ਮਨੁ ਮੰਨੇ ॥

ਮੈ ਹਰਿ ਪ੍ਰਭੁ ਪਿਆਰਾ ਦਸਿ ਗੁਰੁ ਮਿਲਿ ਹਰਿ ਮਨੁ ਮੰਨੇ ॥

mai har parabh pi-aaraa das gur mil har man mannay.

Arrange an audience with my God, who is my true love, O! my
teacher-Guru; meeting Waheguru my mind blossoms with happiness.

ਹਉ ਮੂਰਖੁ ਕਾਰੈ ਲਾਈਆ ਨਾਨਕ ਹਰਿ ਕੰਮੇ ॥੩॥

ਹਉ ਮੂਰਖੁ ਕਾਰੈ ਲਾਈਆ ਨਾਨਕ ਹਰਿ ਕੰਮੇ ॥ ੩ ॥

ha-o moorakh kaarai laa-ee-aa naanak har kammay. ||3||

I am ignorant and immature, but Waheguru has appointed me to
perform His multitude services. ||3||

*Pauri 7 with 2 sloaks
(Guru Nanak 1, Guru Angad 1)*

ਸਲੋਕ ਮਃ ੧ ॥

1. ਹਉ^{੨੭੫} ਵਿਚਿ ਆਇਆ ਹਉ ਵਿਚਿ ਗਇਆ ॥
2. ਹਉ ਵਿਚਿ ਜੰਮਿਆ ਹਉ ਵਿਚਿ ਮੁਆ ॥
3. ਹਉ ਵਿਚਿ ਦਿਤਾ ਹਉ ਵਿਚਿ ਲਇਆ ॥
4. ਹਉ ਵਿਚਿ ਖਟਿਆ ਹਉ ਵਿਚਿ ਗਇਆ^{੨੭੬} ॥
5. ਹਉ ਵਿਚਿ ਸਚਿਆਰੁ^{੨੭੭} ਕੁੜਿਆਰੁ^{੨੭੮} ॥
6. ਹਉ ਵਿਚਿ ਪਾਪ ਪੁੰਨ ਵੀਚਾਰੁ^{੨੭੯} ॥
7. ਹੁ ਵਿਚਿ ਨਰਕਿ ਸੁਰਗਿ ਅਵਤਾਰੁ^{੨੮੦} ॥
8. ਹਉ ਵਿਚਿ ਹਸੈ ਹਉ ਵਿਚਿ ਰੋਵੈ ॥
9. ਹਉ ਵਿਚਿ ਭਰੀਐ^{੨੮੧} ਹਉ ਵਿਚਿ ਧੋਵੈ^{੨੮੨} ॥
10. ਹਉ ਵਿਚਿ ਜਾਤੀ^{੨੮੩} ਜਿਨਸੀ^{੨੮੪} ਖੋਵੈ^{੨੮੫} ॥
11. ਹਉ ਵਿਚਿ ਮੂਰਖੁ ਹਉ ਵਿਚਿ ਸਿਆਣਾ ॥
12. ਮੋਖ^{੨੮੬} ਮੁਕਤਿ^{੨੮੭} ਕੀ ਸਾਰ ਨ ਜਾਣਾ ॥
13. ਹਉ ਵਿਚਿ ਮਾਇਆ^{੨੮੮} ਹਉ ਵਿਚਿ ਛਾਇਆ^{੨੮੯} ॥
14. ਹਉਮੈ ਕਰਿ ਕਰਿ ਜੰਤ ਉਪਾਇਆ <u>੨੯੦</u> ॥
15. ਹਉਮੈ ਬੂਝੈ^{੨੯੧} ਤਾ ਦਰੁ ਸੂਝੈ <u>੨੯੨</u> ॥
16. ਗਿਆਨ ਵਿਹੂਣਾ^{੨੯੩} <u>ਕਥਿ ਕਥਿ ਲੂਝੈ</u> <u>੨੯੪</u> ॥
17. ਨਾਨਕ ਹੁਕਮੀ ਲਿਖੀਐ ਲੇਖੁ ॥
18. <u>ਜੇਹਾ ਵੇਖਹਿ ਤੇਹਾ ਵੇਖੁ</u> <u>੨੯੫</u> ॥ ੧ ॥

---

²⁷⁵ Pride, ego
²⁷⁶ Loss
²⁷⁷ True
²⁷⁸ False
²⁷⁹ Reflection of virtue or sin
²⁸⁰ To fall
²⁸¹ To get soiled

सलोक मः १ ॥

1. हउ^{२७५} विचि आइआ हउ विचि गइआ ॥
2. हउ विचि जंमिआ हउ विचि मुआ ॥
3. हउ विचि दिता हउ विचि लइआ ॥
4. हउ विचि खटिआ हउ विचि गइआ^{२७६} ॥
5. हउ विचि सचिआरु^{२७७} कूड़िआरु^{२७८} ॥
6. हउ विचि पाप पुंन वीचारु^{२७९} ॥
7. हु विचि नरकि सुरगि अवतारु^{२८०} ॥
8. हउ विचि हसै हउ विचि रोवै ॥
9. हउ विचि भरीऐ^{२८१} हउ विचि धोवै^{२८२} ॥
10. हउ विचि जाती^{२८३} जिनसी^{२८४} खोवै^{२८५} ॥
11. हउ विचि मूरखु हउ विचि सिआणा ॥
12. मोख ^{२८६}मुकति^{२८७} की सार न जाणा ॥
13. हउ विचि माइआ^{२८८} हउ विचि छाइआ^{२८९} ॥
14. हउमै करि करि जंत उपाइआ <u>२९०</u> ॥
15. हउमै बूझै^{२९१} ता दरु सूझै <u>२९२</u> ॥
16. गिआन विहूणा^{२९३} <u>कथि कथि लूझै</u> <u>२९४</u> ॥
17. नानक हुकमी लिखीऐ लेखु ॥
18. <u>जेहा वेखहि तेहा वेखु</u> <u>२९५</u> ॥ १ ॥

---

²⁸² To wash off
²⁸³ Castes
²⁸⁴ Clans
²⁸⁵ To change
²⁸⁶ Salvation
²⁸⁷ Emancipation
²⁸⁸ Illusion, maya

Sloak Mehla 1.

1. ha-o²⁷⁵ vich aa-i-aa. ha-o vich ga-i-aa.
2. ha-o vich jammi-aa ha-o vich mu-aa.
3. ha-o vich ditaa ha-o vich la-i-aa.
4. ha-o vich khati-aa ha-o vich ga-i-aa²⁷⁶.
5. ha-o vich sachiaar²⁷⁷ koorhi-aar²⁷⁸.
6. ha-o vich paap punn veechaar²⁷⁹.
7. ha-o vich narak surag avtaar²⁸⁰.
8. ha-o vich hasai ha-o vich rovai.
9. ha-o vich bhaaree-ai²⁸¹ ha-o vich Dhovai²⁸².
10. ha-o vich jaatee²⁸³ jinsee²⁸⁴ khovai²⁸⁵.
11. ha-o vich moorakh ha-o vich si-aanaa.
12. mokh ²⁸⁶mukat kee²⁸⁷ saar na jaanaa.
13. ha-o vich maa-i-aa²⁸⁸ ha-o vich chhaa-i-aa²⁸⁹.
14. ha-umai kar kar jant upaa-i-aa²⁹⁰.
15. ha-umai boojhai²⁹¹ taa dar soojhai²⁹².
16. gi-aan vihoonaa²⁹³ kath kath loojhai²⁹⁴.
17. naanak hukmee likhee-ai laykh.
18. jayhaa vaykheh tayhaa vaykh.²⁹⁵ ||1||

---

²⁸⁹ Delusion
²⁹⁰ To get entangled in transmigration
²⁹¹ To know, to understand
²⁹² Portal of salvation, the house of God
²⁹³ Without knowledge
²⁹⁴ Foul talks and ill-conceived fights
²⁹⁵ To mould one according to one's wish

ਮਹਲਾ ੨ ॥

1. ਹਉਮੈ ਏਹਾ ਜਾਤਿ ਹੈ ²⁹⁶ਹਉਮੈ ਕਰਮ ਕਮਾਹਿ²⁹⁷ ॥
2. ਹੁਮੈ ਏਈ ਬੰਧਨਾ ²⁹⁸ਫਿਰਿ ਫਿਰਿ ਜੋਨੀ ਪਾਹਿ ॥
3. ਹਉਮੈ ਕਿਥਹੁ²⁹⁹ ਉਪਜੈ³⁰⁰ ਕਿਤੁ ਸੰਜਮਿ³⁰¹ ਇਹ ਜਾਇ³⁰² ॥
4. ਹਉਮੈ ਏਹੋ ਹੁਕਮੁ ਹੈ ਪਇਐ ਕਿਰਤਿ³⁰³ ਫਿਰਹਿ³⁰⁴ ॥
5. ਹਉਮੈ ਦੀਰਘ ਰੋਗੁ³⁰⁵ ਹੈ ਦਾਰੂ ਭੀ ਇਸੁ ਮਾਹਿ³⁰⁶ ॥
6. ਕਿਰਪਾ ਕਰੇ ਜੇ ਆਪਣੀ ਤਾ ਗੁਰ ਕਾ ਸਬਦੁ ਕਮਾਹਿ³⁰² ॥
7. ਨਾਨਕੁ ਕਹੈ ਸੁਣਹੁ ਜਨਹੁ ਇਤੁ ਸੰਜਮਿ³⁰⁸ ਦੁਖ ਜਾਹਿ ॥ ੨ ॥

महला २ ॥

1 हउमै इेहा जाति है ²⁹⁶हउमै करम कमाहि²⁹⁷ ॥
2. हुमै इेई बंधना ²⁹⁸फिरि फिरि जोनी पाहि ॥
3. हउमै किथहु²⁹⁹ उपजै³⁰⁰ कितु संजमि³⁰¹ इह जाइ³⁰² ॥
4. हउमै इेहो हुकमु है पइिऐ किरति³⁰³ फिराहि ³⁰⁴ ॥
5. हउमै दीरघ रोगु ³⁰⁵है दारू भी इसु माहि ³⁰⁶ ॥
6. किरपा करे जे आपणी ता गुर का सबदु कमाहि³⁰⁷ ॥
7. नानकु कहै सुणहु जनहु इतु संजमि³⁰⁸ दुख जाहि ॥ २ ॥

Mehla 2.

1. ha-umai ayhaa jaat hai [296]ha-umai karam kamaahi[297].
2. ha-umai ay-ee banDhnaa [298]fir fir jonee paahi.
3. ha-umai kithhu[299] oopjai[300] kit sanjam[301] ih jaa-ay[302].
4. ha-umai ayho hukam hai pa-i-ai kirat[303] firaahi[304].
5. ha-umai deeragh rog [305]hai daaroo bhee is maahi[306].
6. kirpaa karay jay aapnee taa gur kaa sabad kamaah[307].
7. naanak kahai sunhu janhu it sanjam[308] dukh jaah. ||2||

---

[296] The trait of ego
[297] To get involved
[298] Bondage
[299] From where
[300] Life

[301] Cycle of
[302] Death
[303] Karmas
[304] To wander
[305] Cancer

[306] Self-curing medicine
[307] To know
[308] Mode

Theme	Literal Meaning

Sloak Mehla 1

Ego is the main cause of man's separation from God, which then results in pain and grief.

Mehla 2

It is a deadly cancer, which gives unbearable suffering.

Sloak Mehla 1

1. People walk up in ego and fall down in ego.
2. They live in ego and die in ego.
3. They give alms in ego and accept charity in ego.
4. They make livelihood in ego and spend it in ego.
5. They speak truth in ego and utter lie in ego.
6. They reflect virtue in ego and commit sin in ego.
7. They enter hell in ego and go to heaven in ego.
8. They laugh in ego and cry in ego.
9. They get soiled in ego and stay cleaner in ego.
10. They get tangled in caste prejudices and lose the true path.
11. In ego are involved the wise and the foolish.
12. Ego deprives one's hope of deliverance.
13. Ego involves one in maya; in ego does one stay deluded.
14. Ego lets no one to be free from the cycle of transmigration.
15. Those who overcome ego, reach the portal of salvation.
16. Devoid of wisdom one wanders in wilderness.
17. The destiny is shaped by Waheguru's orders.
18. Yet people see whatever they want to see.

Mehla 2

1. It is the inherent roots of ego that one irresistibly gets involved in.
2. It is the bondage of ego that triggers off the cycle of transmigration.
3. From where ego begets? And how does it perish?
4. Ego breeds bad actions and shapes harmful operations.
5. Ego is a cancer and no medicine works on it.
6. It is only with the grace of Waheguru that one is attuned to his Shabad.
7. And it is the shabad that cures the pain of vices.

ਪਉੜੀ ॥

1. ਸੇਵ ਕੀਤੀ ਸੰਤੋਖੀਈਂ ੩੦੯ ਜਿਨੀ ਸਚੋ ਸਚੁ ਧਿਆਇਆ ॥

2. ਉਨੀ੩੧੦ ਮੰਦੈ੩੧੧ ਪੈਰੁ ਨ ਰਖਿਓ ਕਰਿ ਸੁਕ੍ਰਿਤੁ੩੧੨ ਧਰਮੁ ਕਮਾਇਆ ੩੧੩ ॥

3. ਉਨੀ ਦੁਨੀਆ ਤੋੜੇ ਬੰਧਨਾ ੩੧੪ ਅੰਨੁ ਪਾਣੀ ਥੋੜਾ ਖਾਇਆ ॥

4. ਤੂੰ ਬਖਸੀਸੀ ੩੧੫ ਅਗਲਾ੩੧੬ ਨਿਤ ਦੇਵਹਿ ੩੧੭ ਚੜਹਿ ਸਵਾਇਆ ੩੧੮ ॥

5. ਵਡਿਆਈੀ੩੧੯ ਵਡਾ੩੨੦ ਪਾਇਆ ॥ ੭ ॥

ਪਉੜੀ ॥

1. सेव कीती संतोखीईं ੩੦੯ जिनी सचो सचु धिआइआ ॥

2. उनी੩੧੦ मंदै੩੧੧ पैरु न रखिए करि सुक्रितु੩੧੨ धरमु कमाइआ ੩੧੩ ॥

3. उनी दुनीआ तोड़े बंधना ੩੧੪ अंनु पाणी थोड़ा खाइआ ॥

4. तूं बखसीसी ੩੧੫ अगला੩੧੬ नित देवहि ੩੧੭ चड़हि सवाइआ ੩੧੮ ॥

5. वडिआई੩੧੯ वडा੩੨੦ पाइआ ॥ ੭ ॥

Pauri.

1. sayv keetee santokhee-ee[N] [309]jin[H]ee sacho sach Dhi-aa-i-aa.

2. on[H]ee[310] mandai[311] pair na rakhi-o kar sukarit[312] Dharam kamaa-i-aa[313].

3. on[H]ee dunee-aa torhay banDhnaa [314]ann paanee thorhaa khaa-i-aa.

4. too[N] bakhseesee [315]aglaa[316] nit dayveh [317]charheh savaa-i-aa[318].

5. vadi-aa-ee[319] vadaa[320] paa-i-aa. ||7||

Theme

Pauri

The perfect human beings are those who can freely communicate with Waheguru

Literal Meaning

Pauri

1. The devotion of the truthful ones alone meets Waheguru's approval, as that rests on truth and truth alone.
2. They tread not the evil path, and earn their livelihood through honest means.
3. They break all worldly bondage and subsist on meagre provision.
4. Waheguru is the provider of all bounties, he alone bestows these daily on his devotees.
5. It is only by cultivating virtues that people get Waheguru's audience.

---

[309] Contended people
[310] Those
[311] Sin
[312] Virtuous acts

[313] Piety is earned
[314] To break their bondage
[315] The bestower of Grace
[316] Great

[317] Every day
[318] Increase manifolds
[319] Praises of God
[320] Waheguru

ਗੁਰ ਅੰਮ੍ਰਿਤ ਭਿੰਨੀ ਦੇਹੁਰੀ ਅੰਮ੍ਰਿਤੁ ਬੁਰਕੇ ਰਾਮ ਰਾਜੇ ॥

ਗੁਰ ਅੰਮ੍ਰਿਤ ਭਿੰਨੀ ਦੇਹੁਰੀ ਅੰਮ੍ਰਿਤੁ ਬੁਰਕੇ ਰਾਮ ਰਾਜੇ ॥

gur amrit bhinnee dayhuree amrit burkay raam raajay.

Waheguru has a vast reservior of ambrosial nectar;
He sprinkles it upon me, He is indeed King of Kings.

ਜਿਨਾ ਗੁਰਬਾਣੀ ਮਨਿ ਭਾਈਆ ਅੰਮ੍ਰਿਤਿ ਛਕਿ ਛਕੇ ॥

ਜਿਨਾ ਗੁਰਬਾਣੀ ਮਨਿ ਭਾਈਆ ਅੰਮ੍ਰਿਤਿ ਛਕਿ ਛਕੇ ॥

jinaa gurbaanee man bhaa-ee-aa amrit chhak chhakay.

Those whose minds are blessed with the word of the shabad,
they are ever drinking nectar of His name.

ਗੁਰ ਤੁਠੈ ਹਰਿ ਪਾਇਆ ਚੂਕੇ ਧਕ ਧਕੇ ॥

ਗੁਰ ਤੁਠੈ ਹਰਿ ਪਾਇਆ ਚੂਕੇ ਧਕ ਧਕੇ ॥

gur tuthai har paa-i-aa chookay Dhak Dhakay.

If Waheguru himself so wishes only then we realise Him,
and thereafter do not wander in wilderness.

ਹਰਿ ਜਨੁ ਹਰਿ ਹਰਿ ਹੋਇਆ ਨਾਨਕੁ ਹਰਿ ਇਕੇ ॥੪॥੯॥੧੬॥

ਹਰਿ ਜਨੁ ਹਰਿ ਹਰਿ ਹੋਇਆ ਨਾਨਕੁ ਹਰਿ ਇਕੇ ॥ ੪ ॥ ੯ ॥ ੧੬ ॥

har jan har har ho-i-aa naanak har ikay. ||4||9||16||

When a devotee merges in his Master then the diference between
the two is eliminated. ||4||9||16||

*Pauri 8 with 2 sloaks
(Guru Nanak 2)*

ਸਲੋਕ ਮਃ ੧ ॥

1. ਪੁਰਖਾਂ³²¹ ਬਿਰਖਾਂ³²² ਤੀਰਥਾਂ³²³ ਤਟਾਂ³²⁴ ਮੇਘਾਂ³²⁵ ਖੇਤਾਂਹ³²⁶ ॥

2. ਦੀਪਾਂ³²⁷ ਲੋਆਂ³²⁸ ਮੰਡਲਾਂ³²⁹ ਖੰਡਾਂ³³⁰ ਵਰਭੰਡਾਂਹ³³¹ ॥

3. ਅੰਡਜ³³² ਜੇਰਜ³³³ ਉਤਭੁਜਾਂ³³⁴ ਖਾਣੀ³³⁵ ਸੇਤਜਾਂਹ³³⁶ ॥

4. ਸੋ ਮਿਤਿ ³³⁷ਜਾਣੈ ਨਾਨਕਾ ਸਰਾਂ³³⁸ ਮੇਰਾਂ³³⁹ ਜੰਤਾਹ³⁴⁰ ॥

5. ਨਾਨਕ ਜੰਤ ਉਪਾਇ ਕੈ ³⁴¹ਸੰਮਾਲੇ ਸਭਨਾਹ ॥

6. ਜਿਨਿ³⁴² ਕਰਤੈ ਕਰਣਾ ਕੀਆ ਚਿੰਤਾ ਭਿ ਕਰਨੀ ਤਾਹ³⁴³ ॥

7. ਸੋ ਕਰਤਾ ਚਿੰਤਾ ਕਰੇ ਜਿਨਿ ਉਪਾਇਆ ਜਗੁ ॥

8. ਤਿਸੁ ਜੋਹਾਰੀ ³⁴⁴ਸੁਅਸਤਿ³⁴⁵ ਤਿਸੁ ਤਿਸੁ ਦੀਬਾਣੁ³⁴⁶ ਅਭਗੁ³⁴⁷ ॥

9. ਨਾਨਕ ਸਚੇ ਨਾਮ ਬਿਨੁ ਕਿਆ ਟਿਕਾ ³⁴⁸ਕਿਆ ਤਗੁ³⁴⁹ ॥ ੧ ॥

---

³²¹ Human beings
³²² Vegetation
³²³ Holy places
³²⁴ Banks of sacred streams
³²⁵ Clouds
³²⁶ Farms
³²⁷ Islands
³²⁸ Spheres
³²⁹ Universe
³³⁰ Continents

सलोक मः १ ॥

1. पुरखाँ³²¹ बिरखाँ³²² तीरथाँ³²³ तटाँ³²⁴ मेघाँ³²⁵ खेताँह³²⁶ ॥

2. दीपाँ³²⁷ लोआँ³²⁸ मंडलाँ³²⁹ खंडाँ³³⁰ वरभंडाँह³³¹ ॥

3. अंडज³³² जेरज³³³ उतभुजाँ³³⁴ खाणी³³⁵ सेतजाँह³³⁶ ॥

4. सो मिति ³³⁷जाणै नानका सराँ³³⁸ मेराँ³³⁹ जंताह³⁴⁰ ॥

5. नानक जंत उपाइ कै ³⁴¹संमाले सभनाह ॥

6. जिनि³⁴² करतै करणा कीआ चिंता भि करणी ताह³⁴³ ॥

7. सो करता चिंता करे जिनि उपाइआ जगु ॥

8. तिसु जोहारी ³⁴⁴सुअसति³⁴⁵ तिसु तिसु दीबाणु³⁴⁶ अभगु³⁴⁷ ॥

9. नानक सचे नाम बिनु किआ टिका ³⁴⁸किआ तगु³⁴⁹ ॥ १ ॥

---

³³¹ Solar system
³³² Egg-born
³³³ Womb-born
³³⁴ Seed-born
³³⁵ Process of creation
³³⁶ Sweat-born
³³⁷ Their condition
³³⁸ Oceans
³³⁹ Mountains
³⁴⁰ Sentient beings, those who breathe to live

Sloak Mehla 1.

1. purkhaa[N321] birkhaa[N322] teerthaa[N323] tataa[N324] mayghaa[N325] khaytaa[N]h[326].

2. deepaa[N327] lo-aa[N328] mandlaa[N329] khandaa[N330] varbhandaa[N]h[331].

3. andaj[332] jayraj[333] ut-bhujaa[N334] khaanee[335] saytjaa[N]h[336].

4. so mit [337]jaanai naankaa saraa[N338] mayraa[N339] jantaah[340].

5. naanak jant upaa-ay kai [341]sammaalay sabhnaah.

6. jin[342] kartai karnaa kee-aa chintaa bhe karnee taah[343].

7. so kartaa chintaa karay jin upaa-i-aa jag.

8. tis johaaree [344]su-asat tis[345] tis deebaan[346] abhag[347].

9. naanak sachay naam bin ki-aa tikaa [348]ki-aa tag[349]. ||1||

---

³⁴¹ Having created the universe
³⁴² Who
³⁴³ Him
³⁴⁴ Salutation
³⁴⁵ Obeisance
³⁴⁶ Court
³⁴⁷ Imperishable
³⁴⁸ Frontal mark
³⁴⁹ Hindu sacred thread

ਮਃ ੧ ॥

1. ਲਖ ਨੇਕੀਆ ਚੰਗਿਆਈਆ ਲਖ ਪੁੰਨਾ³⁵⁰ ਪਰਵਾਣੁ³⁵¹ ॥

2. ਲਖ ਤਪ ਉਪਰਿ ਤੀਰਥਾਂ³⁵² ਸਹਜ³⁵³ ਜੋਗ³⁵⁴ ਬੇਬਾਣ³⁵⁵ ॥

3. ਲਖ ਸੂਰਤਣ³⁵⁶ ਸੰਗਰਾਮ³⁵⁷ ਰਣ³⁵⁸ ਮਹਿ ਛੁਟਹਿ ਪਰਾਣ ॥

4. ਲਖ ਸੁਰਤੀ³⁵⁹ ਲਖ ਗਿਆਨ ਧਿਆਨ ਪੜੀਅਹਿ ਪਾਠ ਪੁਰਾਣ ॥

5. ਜਿਨਿ ਕਰਤੈ ਕਰਣਾ ਕੀਆ ਲਿਖਿਆ ਆਵਣ ਜਾਣੁ ॥

6. ਨਾਨਕ ਮਤੀ³⁶⁰ ਮਿਥਿਆ³⁶¹ ਕਰਮੁ ਸਚਾ ਨੀਸਾਣੁ³⁶² ॥ ੨ ॥

ਸਃ ੧ ॥

1. लख नेकीआ चंगिआईआ लख पुंना³⁵⁰ परवाणु³⁵¹ ॥

2. लख तप उपरि तीरथाँ³⁵² सहज³⁵³ जोग³⁵⁴ बेबाण³⁵⁵ ॥

3. लख सूरतण³⁵⁶ संगराम³⁵⁷ रण³⁵⁸ महि छुटहि पराण ॥

4. लख सुरती³⁵⁶ लख गिआन धिआन पड़ीअहि पाठ पुराण ॥

5. जिनि करतै करणा कीआ लिखिआ आवण जाणु ॥

6. नानक मती³⁶⁰ मिथिआ³⁶¹ करमु सचा नीसाणु³⁶² ॥ २ ॥

Mehla 1.

1. lakh naykee-aa chang-aa-ee-aa lakh punnaa[350] parvaan[351].

2. lakh tap upar teerthaaN [352]sahj[353] jog[354] baybaan[355].

3. lakh soortan[356] sangraam [357]ran[358] meh chhuteh paraan.

4. lakh surtee[359] lakh gi-aan Dhi-aan parhee-ah paath puraan.

5. jin kartai karnaa kee-aa likhi-aa aavan jaan.

6. naanak matee[360] mithi-aa[361] karam sachaa neesaan. [362] ||2||

---

[350] Charity
[351] Acceptance
[352] Meditation at the holy places
[353] Samadhi, to sit in meditation
[354] Yogic posture

[355] In wilderness, forests, mountains, etc.
[356] Brave men, fighters
[357] Knights
[358] Battleground
[359] Sruti, the Hindu scriptures

[360] Wisdom, knowledge
[361] False
[362] The mark of Grace

Theme	**Literal Meaning**

Theme

Sloak Mehla 1

Waheguru has created the whole Universe and is looking after it with great excitement.

Literal Meaning

Sloak Mehla 1

1. Different races of human beings, different kinds of vegetation, numerous holy places, countless river banks, black and white clouds and varied type of farming lands,
2. Numerous islands, regions, a number of large and small spheres – make the whole universe,
3. Different sources of creation of life – the egg, the womb, the sweat and the seed,
4. The limits of all the above are only known to Waheguru; in addition, there are countless lakes and mountains within where thousand of other varieties of creatures reside.
5. Having created all the lives and objects Waheguru sustains and tends them all.
6. Being the Creator of all he worries about their well-being as well.
7. As the Master of the Cosmos, he looks after its proper functioning.
8. To Him I bow, to Him I pray for grace, his creation is so wondrous.
9. Without the true devotion of Waheguru, the rituals of putting sacred mark on the forehead and wearing of sacred thread around the shoulder and waist are useless.

Mehla 1

All worldly methods of meditation, bravery and wisdom are useless if they are devoid of God's grace.

Mehla 1

1. There are indefinite number of good deeds, acts of piety and countless charities of approved merit.
2. There are numerous counts of penances performed at holy places, and infinite feats of yoga performed in wilderness.
3. There are countless warriors fighting and dying in the battlefield.
4. There are varied modes of controlling mind, different pursuits of knowledge and reciting Puranas (Hindu scriptures)
5. The regulation of all above, to our Master, the designer of birth and death,
6. Are mere child's play. His light pervades in all of them

ਪਉੜੀ ॥

1. ਸਚਾ ਸਾਹਿਬੁ ਏਕੁ ਤੂੰ ਜਿਨਿ ਸਚੋ ਸਚੁ ਵਰਤਾਇਆ ॥
2. ਜਿਸੁ ਤੂੰ ਦੇਹਿ ਤਿਸੁ ਮਿਲੈ ਸਚੁ ਤਾ ਤਿਨੀ ਸਚੁ ਕਮਾਇਆ ॥
3. ਸਤਿਗੁਰਿ ਮਿਲਿਐ ਸਚੁ ਪਾਇਆ ਜਿਨ ਕੈ ਹਿਰਦੈ ਸਚੁ ਵਸਾਇਆ ॥
4. ਮੂਰਖ ਸਚੁ ਨ ਜਾਣਨੀ ਮਨਮੁਖੀ³⁶³ ਜਨਮੁ ਗਵਾਇਆ ॥
5. ਵਿਚਿ ਦੁਨੀਆ ਕਾਹੇ ਆਇਆ ॥ ੮ ॥

ਪਉੜੀ ॥

1. सचा साहिबु इेकु तूं जिनि सचो सचु वरताइआ ॥
2. जिसु तूं देहि तिसु मिलै सचु ता तिनी सचु कमाइआ ॥
3. सतिगुरि मिलिअै सचु पाइआ जिन कै हिरदै सचु वसाइआ ॥
4. मूरख सचु न जाणनी मनमुखी³⁶³ जनमु गवाइआ ॥
5. विचि दुनीआ काहे आइआ ॥ ੮ ॥

Pauri.

1. sachaa saahib ayk too^N jin sacho sach vartaa-i-aa.
2. jis too^N deh tis milai sach taa tin^Hee sach kamaa-i-aa.
3. satgur mili-ai sach paa-i-aa jin^H kai hirdai sach vasaa-i-aa.
4. moorakh sach na $jaanan^H$ee manmukhee³⁶³ janam gavaa-i-aa.
5. vich dunee-aa kaahay aa-i-aa. ||8||

Theme

Pauri

God has many treasures of truth. He gives it to those whom he blesses.

Literal Meaning

Pauri

1. O! Master, you are the only true reality, you have ordained Truth to prevail everywhere.
2. He alone endures with truth, to whom you bless; such blessed ones are alone who dwell in truth.
3. The recipe of truth can be taken from a true teacher, plant truth first in his heart.
4. The fools do not imbibe truth, the non-believers too waste their lives.
5. Their stay on earth is thus laid useless and meaningless.

---

³⁶³ Atheist

ਆਸਾ ਮਹਲਾ ੪ ॥

आसा महला ੪ ॥

Asa Mehla 4.

Asa Mehla 4.

ਹਰਿ ਅੰਮ੍ਰਿਤ ਭਗਤਿ ਭੰਡਾਰ ਹੈ ਗੁਰ ਸਤਿਗੁਰ ਪਾਸੇ ਰਾਮ ਰਾਜੇ ॥

हरि अंम੍रित भगति भंडार है गुर सतिगुर पासे राम राजे ॥

har amrit bhagat bhandaar hai gur satgur paasay raam raajay.

The treasure of nectar is found through the teachings of the Guru-
teacher, Waheguru is indeed the King of Kings.

ਗੁਰੁ ਸਤਿਗੁਰੁ ਸਚਾ ਸਾਹੁ ਹੈ ਸਿਖ ਦੇਇ ਹਰਿ ਰਾਸੇ ॥

गुरु सतिगुरु सचा साहु है सिख देइ हरि रासे ॥

gur satgur sachaa saahu hai sikh day-ay har raasay.

Waheguru, the great Master is our real Banker,
He gives to His devotees the capital of true life.

ਧਨੁ ਧੰਨੁ ਵਣਜਾਰਾ ਵਣਜੁ ਹੈ ਗੁਰੁ ਸਾਹੁ ਸਾਬਾਸੇ ॥

धनु धंनु वणजारा वणजु है गुरु साह साबासे ॥

Dhan Dhan vanjaaraa vanaj hai gur saahu saabaasay.

Blessed, blessed is the trader and the trade;
how wonderful is the Banker, the great Master!

ਜਨੁ ਨਾਨਕੁ ਗੁਰੁ ਤਿਨੀ ਪਾਇਆ ਜਿਨ ਧੁਰਿ ਲਿਖਤੁ ਲਿਲਾਟਿ ਲਿਖਾਸੇ ॥੧॥

जनु नानकु गुरु तिनी पाइआ जिन धुरि लिखतु लिलाटि लिखासे ॥ ੧ ॥

jan naanak gur tinʰee paa-i-aa jin Dhur likhat lilaat likhaasay. ||1||

They alone obtain the audience of Waheguru who qualify for
His Grace through their goodness.

Pauri 9 with 2 sloaks
(Guru Nanak 2)

ਸਲੋਕੁ ਮਃ ੧ ॥

1. ਪੜਿ ਪੜਿ[364] ਗਡੀ ਲਦੀਅਹਿ[365] ਪੜਿ ਪੜਿ ਭਰੀਅਹਿ[366] ਸਾਥ[367] ॥
2. ਪੜਿ ਪੜਿ ਬੇੜੀ ਪਾਈਐ[368] ਪੜਿ ਪੜਿ ਗਡੀਅਹਿ ਖਾਤ[369] ॥
3. ਪੜੀਅਹਿ ਜੇਤੇ ਬਰਸ ਬਰਸ[370] ਪੜੀਅਹਿ ਜੇਤੇ ਮਾਸ[371] ॥
4. ਪੜੀਐ ਜੇਤੀ[372] ਆਰਜਾ[373] ਪੜੀਅਹਿ ਜੇਤੇ ਸਾਸ[374] ॥
5. ਨਾਨਕ ਲੇਖੈ ਇਕ ਗਲ[375] ਹੋਰੁ ਹਉਮੈ[376] ਝਖਣਾ ਝਾਖ[377] ॥ ੧ ॥

ਮਃ ੧ ॥

1. ਲਿਖਿ ਲਿਖਿ ਪੜਿਆ ॥
2. ਤੇਤਾ ਕੜਿਆ[378] ॥
3. ਬਹੁ ਤੀਰਥ ਭਵਿਆ[379] ॥
4. ਤੇਤੋ[380] ਲਵਿਆ[381] ॥
5. ਬਹੁ ਭੇਖ ਕੀਆ[382] ਦੇਹੀ ਦੁਖ ਦੀਆ ॥
6. ਸਹੁ ਵੇ ਜੀਆ[383] ਅਪਣਾ ਕੀਆ ॥

---

[364] Read and study
[365] Cart load of
[366] Multitude of books
[367] All
[368] Fill up a full boat
[369] Fill up a pit
[370] Year upon year

सलोकु मः १ ॥

1. पड़ि पड़ि[364] गडी लदीअहि[365] पड़ि पड़ि भरीअहि[366] साथ[367] ॥
2. पड़ि पड़ि बेड़ी पाइऐ[368] पड़ि पड़ि गडीअहि खात[369] ॥
3. पड़ीअहि जेते बरस बरस[370] पड़ीअहि जेते मास[371] ॥
4. पड़ीऐ जेती[372] आरजा[373] पड़ीअहि जेते सास[374] ॥
5. नानक लेखै इक गल[375] होरु हउमै[376] झखणा झाख[377] ॥ १ ॥

मः १ ॥

1. लिखि लिखि पड़िआ ॥
2. तेता कड़िआ[378] ॥
3. बहु तीरथ भविआ[379] ॥
4. तेतो[380] लविआ[381] ॥
5. बहु भेख कीआ[382] देही दुखु दीआ ॥
6. सहु वे जीआ[383] अपणा कीआ ॥

---

[371] All months in those years
[372] As much, all
[373] Life
[374] Breath
[375] A thing which counts is the name of Waheguru
[376] Ego
[377] Waste

Sloak Mehla 1.

1. parh parh[364] gadee ladee-ah[365] parh parh bharee-ah[366] saath[367].
2. parh parh bayrhee paa-ee-ai[368] parh parh gadee-ah khaat[369].
3. parhee-ah jaytay baras baras[370] parhee-ah jaytay maas[371].
4. parhee-ai jaytee[372] aarjaa[373] parhee-ah jaytay saas[374].
5. naanak laykhai ik gal[375] hor ha-umai[376] jhakh-naa jhaakh[377]. ||1||

Mehla 1.

1. likh likh parhi-aa.
2. taytaa karhi-aa[378].
3. baho tirath bhavi-aa[379].
4. tayto[380] lavi-aa[381].
5. baho bhaykh kee-aa[382] dayhee dukh dee-aa.
6. saho vay jee-aa[383] apnaa kee-aa.

---

[378] Egoistic
[379] Visit to holy places, wander in holy places
[380] That much
[381] To talk superfluous
[382] Changing different apparels, wearing different religious colours
[383] O! my soul endure the results of your acts

Gurmukhi	Devanagari	Transliteration
7. ਅੰਨੁ ਨ ਖਾਇਆ[384] ਸਾਦੁ ਗਵਾਇਆ[385] ॥	7. अंनु न खाइआ[384] सादु गवाइआ[385] ॥	7. ann na khaa-i-aa[384] saad gavaa-i-aa[385].
8. ਬਹੁ ਦੁਖ ਪਾਇਆ ਦੂਜਾ ਭਾਇਆ[386] ॥	8. बहु दुखु पाइआ दूजा भाइआ[386] ॥	8. baho dukh paa-i-aa doojaa bhaa-i-aa[386].
9. ਬਸਤੁ ਨ ਪਹਿਰੈ ॥	9. बसत्र न पहिरै ॥	9. bastar na pahirai.
10. ਅਹਿਨਿਸਿ[387] ਕਹਰੈ[388] ॥	10. अहिनिसि[387] कहरै[388] ॥	10. ahinis[387] kahrai[388].
11. ਮੋਨਿ ਵਿਗੂਤਾ[389] ॥	11. मोनि विगूता[389] ॥	11. mon vigootaa[389].
12. ਕਿਉ ਜਾਗੈ ਗੁਰ ਬਿਨੁ[390] ਸੂਤਾ ॥	12. किउ जागै गुर बिनु[390] सूता ॥	12. ki-o jaagai gur bin[390] sootaa.
13. ਪਗ[391] ਉਪੇਤਾਨਾ[392] ॥	13. पग[391] उपेताना[392] ॥	13. pag[391] upaytaanaa[392].
14. ਅਪਨਾ ਕੀਆ ਕਮਾਨਾ ॥	14. अपना कीआ कमाना ॥	14. apnaa kee-aa kamaanaa.
15. ਅਲੁ ਮਲੁ ਖਾਈ[393] ਸਿਰਿ ਛਾਈ[394] ਪਾਈ ॥	15. अलु मलु खाई[393] सिरि छाई[394] पाई ॥	15. al mal khaa-ee[393] sir chhaa-ee[394] paa-ee.
16. ਮੂਰਖਿ ਅੰਧੈ ਪਤਿ[395] ਗਵਾਈ ॥	16. मूरखि अंधै पति[395] गवाई ॥	16. moorakh anDhai pat[395] gavaa-ee.
17. ਵਿਣੁ ਨਾਵੈ ਕਿਛੁ ਥਾਇ ਨ ਪਾਈ ॥	17. विणु नावै किछु थाइ न पाई ॥	17. vin naavai kichh thaa-ay na paa-ee.
18. ਰਹੈ ਬੇਬਾਨੀ[396] ਮੜੀ[397] ਮਸਾਨੀ[398] ॥	18. रहै बेबानी[396] मड़ी[397] मसानी[398] ॥	18. rahai baybaanee[396] marhee[397] masaanee[398].
19. ਅੰਧੁ[399] ਨ ਜਾਨੈ ਫਿਰਿ ਪਛੁਤਾਨੀ ॥	19. अंधु[399] न जाणै फिरि पछुताणी ॥	19. anDh[399] na jaanai fir pachhutaanee.
20. ਸਤਿਗੁਰੁ ਭੇਟੇ ਸੋ ਸੁਖੁ ਪਾਏ ॥	20. सतिगुरु भेटे सो सुखु पाइ ॥	20. satgur bhaytay so sukh paa-ay.
21. ਹਰਿ ਕਾ ਨਾਮੁ ਮੰਨਿ ਵਸਾਏ ॥	21. हरि का नामु मंनि वसाइ ॥	21. har kaa naam man vasaa-ay.
22. ਨਾਨਕ ਨਦਰਿ ਕਰੇ ਸੋ ਪਾਏ ॥	22. नानक नदरि करे सो पाइ ॥	22. naanak nadar karay so paa-ay.
23. ਆਸ[400] ਅੰਦੇਸੇ[401] ਤੇ ਨਿਹਕੇਵਲੁ[402] ਹਉਮੈ ਸਬਦਿ ਜਲਾਏ[403] ॥ ੨ ॥	23. आस[400] अंदेसे[401] ते निहकेवलु[402] हउमै सबदि जलाइ[403] ॥ २ ॥	23. aas[400] andaysay[401] tay nihkayval[402] ha-umai sabad jalaa-ay.[403] ||2||

---

384 Fasting
385 To lose the taste of life
386 If and when you run after others
387 Day and night
388 To live in agony
389 To ruin
390 Without a teacher-Guru
391 Feet
392 Bare feet
393 To eat filth
394 Ashes
395 Honour, chastity
396 Wilderness
397 Graveyards
398 Cremation ground
399 A blind man
400 Hope
401 Fear
402 Being free from
403 Ego is burnt with the heat of *Nam*

Theme

Sloak Mehla 1

That learning is of no avail, which does not glorify the qualities of Waheguru.

Mehla 1

If knowledge breeds ego then the name of Waheguru burns the ego.

Literal Meaning

Sloak Mehla 1

1. One who reads cart-load of books, and scans countless files.
2. One who browses through boat-load of folders, and fills up cellars with reading material.
3. One who reads year upon year and does not waste (any month) even a single moment unread,
4. One who reads all his life, even up to his/her last breath.
5. But all these readings are sheer waste of time if they do not involve the comprehension of true love and sweet remembrance of Waheguru's name.

Mehla 1

1. The more one reads and writes,
2. The worst torn with doubts is one within oneself.
3. The more one visits the holy places,
4. The worse incoherent talker one becomes.
5. The more one wanders from cult to cult, the worse does one grieve for oneself.
6. The indulgence in above activities leads to suffering and grief.
7. One who gives up food (rigorous fasting), and denies himself/herself the tastes of life,
8. One who gets involved in duality (worship of gods and goddesses), and ruins the very purpose of life,
9. One who chooses to live naked (a Jain cult)
10. And torment his/her body, and
11. One who chooses not to speak (prolonged silence),
12. They all need the guidance of teacher-Guru (for all these ways do not lead to the house of God)

13. One who prefers to walk barefoot,
14. And suffer in remorse.
15. One who eats rotten food and disfigures his/her body,
16. These people are also stupid blind people who lose their dignity of living.
17. For without recourse to Waheguru's name all other rituals and acts of tormentation and penances are of no avail.
18. One who lives in barren places or in graveyards,
19. One who first turns blind eye to worldly comforts and then repents.
20. All these get true happiness firstly, with the help of teacher-Guru.
21. Secondly, with imbibing Waheguru's name deep in their minds, and
22. Thirdly, by invoking Waheguru's Grace.
23. In this way they will be freed from false hopes and fears, and with the power of Waheguru's *Nam* (Shabad) they will burn their ego.

ਪਉੜੀ ॥

1. ਭਗਤ ਤੇਰੈ ਮਨਿ ਭਾਵਦੇ ਦਰਿ ਸੋਹਨਿ⁴⁰⁴ ਕੀਰਤਿ ਗਾਵਦੇ ॥
2. ਨਾਨਕ ਕਰਮਾ ਬਾਹਰੇ⁴⁰⁵ ਦਰਿ ਢੋਅ ਨ ਲਹਨੀ⁴⁰⁶ ਧਾਵਦੇ⁴⁰⁷ ॥
3. ਇਕਿ ਮੂਲ ਨ ਬੁਝਨਿ ਆਪਣਾ ਅਣਹੋਦਾ⁴⁰⁸ ਆਪੁ ਗਣਾਇਦੇ⁴⁰⁹ ॥
4. ਹਉ ⁴¹⁰ਢਾਢੀ ਕਾ ਨੀਚੁ ਜਾਤਿ ਹੋਰਿ ਉਤਮ ਜਾਤਿ ਸਦਾਇਦੇ⁴¹¹ ॥
5. ਤਿਨ ਮੰਗਾ⁴¹² ਜਿ ਤੁਝੈ ਧਿਆਇਦੇ ॥ ੯ ॥

पउड़ी ॥

1. भगत तेरै मनि भावदे दरि सोहनि⁴⁰⁴ कीरति गावदे ॥
2. नानक करमा बाहरे⁴⁰⁵ दरि ढोअ न लहनी⁴⁰⁶ धावदे⁴⁰⁷ ॥
3. इकि मूलु न बुझनि आपणा अणहोदा⁴⁰⁸ आपु गणाइदे⁴⁰⁹ ॥
4. हउ ⁴¹⁰ढाढी का नीचु जाति होरि उतम जाति सदाइदे⁴¹¹ ॥
5. तिन मंगा⁴¹² जि तुझै धिआइदे ॥ ६ ॥

Pauri.

1. bhagat tayrai man bhaavday dar sohan[404] keerat gaavday.
2. naanak karmaa baahray[405] dar dho-a na lehnHee[406] Dhaavday[407].
3. ik mool na bujhniH aapnaa anhodaa[408] aap ganaa-iday[409].
4. ha-o [410]dhaadhee kaa neech jaat hor utam jaat sadaa-iday[411].
5. tihH mangaa[412] je tujhai Dhi-aa-iday. ||9||

Theme

Pauri

Waheguru loves his true devotees. In his court the caste does not count.

Literal Meaning

Pauri

1. O! Waheguru, your devotees are dear to you, when they sing your glories their faces shine with glow.
2. But those who do not qualify for your grace are not permitted to go through the gate which leads to your dwelling.
3. These people break away from their roots and are lost in the whirlpool of existence.
4. O! Waheguru, I am your minstrel, considered low caste by hypocrites who pretend to be of high caste.
5. But my only ambition is to live with those who are absorbed in your name.

---

[404] Standing in your beautiful courtyard
[405] Devoid of Waheguru's Grace
[406] To find no shelter
[407] To wander aimlessly
[408] Without a cause
[409] To sing one's own praises
[410] I am
[411] Others boast of their high caste
[412] I want the company of those

ਸਚੁ ਸਾਹੁ ਹਮਾਰਾ ਤੂੰ ਧਨੀ ਸਭ ਜਗਤੁ ਵਣਜਾਰਾ ਰਾਮ ਰਾਜੇ ॥

ਸਚੁ ਸਾਹੁ ਹਮਾਰਾ ਤੂੰ ਧਣੀ ਸਭੁ ਜਗਤੁ ਵਣਜਾਰਾ ਰਾਮ ਰਾਜੇ ॥

sach saahu hamaaraa too^N Dhanee sabh jagat vanjaaraa raam raajay.

You are my true Banker, O my Master; the whole world is
pursuing your trade, O King of Kings.

ਸਭ ਭਾਂਡੇ ਤੁਧੈ ਸਾਜਿਆ ਵਿਚਿ ਵਸਤੁ ਹਰਿ ਥਾਰਾ ॥

ਸਭ ਭਾਂਡੇ ਤੁਧੈ ਸਾਜਿਆ ਵਿਚਿ ਵਸਤੁ ਹਰਿ ਥਾਰਾ ॥

sabh bhaa^Nday tuDhai saaji-aa vich vasat har thaaraa.

You fashioned all vessels, and that which dwells
within there is also Your own creation.

ਜੋ ਪਾਵਹਿ ਭਾਂਡੇ ਵਿਚਿ ਵਸਤੁ ਸਾ ਨਿਕਲੈ ਕਿਆ ਕੋਈ ਕਰੇ ਵੇਚਾਰਾ ॥

ਜੋ ਪਾਵਹਿ ਭਾਂਡੇ ਵਿਚਿ ਵਸਤੁ ਸਾ ਨਿਕਲੈ ਕਿਆ ਕੋਈ ਕਰੇ ਵੇਚਾਰਾ ॥

*jo paavahi bhaa^Nday vich vasat saa niklai ki-aa ko-ee karay
vaychaaraa.*

Whatever You place in those vessels, that alone comes out
from within. What can the poor creatures do?

ਜਨ ਨਾਨਕ ਕਉ ਹਰਿ ਬਖਸਿਆ ਹਰਿ ਭਗਤਿ ਭੰਡਾਰਾ ॥੨॥

ਜਨ ਨਾਨਕ ਕਉ ਹਰਿ ਬਖਸਿਆ ਹਰਿ ਭਗਤਿ ਭੰਡਾਰਾ ॥ ੨ ॥

jan naanak ka-o har bakhsi-aa har bhagat bhandaaraa. ||2||

Waheguru has given the treasure of His devotional
worship to us all. ||2||

Pauri 10 with 2 sloaks
(Guru Nanak 2)

ਸਲੋਕੁ ਮਃ ੧ ॥

1. ਕੂੜੁ[413] ਰਾਜਾ ਕੂੜੁ ਪਰਜਾ ਕੂੜੁ ਸਭੁ ਸੰਸਾਰੁ ॥
2. ਕੂੜੁ ਮੰਡਪ[414] ਕੂੜੁ ਮਾੜੀ[415] ਕੂੜੁ ਬੈਸਣਹਾਰੁ[416] ॥
3. ਕੂੜੁ ਸੁਇਨਾ[417] ਕੂੜੁ ਰੁਪਾ[418] ਕੂੜੁ ਪੈਨਣਹਾਰ ॥
4. ਕੂੜੁ ਕਾਇਆ[419] ਕੂੜੁ ਕਪੜੁ[420] ਕੂੜੁ ਰੂਪੁ ਅਪਾਰ ॥
5. ਕੂੜੁ ਮੀਆ ਕੂੜੁ ਬੀਬੀ ਖਪਿ[421] ਹੋਏ ਖਾਰੁ [422] ॥
6. ਕੂੜਿ[423] ਕੂੜੈ[424] ਨੇਹੁ ਲਗਾ ਵਿਸਰਿਆ ਕਰਤਾਰੁ ॥
7. ਕਿਸੁ ਨਾਲਿ ਕੀਚੈ ਦੋਸਤੀ ਸਭੁ ਜਗੁ ਚਲਣਹਾਰੁ ॥
8. ਕੂੜੁ ਮਿਠਾ ਕੂੜੁ ਮਾਖਿਉ[424] ਕੂੜੁ ਡੋਬੇ ਪੂਰੁ[426] ॥
9. ਨਾਨਕੁ ਵਖਾਣੈ ਬੇਨਤੀ[427] ਤੁਧੁ ਬਾਝੁ ਕੂੜੋ ਕੂੜੁ ॥ ੧ ॥

सलोकु मः १ ॥

1. कूड़ु[413] राजा कूड़ु परजा कूड़ु सभु संसारु ॥
2. कूड़ु मंडप[414] कूड़ु माड़ी[415] कूड़ु बैसणहारु[416] ॥
3. कूड़ु सुइना[417] कूड़ु रुपा[418] कूड़ु पैनणहारु ॥
4. कूड़ु काइआ[419] कूड़ु कपड़ु[420] कूड़ु रूप अपार ॥
5. कूड़ु मीआ कूड़ु बीबी खपि[421] होइ.खारु [422] ॥
6. कूड़ि[423] कूड़ै[424] नेहु लगा विसरिआ करतारु ॥
7. किसु नालि कीचै दोसती सभु जगु चलनहारु ॥
8. कूड़ु मिठा कूड़ु माखिउ[425] कूड़ु डोबे पूरु[426] ॥
9. नानकु वखाणै बेनती[427] तुधु बाझु कूड़ो कूड़ु ॥ १ ॥

Sloak Mehla 1.

1. koo<u>rh</u>[413] raajaa koo<u>rh</u> parjaa koo<u>rh</u> sabh sansaar.
2. koo<u>rh</u> mandap[414] koo<u>rh</u> maa<u>rh</u>ee[415] koo<u>rh</u> baisanhaar[416].
3. koo<u>rh</u> su-inaa[417] koo<u>rh</u> rupaa[418] koo<u>rh</u> pain^Hanhaar.
4. koo<u>rh</u> kaa-i-aa[419] koo<u>rh</u> kaparh[420] koo<u>rh</u> roop apaar.
5. koo<u>rh</u> mee-aa koo<u>rh</u> beebee <u>kh</u>ap[421] ho-ay <u>kh</u>aar[422].
6. koo<u>rh</u>[423] koo<u>rh</u>ai[424] nayhu lagaa visri-aa kartaar.
7. kis naal keechai <u>d</u>os<u>t</u>ee sa<u>bh</u> jag chalanhaar.
8. koo<u>rh</u> mithaa koo<u>rh</u> maa<u>kh</u>i-o[425] koo<u>rh</u> dobay poor[426].
9. naanak vakhaanai bayn<u>t</u>ee[427] <u>t</u>u<u>Dh</u> baa<u>jh</u> koo<u>rh</u>o koo<u>rh</u>. ||1||

---

[413] Illusion, transitory
[414] Large marquee
[415] Palaces
[416] Inhabitants
[417] Gold

[418] Silver (Jewellery)
[419] Physical body
[420] Clothing
[421] Pine away, excitement, struggling in vain
[422] Lost, to wander without a definite destination

[423] One involved in falsehood
[424] False person, a person involved in falsehood
[425] Honey
[426] Boat full of, the whole life
[427] To make a request

ਮਃ ੧ ॥

1. ਸਚੁ ਤਾ ਪਰੁ ਜਾਣੀਐ ਜਾ ਰਿਦੈ ਸਚਾ ਹੋਇ ੪੨੮ ॥
2. ਕੂੜ ਕੀ ਮਲੁ ਉਤਰੈ ਤਨੁ ਕਰੇ ਹਛਾ ਧੋਇ ॥
3. ਸਚੁ ਤਾ ਪਰੁ ਜਾਣੀਐ ਜਾ ਸਚਿ ਧਰੇ ਪਿਆਰੁ ੪੨੯ ॥
4. ਨਾਉ ਸੁਣਿ ਮਨੁ ਰਹਸੀਐ ਤਾ ਪਾਏ ਮੋਖ ਦੁਆਰੁ ॥
5. ਸਚੁ ਤਾ ਪਰੁ ਜਾਣੀਐ ਜਾ ਜੁਗਤਿ ਜਾਣੈ ਜੀਉ ੪੩੦ ॥
6. ਧਰਤਿ ਕਾਇਆ ਸਾਧ ਕੈ ੪੩੧ ਵਿਚਿ ਦੇਇ ਕਰਤਾ ਬੀਉ ੪੩੨ ॥
7. ਸਚੁ ਤਾ ਪਰੁ ਜਾਣੀਐ ਜਾ ਸਿਖ ਸਚੀ ਲੇਇ ॥੪੩੩
8. ਦਇਆ ਜਾਣੈ ਜੀਅ ਕੀ ਕਿਛੁ ਪੁੰਨੁ ਦਾਨੁ ਕਰੇਇ ॥
9. ਸਚੁ ਤਾਂ ਪਰੁ ਜਾਣੀਐ ਜਾ ਆਤਮ ਤੀਰਥਿ ਕਰੇ ਨਿਵਾਸੁ ੪੩੪ ॥
10. ਸਤਿਗੁਰੂ ਨੋ ਪੁਛਿ ਕੈ ਬਹਿ ਰਹੈ ਕਰੇ ਨਿਵਾਸੁ ॥
11. ਸਚੁ ਸਭਨਾ ਹੋਇ ਦਾਰੂ ਪਾਪ ਕਢੈ ਧੋਇ ॥
12. ਨਾਨਕੁ ਵਖਾਣੈ ਬੇਨਤੀ ਜਿਨ ਸਚੁ ਪਲੈ ਹੋਇ ੪੩੫ ॥ ੨ ॥

Mehla 1.

1. sach taa par jaanee-ai jaa ridai sachaa ho-ay[428].
2. koorh kee mal utrai tan karay hachhaa Dho-ay.
3. sach taa par jaanee-ai jaa sach Dharay pi-aar[429].
4. naa-o sun man rehsee-ai taa paa-ay mokh du-aar.
5. sach taa par jaanee-ai jaa jugat jaanai jee-o[430].
6. Dharat kaa-i-aa saaDh kai[431] vich day-ay kartaa bee-o[432].
7. sach taa par jaanee-ai jaa sikh sachee lay-ay[433].
8. da-i-aa jaanai jee-a kee kichh punn daan karay-i.
9. sach taa^N par jaanee-ai jaa aatam tirath karay nivaas[434].
10. satguroo no puchh kai bahi rahai karay nivaas.
11. sach sabhnaa ho-ay daaroo paap kadhai Dho-ay.
12. naanak vakhaanai bayntee jin sach palai ho-ay[435]. ||2||

---

[428] If intentions are honest
[429] If one bears love to the loved one, to love truly
[430] If one understands the way of truthful living
[431] To prepare the body for the heavenly seed
[432] Seed
[433] If one gets the right type of instructions
[434] If one makes his heart as a pilgrimage
[435] One who has earned a lot of truth in life

Theme	_Literal Meaning_

Sloak Mehla 1

Everything in this world, though is reality, but is transitory, only Waheguru's name is permanent

Sloak Mehla 1

1. The tenure of every ruler is for a limited period and so is of his/her subjects; the living days of all other worldly objects is also numbered.
2. The physical life span of mansions, palaces and all their inhabitants is also limited.
3. Illusionary are precious metals like gold and silver and so are their users.
4. Illusionary is the body made of five perishable elements, so are robes, which cover those bodies, and in vain is their astounding beauty.
5. The company of husband and wife is also temporary. They get disgraced when they separate from each other.
6. Human beings are involved in loving transitory relationships, and have forgotten their true and permanent friend 'Waheguru'.
7. With whom can you make friends when every thing is transitory?
8. Sugar and honey are also tasteless when compared with the sweetness of Waheguru. The ignorant have never understood this secret.
9. Let us pray to only one Reality, except whom everything else is an illusion and is transitory.

Theme	*Literal Meaning*

Mehla 1

The truth is not only words but the intention of the doer

Mehla 1

1. Truth does abide in it, when the conscious is clear.
2. When the filth of sin is washed away and both mind and body are clean.
3. Truth does abide in it, when human heart is filled with love (not hatred).
4. When the mind is engrossed in Waheguru's name, then the door of deliverance is not far away.
5. Truth does abide in it, when the mind chooses the virtuous path.
6. When soul worships Waheguru, and earth helps the seed of love to sprout.
7. Truth does abide in it, when the true teaching is followed.
8. When one is compassionate and offers one's share in charity.
9. Truth does abide in it, when one washes and purifies one's inner self, and
10. When one settles in one's heart the light of Waheguru.
11. Truth is the medicine which cures all sins.
12. Let us pray to the Almighty with truth and nothing, but the truth filled in our heart.

ਪਉੜੀ ॥

1. ਦਾਨੁ ਮਹਿੰਡਾ⁴³⁶ ਤਲੀ ਖਾਕੁ⁴³⁷ ਜੇ ਮਿਲੈ ਤ ਮਸਤਕਿ ਲਾਈਐ ॥
2. ਕੂੜਾ ਲਾਲਚੁ ਛਡੀਐ ਹੋਇ ਇਕ ਮਨਿ ਅਲਖੁ⁴³⁸ ਧਿਆਈਐ ॥
3. ਫਲੁ ਤੇਵਹੋ ਪਾਈਐ ਜੇਵੇਹੀ ਕਾਰ ਕਮਾਈਐ ॥
4. ਜੇ ਹੋਵੈ ਪੂਰਬਿ⁴³⁹ ਲਿਖਿਆ ਤਾ ਧੂੜਿ ਤਿਨਾ ਦੀ ਪਾਈਐ ॥
5. ਮਤਿ ਥੋੜੀ⁴⁴⁰ ਸੇਵ ਗਵਾਈਐ ⁴⁴¹ ॥ ੧੦ ॥

पउड़ी ॥

1. दानु महिंडा⁴³⁶ तली खाकु⁴³⁷ जे मिलै त मसतकि लाईऐ ॥
2. कूड़ा लालचु छडीऐ होइ इक मनि अलखु⁴³⁸ धिआईऐ ॥
3. फलु तेवहो पाईऐ जेवेही कार कमाईऐ ॥
4. जे होवै पूरबि⁴³⁹ लिखिआ ता धूड़ि तिना दी पाईऐ ॥
5. मति थोड़ी⁴⁴⁰ सेव गवाईऐ ⁴⁴¹ ॥ १० ॥

Pauri.

1. daan mahindaa[436] talee <u>kh</u>aak[437] jay milai ta mas<u>t</u>ak laa-ee-ai.
2. koo<u>rh</u>aa laalach <u>chh</u>adee-ai ho-ay ik man ala<u>kh</u>[438] <u>Dh</u>i-aa-ee-ai.
3. fal <u>t</u>ayvayho paa-ee-ai jayvayhee kaar kamaa-ee-ai.
4. jay hovai poorab[439] li<u>kh</u>i-aa <u>t</u>aa <u>Dh</u>oo<u>rh</u> <u>t</u>in^Haa <u>d</u>ee paa-ee-ai.
5. ma<u>t</u> <u>th</u>o<u>rh</u>ee[440] sayv gavaa-ee-ai. [441]||10||

Theme

Pauri
A true devotee longs for the dust of the feet of the holy

Literal Meaning

Pauri
1. Most cherished gift for me is the dust consecrated by the feet of the true saints. If I were to get it, I will apply it on my forehead.
2. Let us all shed blind greed and meditate on the Shabad, the word of Ineffable God.
3. We are rewarded or punished according to our actions, this is the dictum of karma principle.
4. According to one's destiny (made up by one's own karma) one attains the company and teaching of pure people.
5. When our intellect is clouded with the filth of ego, we lose sight of the merit of selfless service.

---

[436] The gift which I need
[437] The dust of the feet of the holy

[438] With absolute concentration
[439] Pre-destined, beginning

[440] Due to limited intellect
[441] To lose the value of real service

ਹਮ ਕਿਆ ਗੁਣ ਤੇਰੇ ਵਿਥਰਹ ਸੁਆਮੀ ਤੂੰ ਅਪਰ ਅਪਾਰੋ ਰਾਮ ਰਾਜੇ ॥

हम किआ गुण तेरे विथरह सुआमी तूं अपर अपारो राम राजे ॥

ham ki-aa gun tayray vithreh su-aamee too^N apar apaaro raam raajay.

What glorious virtues of Yours can I describe, O my Master? You are
the most infinite of the infinite, O King of the Kings.

ਹਰਿ ਨਾਮੁ ਸਾਲਾਹਹ ਦਿਨੁ ਰਾਤਿ ਏਹਾ ਆਸ ਆਧਾਰੋ ॥

हरि नामु सालाहह दिनु राति इेहा आस आधारो ॥

har naam saalaahah din raat ayhaa aas aaDhaaro.

I praise the Name of Waheguru, day and night;
this alone is my hope and support.

ਹਮ ਮੂਰਖ ਕਿਛੂਅ ਨ ਜਾਣਹਾ ਕਿਵ ਪਾਵਹ ਪਾਰੋ ॥

हम मूरख किछूअ न जाणहा किव पावह पारो ॥

ham moorakh kichhoo-a na jaanhaa kiv paavah paaro.

I am ignorant and immature, and I know nothing. How can I find
Your limits?

ਜਨੁ ਨਾਨਕੁ ਹਰਿ ਕਾ ਦਾਸੁ ਹੈ ਹਰਿ ਦਾਸ ਪਨਿਹਾਰੋ ॥੩॥

जनु नानकु हरि का दासु है हरि दास पनिहारो ॥ ३ ॥

jan naanak har kaa daas hai har daas panihaaro. ||3||

I am your slave and also a slave of the devotees of Waheguru. ||3||

Pauri 11 with 3 sloaks (Guru Nanak 3)

ਸਲੋਕੁ ਮਃ ੧ ॥

1. ਸਚਿ ਕਾਲੁ[442] ਕੂੜੁ ਵਰਤਿਆ[443] ਕਲਿ[444] ਕਾਲਖ ਬੇਤਾਲ[445] ॥

2. ਬੀਉ ਬੀਜਿ ਪਤਿ ਲੈ ਗਏ [446] ਅਬ ਕਿਉ ਉਗਵੈ[447] ਦਾਲਿ[448] ॥

3. ਜੇ ਇਕੁ ਹੋਇ[449] ਤ ਉਗਵੈ[450] ਰੁਤੀ ਹੂ ਰੁਤਿ ਹੋਇ[451] ॥

4. ਨਾਨਕ ਪਾਹੈ[452] ਬਾਹਰਾ[453] ਕੋਰੈ[454] ਰੰਗੁ ਨ ਸੋਇ ॥

5. ਭੈ[455] ਵਿਚਿ ਖੁੰਬਿ ਚੜਾਈਐ[456] ਸਰਮੁ ਪਾਹੁ[457] ਤਨਿ ਹੋਇ ॥

6. ਨਾਨਕ ਭਗਤੀ ਜੇ ਰਪੈ[458] ਕੂੜੈ ਸੋਇ[459] ਨ ਕੋਇ ॥ ੧ ॥

सलोकु मः १ ॥

1. सचि कालु[442] कूड़ु वरतिआ[443] कलि[444] कालख बेताल[445] ॥

2. बीउ बीजि पति लै गइ [446] अब किउ उगवै[447] दालि[448] ॥

3. जे इकु होइ[449] त उगवै[450] रुती हू रुति होइ[451] ॥

4. नानक पाहै[452] बाहरा[453] कोरै[454] रंगु न सोइ ॥

5. भै[455] विचि खुंबि चड़ाईऐ[456] सरमु पाहु[457] तनि होइ ॥

6. नानक भगती जे रपै[458] कूड़ै सोइ[459] न कोइ ॥ १ ॥

Sloak Mehla 1.

1. sach kaal[442] koorh varti-aa[443] kal[444] kaalakh baytaal[445].

2. bee-o beej pat lai ga-ay [446]ab ki-o ugvai[447] daal[448].

3. jay ik ho-ay[449] ta ugvai[450] rutee hoo rut ho-ay[451].

4. naanak paahai[452] baahraa[453] korai[454] rang na so-ay.

5. bhai[455] vich khumb charhaa-ee-ai[456] saram paahu[457] tan ho-ay.

6. naanak bhagtee jay rapai[458] koorhai so-ay[459] na ko-ay. ||1||

---

[442] Famine, scarcity
[443] To prevail
[444] Kalyug
[445] Demons
[446] Those who had sown the seed of name they have gone with the earned honour
[447] Sprout

[448] Broken seed
[449] Whole seed
[450] To germinate
[451] In the right season
[452] A substance used for dyeing
[453] Without
[454] Brand new

[455] Fear
[456] To put into a big tub of boiling water for cleaning
[457] If dyeing substance is made of modesty
[458] Dyed
[459] Reputation

ਮਃ ੧ ॥

1. ਲਬੁ⁴⁶⁰ ਪਾਪੁ ਦੁਇ ਰਾਜਾ ਮਹਤਾ⁴⁶¹ ਕੂੜੁ ਹੋਆ ਸਿਕਦਾਰੁ⁴⁶² ॥
2. ਕਾਮੁ⁴⁶³ ਨੇਬੁ⁴⁶⁴ ਸਦਿ⁴⁶⁵ ਪੁਛੀਐ ਬਹਿ ਬਹਿ ਕਰੇ ਬੀਚਾਰੁ ॥
3. ਅੰਧੀ ਰਜਤਿ⁴⁶⁶ ਗਿਆਨ ਵਿਹੂਣੀ⁴⁶⁷ ਭਾਹਿ ਭਰੇ⁴⁶⁸ ਮੁਰਦਾਰੁ⁴⁶⁹ ॥
4. ਗਿਆਨੀ ਨਚਹਿ ਵਾਜੇ ਵਾਵਹਿ ਰੂਪ ਕਰਹਿ ਸੀਗਾਰੁ ॥
5. ਉਚੇ ਕੂਕਹਿ⁴⁷⁰ ਵਾਦਾ⁴⁷¹ ਗਾਵਹਿ ਜੋਧਾ ਕਾ ਵੀਚਾਰੁ ॥
6. ਮੂਰਖ ਪੰਡਿਤ ਹਿਕਮਤਿ⁴⁷² ਹੁਜਤਿ⁴⁷³ ਸੰਜੈ⁴⁷⁴ ਕਰਹਿ ਪਿਆਰੁ ॥
7. ਧਰਮੀ ਧਰਮੁ ਕਰਹਿ ਗਾਵਾਵਹਿ ਮੰਗਹਿ ਮੋਖ ਦੁਆਰੁ ॥
8. ਜਤੀ⁴⁷⁵ ਸਦਾਵਹਿ ਜੁਗਤਿ ਨ ਜਾਨਹਿ ਛਡਿ ਬਹਹਿ ਘਰ ਬਾਰੁ ॥
9. ਸਭੁ ਕੋ ਪੂਰਾ ਆਪੇ ਹੋਵੈ ਘਟਿ ਨ ਕੋਈ ਆਖੈ ॥
10. ਪਤਿ ਪਰਵਾਣਾ⁴⁷⁶ ਪਿਛੈ ਪਾਈਐ ਤਾ ਨਾਨਕ ਤੋਲਿਆ ਜਾਪੈ⁴⁷⁷ ॥ ੨ ॥

ਮਃ ੧ ॥

1. ਲਬੁ⁴⁶⁰ ਪਾਪੁ ਦੁਇ ਰਾਜਾ ਮਹਤਾ⁴⁶¹ ਕੂੜੁ ਹੋਆ ਸਿਕਦਾਰੁ⁴⁶² ॥
2. ਕਾਮੁ⁴⁶³ ਨੇਬੁ⁴⁶⁴ ਸਦਿ⁴⁶⁵ ਪੁਛੀਐ ਬਹਿ ਬਹਿ ਕਰੇ ਬੀਚਾਰੁ ॥
3. ਅੰਧੀ ਰਯਤਿ⁴⁶⁶ ਗਿਆਨ ਵਿਹੂਣੀ⁴⁶⁷ ਭਾਹਿ ਭਰੇ⁴⁶⁸ ਮੁਰਦਾਰੁ⁴⁶⁹ ॥
4. ਗਿਆਨੀ ਨਚਹਿ ਵਾਜੇ ਵਾਵਹਿ ਰੂਪ ਕਰਹਿ ਸੀਗਾਰੁ ॥
5. ਤੂਚੇ ਕੂਕਹਿ⁴⁷⁰ ਵਾਦਾ⁴⁷¹ ਗਾਵਹਿ ਜੋਧਾ ਕਾ ਵੀਚਾਰੁ ॥
6. ਮੂਰਖ ਪੰਡਿਤ ਹਿਕਮਤਿ⁴⁷² ਹੁਜਤਿ⁴⁷³ ਸੰਜੈ⁴⁷⁴ ਕਰਹਿ ਪਿਆਰੁ ॥
7. ਧਰਮੀ ਧਰਮੁ ਕਰਹਿ ਗਾਵਾਵਹਿ ਮੰਗਹਿ ਮੋਖ ਦੁਆਰੁ ॥
8. ਜਤੀ⁴⁷⁵ ਸਦਾਵਹਿ ਜੁਗਤਿ ਨ ਜਾਣਹਿ ਛਡਿ ਬਹਹਿ ਘਰ ਬਾਰੁ ॥
9. ਸਭੁ ਕੋ ਪੂਰਾ ਆਪੇ ਹੋਵੈ ਘਟਿ ਨ ਕੋਈ ਆਖੈ ॥
10. ਪਤਿ ਪਰਵਾਣਾ⁴⁷⁶ ਪਿਛੈ ਪਾਈਐ ਤਾ ਨਾਨਕ ਤੋਲਿਆ ਜਾਪੈ⁴⁷⁷ ॥ ੨ ॥

Mehla 1.

1. lab⁴⁶⁰ paap du-ay raajaa mahtaa⁴⁶¹ koorh ho-aa sikdaar⁴⁶².
2. kaam⁴⁶³ nayb⁴⁶⁴ sad⁴⁶⁵ puchhee-ai bahi bahi karay beechaar.
3. anDhee rayat⁴⁶⁶ gi-aan vihoonee⁴⁶⁷ bhaahi bharay⁴⁶⁸ murdaar⁴⁶⁹.
4. gi-aanee nacheh vaajay vaaveh roop karahi seegaar.
5. oochay kookeh⁴⁷⁰ vaadaa⁴⁷¹ gaavahi joDhaa kaa veechaar.
6. moorakh pandit hikmat⁴⁷² hujat⁴⁷³ sanjai⁴⁷⁴ karahi pi-aar.
7. Dharmee Dharam karahi gaavaaveh mangeh mokh du-aar.
8. jatee⁴⁷⁵ sadaaveh jugat na jaaneh chhad baheh ghar baar.
9. sabh ko pooraa aapay hovai ghat na ko-ee aakhai.
10. pat parvaanaa⁴⁷⁶ pichhai paa-ee-ai taa naanak toli-aa jaapai. ⁴⁷⁷||2||

---

⁴⁶⁰ Greed
⁴⁶¹ Minister
⁴⁶² Master of a mint
⁴⁶³ Passion
⁴⁶⁴ Assistant administrator
⁴⁶⁵ Summoned

⁴⁶⁶ Subjects, people
⁴⁶⁷ Devoid of
⁴⁶⁸ To satisfy the fire of greed
⁴⁶⁹ Bribe
⁴⁷⁰ To shout aloud
⁴⁷¹ Poems

⁴⁷² Cunning devices
⁴⁷³ Petty objections
⁴⁷⁴ To collect wealth
⁴⁷⁵ Continent
⁴⁷⁶ The weight of honour
⁴⁷⁷ Proper weight

ਮਃ ੧ ॥

1. ਵਦੀ[478] ਸੁ ਵਜਗਿ[479] ਨਾਨਕਾ ਸਚਾ ਵੇਖੈ ਸੋਇ[480] ॥
2. ਸਭਨੀ ਛਾਲਾ ਮਾਰੀਆ[481] ਕਰਤਾ ਕਰੇ ਸੁ ਹੋਇ ॥
3. ਅਗੈ ਜਾਤਿ ਨ ਜੋਰੁ ਹੈ ਅਗੈ ਜੀਉ ਨਵੇ[482] ॥
4. ਜਿਨ ਕੀ ਲੇਖੈ ਪਤਿ [483]ਪਵੈ ਚੰਗੇ ਸੇਈ ਕੇਇ ॥ ੩ ॥

ਮਃ ੧ ॥

1. ਵਦੀ[478] ਸੁ ਵਜਗਿ[479] ਨਾਨਕਾ ਸਚਾ ਵੇਖੈ ਸੋਇ[480] ॥
2. ਸਭਨੀ ਛਾਲਾ ਮਾਰੀਆ[481] ਕਰਤਾ ਕਰੇ ਸੁ ਹੋਇ ॥
3. ਅਗੈ ਜਾਤਿ ਨ ਜੋਰੁ ਹੈ ਅਗੈ ਜੀਉ ਨਵੇ[482] ॥
4. ਜਿਨ ਕੀ ਲੇਖੈ ਪਤਿ [483]ਪਵੈ ਚੰਗੇ ਸੇਈ ਕੇਇ ॥ ੩ ॥

Mehla 1.

1. vadee[478] so vajag[479] naankaa sachaa vaykhai so-ay[480].
2. sabhnee chhaalaa maaree-aa[481] kartaa karay so ho-ay.
3. agai jaat na jor hai agai jee-o navay[482].
4. jin kee laykhai pat [483]pavai changay say-ee kay-ay. ||3||

---

[478] Wickedness
[479] Well-known
[480] Waheguru is watching every thing
[481] Every one has jumped (for higher status), hypocrisy
[482] In after world they meet new people
[483] Those whose honour is counted by Waheguru

Theme

Sloak Mehla 1

The dye of Waheguru's shabad is the real colourant. The real honour is one which is acceptable to Waheguru

Mehla 1

The world is engrossed in hypocritical acts. The vices have taken over the virtues.

Literal Meaning

Sloak Mehla 1

1. Truth is hard to find and falsehood is ruling the roost; people smeared with the soot of evil are dancing in devil's steps.
2. Those who sowed unbroken seeds, they harvested its crop; but those whose seed has lost its embryonic cell, will fail to harvest any crop.
3. The seed can sprout only if it is unbroken and is sowed in the right season.
4. Like the unbleached cloth, which, without proper processing would take no colouring; in the same way an unprepared soul would fail to accept the colouring of truth.
5. A soul needs to have fear of God and be seasoned with humility.
6. When a person gets drenched with the love of God, he/she is purged from all falsehood.

Mehla 1

1. Greed and sin, the two are the monarch and the chief minister, with falsehood itself is their chief clerk.
2. Lust, their deputy, is their prime counsellor. He is consulted by them on every account.
3. The people so governed, the subjects, are extremely ignorant. They are absolutely dumb and have no awareness.
4. The gnostics dance, play harmonium and put on makeup and jewellery.
5. They shout and sing aloud the heroic deeds of the knights.
6. The stupid priest pretends to be clever, he displays odd tricks; and longs for material gains.

7. The so called religious people, belonging to various cults, practise various rituals and destroy their good deeds by setting their heart on salvation.
8. There are others who also pretend to practise continence and yet they know nothing about it. They choose to renounce world.
9. They all think they are right, and all others wrong.
10. In the court of Waheguru, the court of final judgement, only those will be acquitted whose accounts He himself audits.

Mehla 1

1. Whatever is destined, that is bound to happen. Waheguru observes all that one does.
2. Howsoever hard one tries, it is God's writ that shall prevail.
3. Neither caste nor power shall be considered in the life hereafter. There you will meet people of different order.
4. Only those will be spared from the chains of *yamas* who carry pious deeds of honour with them.

Mehla 1

People try to do impossible and fail. Wickedness has overtaken compassion and goodness.

ਪਉੜੀ ॥

1. ਧੁਰਿ ਕਰਮ ਜਿਨਾ ਕਉ ਤੁਧੁ ਪਾਇਆ ਤਾ ਤਿਨੀ ਖਸਮੁ ਧਿਆਇਆ ॥
2. ਏਨਾ ਜੰਤਾ ਕੈ ਵਸਿ ਕਿਛੁ ਨਾਹੀ ਤੁਧੁ ਵੇਕੀ⁴⁸⁴ ਜਗਤੁ ਉਪਾਇਆ ॥
3. ਇਕਨਾ ਨੋ ਤੂੰ ਮੇਲਿ ਲੈਹਿ ਇਕਿ ਆਪਹੁ ਤੁਧੁ ਖੁਆਇਆ ⁴⁸⁵ ॥
4. ਗੁਰ ਕਿਰਪਾ ਤੇ ਜਾਨਿਆ ਜਿਥੈ ਤੁਧੁ ਆਪੁ ਬੁਝਾਇਆ ॥
5. ਸਹਜੇ ਹੀ ਸਚਿ ਸਮਾਇਆ⁴⁸⁶ ॥ ੧੧ ॥

पउड़ी ॥

1. धुरि करमु जिना कउ तुधु पाइआ ता तिनी खसमु धिआइआ ॥
2. इना जंता कै वसि किछु नाही तुधु वेकी⁴⁸⁴ जगतु उपाइआ ॥
3. इकना नो तूं मेलि लैहि इकि आपहु तुधु खुआइआ ⁴⁸⁵ ॥
4. गुर किरपा ते जानिआ जिथै तुधु आपु बुझाइआ ॥
5. सहजे ही सचि समाइआ⁴⁸⁶ ॥ ११ ॥

Pauri.

1. $\underline{Dh}$ur karam jinaa ka-o $\underline{tuDh}$ paa-i-aa $\underline{t}$aa $\underline{t}$inee $\underline{kh}$asam $\underline{Dh}$i-aa-i-aa.
2. aynaa jan$\underline{t}$aa kai vas ki$\underline{chh}$ naahee $\underline{tuDh}$ vaykee⁴⁸⁴ jaga$\underline{t}$ upaa-i-aa.
3. iknaa no $\underline{t}$oo^N mayl laihi ik aaphu $\underline{tuDh}$ $\underline{kh}$u-aa-i-aa⁴⁸⁵.
4. gur kirpaa $\underline{t}$ay jaa$\underline{n}$i-aa jithai $\underline{tuDh}$ aap bu$\underline{jh}$aa-i-aa.
5. sehjay hee sach samaa-i-aa⁴⁸⁶. ||11||

Theme

Pauri
People meet and separate according to their karmas and Waheguru's writ

Literal Meaning

Pauri

1. Only those meditate on your name who are destined to do it (they become qualified to meditate by their previous good karmas and your grace).
2. Your creatures have no power of their own; all power rests with you. You have created world of many hues and colours.
3. Those who qualify for your grace, they go closer to you and others whom you forsake, they go astray.
4. God is realised through his own grace and his own writ.
5. It is through Truth that people realise you.

---

⁴⁸⁴ Diverse

⁴⁸⁵ Separation

⁴⁸⁶ Absorbed

ਜਿਉ ਭਾਵੈ ਤਿਉ ਰਾਖਿ ਲੈ ਹਮ ਸਰਨਿ ਪ੍ਰਭ ਆਏ ਰਾਮ ਰਾਜੇ ॥

जिउ भावै तिउ राखि लै हम सरणि प्रभ आइे राम राजे ॥

ji-o bhaavai ti-o raakh lai ham saran parabh aa-ay raam raajay.

As it pleases You, You save me; I have come seeking Your sanctuary,
O God, the King of the Kings.

ਹਮ ਭੂਲਿ ਵਿਗਾੜਹ ਦਿਨਸੁ ਰਾਤਿ ਹਰਿ ਲਾਜ ਰਖਾਏ ॥

हम भूलि विगाड़ह दिनसु राति हरि लाज रखाइे ॥

ham bhool vigaarhah dinas raat har laaj rakhaa-ay.

I am wandering around, ruining myself day and night;
O my Master, please save my honour!

ਹਮ ਬਾਰਿਕ ਤੂੰ ਗੁਰੁ ਪਿਤਾ ਹੈ ਦੇ ਮਤਿ ਸਮਝਾਏ ॥

हम बारिक तूं गुरु पिता है दे मति समझाइे ॥

ham baarik too^N gur pitaa hai day mat samjhaa-ay.

I am just a child; You, O greatest of the great, are my father.
Please give me understanding and instruction.

ਜਨੁ ਨਾਨਕੁ ਦਾਸੁ ਹਰਿ ਕਾਂਢਿਆ ਹਰਿ ਪੈਜ ਰਖਾਏ ॥੪॥੧੦॥੧੨॥

जनु नानकु दासु हरि काँढिआ हरि पैज रखाइे ॥ ४ ॥ १० ॥ १७ ॥

jan naanak daas har kaa^Ndhi-aa har paij rakhaa-ay. ||4||10||17||

I am your slave; O Master, please preserve his honour! ||4||10||17||

Pauri 12 with 4 sloaks
(Guru Nanak 2, Guru Angad 2)

ਸਲੋਕੁ ਮਃ ੧ ॥

1. ਦੁਖੁ ਦਾਰੂ ਸੁਖੁ ਰੋਗੁ ਭਇਆ ਜਾ ਸੁਖੁ ਤਾਮਿ[੪੮੭] ਨ ਹੋਈ ॥
2. ਤੂੰ ਕਰਤਾ ਕਰਣਾ ਮੈ ਨਾਹੀ ਜਾ ਹਉ ਕਰੀ ਨ ਹੋਈ ॥ ੧ ॥
3. ਬਲਿਹਾਰੀ ਕੁਦਰਤਿ ਵਸਿਆ ॥
4. ਤੇਰਾ ਅੰਤੁ ਨ ਜਾਈ ਲਖਿਆ[੪੮੮] ॥ ੧ ॥ ਰਹਾਉ ॥
5. ਜਾਤਿ[੪੮੯] ਮਹਿ ਜੋਤਿ ਜੋਤਿ ਮਹਿ ਜਾਤਾ[੪੯੦] ਅਕਲ ਕਲਾ[੪੯੧] ਭਰਪੂਰਿ ਰਹਿਆ ॥
6. ਤੂੰ ਸਚਾ ਸਾਹਿਬੁ ਸਿਫਤਿ ਸੁਆਲ੍ਹਿਉ ਜਿਨਿ ਕੀਤੀ[੪੯੨] ਸੋ ਪਾਰਿ ਪਇਆ ॥
7. ਕਹੁ ਨਾਨਕ ਕਰਤੇ ਕੀਆ ਬਾਤਾ ਜੋ ਕਿਛੁ ਕਰਣਾ ਸੁ ਕਰਿ ਰਹਿਆ ॥ ੨ ॥

सलोकु मः १ ॥

1. दुखु दारू सुखु रोगु भइआ जा सुखु तामि[४८७] न होइी ॥
2. तूं करता करणा मै नाही जा हउ करी न होइी ॥ १ ॥
3. बलिहारी कुदरति वसिआ ॥
4. तेरा अंतु न जाइी लखिआ[४८८] ॥ १ ॥ रहाउ ॥
5. जाति[४८९] महि जोति जोति महि जाता[४९०] अकल कला[४९१] भरपूरि रहिआ ॥
6. तूं सचा साहिबु सिफति सुआलि्उ जिनि कीती[४९२] सो पारि पइिआ ॥
7. कहु नानक करते कीआ बाता जो किछु करणा सु करि रहिआ ॥ २ ॥

Sloak Mehla 1.

1. dukh daaroo sukh rog bha-i-aa jaa sukh taam[487] na ho-ee.
2. too^{N} kartaa karnaa mai naahee jaa ha-o karee na ho-ee. ||1||
3. balihaaree kudrat vasi-aa.
4. tayraa ant na jaa-ee lakhi-aa[488]. ||1|| rahaa-o.
5. jaat[489] meh jot jot meh jaataa[490] akal kalaa[491] bharpoor rahi-aa.
6. too^{N} sachaa saahib sifat su-aaliha-o jin keetee[492] so paar pa-i-aa.
7. kaho naanak kartay kee-aa baataa jo kichh karnaa so kar rahi-aa. ||2||

---

487 Desire, grief, darkness
488 To comprehend
489 The whole creation
490 To be in, contained
491 Complete with all skills
492 Those who have sung Waheguru's glories

ਮਃ ੨ ॥

1. ਜੋਗ[493] ਸਬਦੰ[494] ਗਿਆਨ ਸਬਦੰ ਬੇਦ[495] ਸਬਦੰ ਬ੍ਰਹਮਣਹ ॥
2. ਖਤ੍ਰੀ ਸਬਦੰ ਸੂਰ[496] ਸਬਦੰ ਸੂਦ੍ ਸਬਦੰ ਪਰਾਕ੍ਰਿਤਹ[497] ॥
3. ਸਰਬ ਸਬਦੰ ਏਕ ਸਬਦੰ ਜੇ ਕੋ ਜਾਣੈ ਭੇਉ[498] ॥
4. ਨਾਨਕੁ ਤਾ ਕਾ ਦਾਸੁ ਹੈ ਸੋਈ ਨਿਰੰਜਨ ਦੇਉ ॥ ੩ ॥

मः २ ॥

1. जोग[493] सबदं[494] गिआन सबदं बेद[495] सबदं ब्राहमणह ॥
2. खत्री सबदं सूर[496] सबदं सूद सबदं पराक्रितह[497] ॥
3. सरब सबदं ऐक सबदं जे को जाणै भेउ[498] ॥
4. नानकु ता का दासु है सोई निरंजन देउ ॥ ३ ॥

Mehla 2.

1. jog[493] sabda^N[494] gi-aan sabda^N bayd[495] sabda^N baraahmaneh.
2. khatree sabda^N soor[496] sabda^N soodar sabda^N paraa kirteh[497].
3. sarab sabda^N ayk sabda^N jay ko jaanai bhay-o[498].
4. naanak taa kaa daas hai so-ee niranjan day-o. ||3||

---

[493] Union with God
[494] Dharam, duty
[495] Vedas
[496] Bravery
[497] Service of humanity
[498] Secret

ਮਃ ੨ ॥

1. ਏਕ ਕ੍ਰਿਸਨੰ[N499] ਸਰਬ ਦੇਵਾ[500] ਦੇਵ ਦੇਵਾ ਤ ਆਤਮਾ[501] ॥
2. ਆਤਮਾ ਬਾਸੁਦੇਵਸਿ੍[502] ਜੇ ਕੋ ਜਾਣੈ ਭੇਉ ॥
3. ਨਾਨਕੁ ਤਾ ਕਾ ਦਾਸੁ ਹੈ ਸੋਈ ਨਿਰੰਜਨ[503] ਦੇਉ ॥ ੪ ॥

ਮਃ ੧ ॥

1. ਕੁੰਭੇ [504] ਬਧਾ ਜਲੁ ਰਹੈ ਜਲ ਬਿਨੁ ਕੁੰਭੁ ਨ ਹੋਇ ॥
2. ਗਿਆਨ ਕਾ ਬਧਾ ਮਨੁ ਰਹੈ ਗੁਰ ਬਿਨੁ ਗਿਆਨੁ ਨ ਹੋਇ ॥ ੫ ॥

मः २ ॥

1. ऐक क्रिसनं[466म] सरब देवा[500] देव देवा त आतमा[501] ॥
2. आतमा बासुदेवसि[502] जे कॊ जाणै भेतु ॥
3. नानकु ता का दासु है सोई निरंजन[503] देतु ॥ ४ ॥

मः १ ॥

1. कुंभे [508] बधा जलु रहै जल बिनु कुंभु न होइ ॥
2. गिआन का बधा मनु रहै गुर बिनु गिआनु न होइ ॥ ५ ॥

Mehla 2.

1. ayk krisan[N499] sarab dayvaa[500] dayv dayvaa ta aatmaa[501].
2. aatmaa baasdayvsi-y[502] jay ko jaanai bhay-o.
3. naanak taa kaa daas hai so-ee niranjan[503] day-o. ||4||

Mehla 1.

1. kumbhay[504] baDhaa jal rahai jal bin kumbh na ho-ay.
2. gi-aan kaa baDhaa man rahai gur bin gi-aan na ho-ay. ||5||

---

[499] Waheguru
[500] All gods
[501] The soul of gods
[502] Omnipresent
[503] Without stains, great
[504] Pitcher

Theme

Sloak Mehla 1

In this materialistic world, sometimes, grief and pain brings you closer to God, whereas comforts allure you away from him.

Mehla 2

God is realised by performing honest and loyal duties of one's chosen profession, where scholars find him through knowledge, the soldiers find him through bravery and servants find him through honest service.

Literal Meaning

Sloak Mehla 1

1. (Sometimes) pain works as a blessing and pleasure as an (illness), for pleasure allures you to go away from God, whereas pain and grief bring you closer to him).
2. You (God) are the creator, I am unable to do anything. Even when I try to do something positive (worthwhile) I fail.
3. I am a sacrifice to the Master of the world who abides in his creation and whose limits cannot be apprehended.
4. Your light pervades in the creation and through that light we perceive you. You are the master of all skills which are reflected in your creation.
5. You are the true Master and inspiring are your sweet glories. Those who immerse in your Shabad, he/she is redeemed.
6. Dwell on the name of the Creator, for all that he wills, that comes to pass.

Mehla 2

1. The dharma of a yogi is the pursuit of knowledge, whereas the duty of a Brahmin is the interpretation of Vedas.
2. The dharma of a Kshatriya is the action of bravery and the duty of a shudra is the service of the rest.
3. The teachings of all religions lead to the Word Divine, only one is to realise this truth.
4. Let us be slaves to those who realise the above truth, for they are immersed in the spirit immaculate.

Theme	Literal Meaning

Mehla 2

God is the supreme devta. His light pervades in all humans and *devtas*.

Mehla 1

The real wisdom comes through: control of mind and teachings of a Guru-teacher.

Mehla 2

1. There is one God, the master of all gods and everything else that exists. He is also the designer and controller of all souls.
2. The prime secret is that the Soul and omnipresent God are in essence one.
3. Let us be slaves to those who realise the above truth, for they are immersed in the spirit immaculate.

Mehla 1

1. The pitcher holds water, yet the pitcher itself would not be shaped without water.
2. Though divine knowledge disciplines human mind, but knowledge itself cannot be had without the support of Guru-teacher.

ਪਉੜੀ ॥

1. ਪੜਿਆ ਹੋਵੈ ਗੁਨਹਗਾਰੁ ਤਾ ਓਮੀ[505] ਸਾਧੁ ਨ ਮਾਰੀਐ ॥
2. ਜੇਹਾ ਘਾਲੇ[506] ਘਾਲਣਾ ਤੇਵੇਹੋ ਨਾਉ ਪਚਾਰੀਐ[507] ॥
3. ਐਸੀ ਕਲਾ ਨ ਖੇਡੀਐ ਜਿਤੁ ਦਰਗਹ ਗਇਆ ਹਾਰੀਐ ॥
4. ਪੜਿਆ ਅਤੈ ਓਮੀਆ ਵੀਚਾਰੁ ਅਗੈ[508] ਵੀਚਾਰੀਐ ॥
5. ਮੁਹਿ ਚਲੈ[509] ਸੁ ਅਗੈ[510] ਮਾਰੀਐ ॥ ੧੨ ॥

ਪਉੜੀ ॥

1. ਪੜਿਆ ਆ ਹੋਵੈ ਗੁਨਹਾਗਾਰੁ ਤਾ ਏਮੀ[505] ਸਾਧੁ ਨ ਮਾਰੀਐ ॥
2. ਜੇਹਾ ਘਾਲੇ[506] ਘਾਲਣਾ ਤੇਵੇਹੋ ਨਾਉ ਪਚਾਰੀਐ[507] ॥
3. ਐਸੀ ਕਲਾ ਨ ਖੇਡੀਐ ਜਿਤੁ ਦਰਗਹ ਗਇਆ ਹਾਰੀਐ ॥
4. ਪੜਿਆ ਅਤੈ ਏਮੀਆ ਵੀਚਾਰੁ ਅਗੈ[508] ਵੀਚਾਰੀਐ ॥
5. ਮੁਹਿ ਚਲੈ[509] ਸੁ ਅਗੈ[510] ਮਾਰੀਐ ॥ ੧੨ ॥

Pauri.

1. parhi-aa hovai gunahgaar taa omee[505] saaDh na maaree-ai.
2. jayhaa ghaalay[506] ghaalnaa tayvayho naa-o pachaaree-ai[507].
3. aisee kalaa na khaydee-ai jit dargeh ga-i-aa haaree-ai.
4. parhi-aa atai omee-aa veechaar agai[508] veechaaree-ai.
5. muhi[509] chalai so agai[510] maaree-ai. ||12||

Theme

Pauri

One reaps whatever one sows. The Divine justice is impartial and does not distinguish between high and low.

Literal Meaning

Pauri

1. It is not fair that if a literate person be a sinner, then an illiterate saint be punished (for literate person's sin).
2. As one acts, so does one receive the reward.
3. One should not act in a subversive manner wherefore, one loses face at the court of God.
4. Divine judgement shall be pronounced for both wise and ignorant in the life-hereafter.
5. The foul-mouth (head strong) talkers shall receive blunt rejection in the next world.

---

[505] Illiterate
[506] Deeds

[507] To acquire
[508] In the next world

[509] Headstrong
[510] Next world

ਆਸਾ ਮਹਲਾ ੪ ॥

आसा महला ४ ॥

Asa Mehla 4.

Asa Mehla 4.

ਜਿਨ ਮਸਤਕਿ ਧੁਰਿ ਹਰਿ ਲਿਖਿਆ ਤਿਨਾ ਸਤਿਗੁਰੁ ਮਿਲਿਆ ਰਾਮ ਰਾਜੇ ॥

जिन मसतकि धुरि हरि लिखिआ तिना सतिगुरु मिलिआ राम राजे ॥

jin mastak Dhur har likhi-aa tinaa satgur mili-aa raam raajay.

Those who have performed good karmas and have been blessed they meet Waheguru, the King of Kings.

ਅਗਿਆਨ ਅੰਧੇਰਾ ਕਟਿਆ ਗੁਰ ਗਿਆਨ ਘਟਿ ਬਲਿਆ ॥

अगिआनु अंधेरा कटिआ गुर गिआनु घटि बलिआ ॥

agi-aan anDhayraa kati-aa gur gi-aan ghat bali-aa.

The Master removes the darkness of ignorance, and spiritual wisdom illuminates hearts.

ਹਰਿ ਲਧਾ ਰਤਨੁ ਪਦਾਰਥੋ ਫਿਰਿ ਬਹੁੜਿ ਨ ਚਲਿਆ ॥

हरि लधा रतनु पदारथो फिरि बहुड़ि न चलिआ ॥

har laDhaa ratan padaaratho fir bahurh na chali-aa.

Those who find the wealth of the jewel of Waheguru they do not wander any longer.

ਜਨ ਨਾਨਕ ਨਾਮੁ ਆਰਾਧਿਆ ਆਰਾਧਿ ਹਰਿ ਮਿਲਿਆ ॥੧॥

जन नानक नामु आराधिआ आराधि हरि मिलिआ ॥ १ ॥

jan naanak naam aaraaDhi-aa aaraaDh har mili-aa. ||1||

Those who meditate on the Nam, the Name of Waheguru, they in their deep meditation meet Waheguru. ||1||

Pauri 13 with 2 sloaks
(Guru Nanak 2)

ਸਲੋਕੁ ਮਃ ੧ ॥

1. ਨਾਨਕ ਮੇਰੁ^{੫੧੧} ਸਰੀਰ ਕਾ ਇਕੁ ਰਥੁ^{੫੧੨} ਇਕੁ ਰਥਵਾਹੁ^{੫੧੩} ॥
2. ਜੁਗ ਜੁਗ ਫੇਰਿ ਵਟਾਈਅਹਿ^{੫੧੪} ਗਿਆਨੀ ਬੁਝਹਿ ਤਾਹਿ ॥
3. ਸਤਜੁਗਿ ਰਥੁ ਸੰਤੋਖੁ^{੫੧੫} ਕਾ ਧਰਮੁ^{੫੧੬} ਅਗੈ ਰਥਵਾਹੁ ॥
4. ਤ੍ਰੇਤੈ ਰਥੁ ਜਤੈ^{੫੧੭} ਕਾ ਜੋਰੁ^{੫੧੮} ਅਗੈ ਰਥਵਾਹੁ ॥
5. ਦੁਆਪੁਰਿ ਰਥੁ ਤਪੈ^{੫੧੯} ਕਾ ਸਤੁ^{੫੨੦} ਅਗੈ ਰਥਵਾਹੁ ॥
6. ਕਲਜੁਗਿ ਰਥੁ ਅਗਨਿ ਕਾ ਕੂੜੁ ਅਗੈ ਰਥਵਾਹੁ ॥ ੧ ॥

सलोकु मः १ ॥

1. नानक मेरु^{५११} सरीर का इकु रथु^{५१२} इकु रथवाहु^{५१३} ॥
2. जुगु जुगु फेरि वटाईअहि^{५१४} गिआनी बुझहि ताहि ॥
3. सतजुगि रथु संतोखु^{५१५} का धरमु^{५१६} अगै रथवाहु ॥
4. त्रेते रथु जतै^{५१७} का जोरु^{५१८} अगै रथवाहु ॥
5. दुआपुरि रथु तपै^{५१९} का सतु^{५२०} अगै रथवाहु ॥
6. कलजुगि रथु अगनि का कूड़ु अगै रथवाहु ॥ १ ॥

Sloak Mehla 1.

1. naanak mayr[511] sareer kaa ik rath[512] ik rathvaahu[513].
2. jug jug fayr vataa-ee-ah[514] gi-aanee bujheh taahi.
3. satjug rath santokh[515] kaa Dharam[516] agai rathvaahu.
4. taraytai rath jatai[517] kaa jor[518] agai rathvaahu.
5. du-aapur rath tapai[519] kaa sat[520] agai rathvaahu.
6. kaljug rath agan kaa koorh agai rathvaahu. ||1||

---

[511] Prime, as the legendary Mer mountain is the pivot of all stars, so is the human body amongst the whole creation.
[512] Chariot
[513] Charioteer
[514] To change
[515] Compassion
[516] Piety
[517] Continence, abstention
[518] Power
[519] Penances
[520] Truth

ਮਃ ੧ ॥

1. ਸਾਮ[੫੨੧] ਕਹੈ ਸੇਤੰਬਰੁ[੫੨੨] ਸੁਆਮੀ ਸਚ ਮਹਿ ਆਛੈ ਸਾਚਿ ਰਹੇ ॥
2. ਸਭੁ ਕੋ ਸਚਿ ਸਮਾਵੈ ॥
3. ਰਿਗੁ[੫੨੩] ਕਹੈ ਰਹਿਆ ਭਰਪੂਰਿ[੫੨੪] ॥
4. ਰਾਮ ਨਾਮੁ ਦੇਵਾ ਮਹਿ ਸੂਰੁ[੫੨੫] ॥
5. ਨਾਇ ਲਇਐ ਪਰਾਛਤ[੫੨੬] ਜਾਹਿ ॥
6. ਨਾਨਕ ਤਉ ਮੋਖੰਤਰੁ ਪਾਹਿ ॥
7. ਜੁਜ[੫੨੭] ਮਹਿ ਜੋਰਿ ਛਲੀ ਚੰਦ੍ਰਾਵਲਿ[੫੨੮] ਕਾਨ੍ ਕ੍ਰਿਸਨੁ ਜਾਦਮੁ[੫੨੯] ਭਇਆ ॥
8. ਪਾਰਜਾਤੁ[੫੩੦] ਗੋਪੀ ਲੈ ਆਇਆ[੫੩੧] ਬਿੰਦ੍ਰਾਬਨ ਮਹਿ ਰੰਗੁ ਕੀਆ[੫੩੨] ॥
9. ਕਲਿ ਮਹਿ ਬੇਦੁ ਅਥਰਬਣੁ[੫੩੩] ਹੂਆ ਨਾਉ ਖੁਦਾਈ ਅਲਹੁ ਭਇਆ[੫੩੪] ॥
10. ਨੀਲ ਬਸਤ੍ਰ ਲੇ ਕਪੜੇ[੫੩੫] ਪਹਿਰੇ ਤੁਰਕ ਪਠਾਣੀ ਅਮਲੁ ਕੀਆ[੫੩੬] ॥
11. ਚਾਰੇ ਵੇਦ ਹੋਏ ਸਚਿਆਰ ॥
12. ਪੜਹਿ ਗੁਣਹਿ ਤਿਨ੍ ਚਾਰ ਵੀਚਾਰ[੫੩੭] ॥
13. ਭਉ[੫੩੮] ਭਗਤਿ ਕਰਿ ਨੀਚੁ[੫੩੯] ਸਦਾਏ ॥
14. ਤਉ ਨਾਨਕ ਮੋਖੰਤਰੁ ਪਾਏ ॥ ੨ ॥

मः १ ॥

1. साम[५२१] कहै सेतंबरु[५२२] सुआमी सच महि आछै साचि रहे ॥
2. सभु को सचि समावै ॥
3. रिगु[५२३] कहै रहिआ भरपूरि[५२४] ॥
4. राम नामु देवा महि सूरु[५२५] ॥
5. नाइ लइऐ पराछत[५२६] जाहि ॥
6. नानक तउ मोखंतरु पाहि ॥
7. जुज[५२७] महि जोरि छली चंद्रावलि[५२८] कान्ह क्रिसनु जादमु[५२९] भइआ ॥
8. पारजातु[५३०] गोपी लै आइआ[५३१] बिंद्राबन महि रंगु कीआ[५३२] ॥
9. कलि महि बेदु अथरबणु[५३३] हूआ नाउ खुदाई अलहु भइआ[५३४] ॥
10. नील बसत्र ले कपड़े[५३५] पहिरे तुरक पठाणी अमलु कीआ[५३६] ॥
11. चारे वेद होए सचिआर ॥
12. पड़हि गुणहि तिन्ह चार वीचार[५३७] ॥
13. भउ[५३८] भगति करि नीचु[५३९] सदाए ॥
14. तउ नानक मोखंतरु पाए ॥ २ ॥

Mehla 1.

1. saam[521] kahai saytambar[522] su-aamee sach meh aachhai saach rahay.
2. sabh ko sach samaavai.
3. rig[523] kahai rahi-aa bharpoor[524].
4. raam naam dayvaa meh soor[525].
5. naa-ay la-i-ai paraachhat[526] jaahi.
6. naanak ta-o mokhantar paahi.
7. juj[527] meh jor chhalee chandraaval[528] kaan[H] krisan jaadam[529] bha-i-aa.
8. paarjaat[530] gopee lai aa-i-aa[531] bindraaban meh rang kee-aa[532].
9. kal meh bayd atharban[533] hoo-aa naa-o khudaa-ee alhu bha-i-aa[534].
10. neel bastar lay kaprhay[535] pahiray turak pathaanee amal kee-aa[536].
11. chaaray vayd ho-ay sachiaar.
12. parheh guneh tin[H] chaar veechaar[537].
13. bhaa-o[538] bhagat kar neech[539] sadaa-ay.
14. ta-o naanak mokhantar paa-ay. ||2||

521 Samveda
522 White-robed
523 Rigveda
524 Omnipresence
525 To exalt
526 Sins
527 Yujarveda
528 By force Chandrawal is seduced
529 Yadav
530 Elysian tree
531 For the milkmaids
532 Revel, merrymaking
533 Atharvaveda
534 God was named as Allah
535 Selected people wore blue robes
536 To rule (Muslims-Turks ruled)
537 Four doctrines
538 Love
539 Meek

Theme

Sloak Mehla 1

Human body is a chariot and it is driven by its soul as a charioteer. Both chariot and charioteer have changed in character and deeds in different eras.

Mehla 1

The four Vedas represent different eras and their character.

Literal Meaning

Sloak Mehla 1

1. Human life is borne by a chariot and a charioteer.
2. These two have been changing in every era – the wise do know this.
3. In the Satyuga the chariot was **Contentment**, and the charioteer was **Righteousness**.
4. In the Tretayuga the chariot was **Penance** (Continence) and charioteer was **Power.**
5. In the Dwaparyuga the chariot was **Austerity** and the charioteer was **Purity of life**.
6. In the Kalyuga the chariot is **Flame of Passion** and the charioteer is **Falsehood**.

Mehla 1

1. The Samveda affirms that in the Satyuga white-clad Waheguru abided in Truth.
2. Truth prevailed everywhere.
3. The Rigveda affirms, in Tretayuga, that God is omnipresent.
4. Rama emerged as a shining star amongst gods.
5. God's name wipes off all sins.
6. And human beings are lead to the gates of liberation.
7. The Yajurveda affirms, in Dwaparyuga, that Krishna of Yadav tribe seduced Chandravali.
8. He courted Satya Bhama, brought Parjat tree from heavens and enjoyed a colourful time in Vrindaban.
9. The Atharvaveda affirms, in Kaliyuga, that God was known as Allah.
10. The chosen people, in this age, wore blue robes and adopted the stance of Muslims and Turks.
11. All four Vedas affirm things in their own way.
12. Those who read and search deeply, they find these four affirmations.
13. The vital truth of life is, that those who love God, and remain humblest of the humble,
14. They alone attain liberation.

ਪਉੜੀ ॥

1. ਸਤਿਗੁਰ ਵਿਟਹੁ[540] ਵਾਰਿਆ ਜਿਤੁ ਮਿਲਿਐ ਖਸਮੁ[541] ਸਮਾਲਿਆ[542] ॥

2. ਜਿਨਿ ਕਰਿ ਉਪਦੇਸੁ ਗਿਆਨ ਅੰਜਨੁ[543] ਦੀਆ ਇਨੀ ਨੇਤ੍ਰੀ ਜਗਤੁ ਨਿਹਾਲਿਆ ॥

3. ਖਸਮੁ ਛੋਡਿ ਦੂਜੈ ਲਗੇ ਡੁਬੇ ਸੇ ਵਣਜਾਰਿਆ[544] ॥

4. ਸਤਿਗੁਰੁ ਹੈ ਬੋਹਿਥਾ[545] ਵਿਰਲੈ ਕਿਨੈ ਵੀਚਾਰਿਆ ॥

5. ਕਰਿ ਕਿਰਪਾ ਪਾਰਿ ਉਤਾਰਿਆ ॥ ੧੩ ॥

ਪਉੜੀ ॥

1. ਸਤਿਗੁਰ ਵਿਟਹੁ[540] ਵਾਰਿਆ ਜਿਤੁ ਮਿਲਿਐ ਖਸਮੁ[541] ਸਮਾਲਿਆ[542] ॥

2. ਜਿਨਿ ਕਰਿ ਉਪਦੇਸੁ ਗਿਆਨ ਅੰਜਨੁ[543] ਦੀਆ ਇਨੀ ਨੇਤ੍ਰੀ ਜਗਤੁ ਨਿਹਾਲਿਆ ॥

3. ਖਸਮੁ ਛੋਡਿ ਦੂਜੈ ਲਗੇ ਡੁਬੇ ਸੇ ਵਣਜਾਰਿਆ[544] ॥

4. ਸਤਿਗੁਰੂ ਹੈ ਬੋਹਿਥਾ[545] ਵਿਰਲੈ ਕਿਨੈ ਵੀਚਾਰਿਆ ॥

5. ਕਰਿ ਕਿਰਪਾ ਪਾਰਿ ਉਤਾਰਿਆ ॥ ੧੩ ॥

Pauri.

1. satgur vitahu[540] vaari-aa jit mili-ai khasam[541] samaali-aa[542].

2. jin kar updays gi-aan anjan[543] dee-aa inHee naytree jagat nihaali-aa.

3. khasam chhod doojai lagay dubay say vanjaari-aa[544].

4. satguroo hai bohithaa[545] virlai kinai veechaari-aa.

5. kar kirpaa paar utaari-aa. ||13||

Theme

Pauri

One can swim the worldly ocean only with the Grace of Waheguru.

Literal Meaning

Pauri

1. May I be a sacrifice unto my true Guru-teacher, whose grace has inculcated into me the Divine Spirit.

2. Whose teachings have lent me the soot of my eyes, which has enabled me to have true vision of this wonderful world.

3. I now know that those who have forsaken their Master and have turned to evil, they all are doomed.

4. The true Guru-teacher is the boat that will ferry us across the turbulent ocean of life.

5. Only a few know that those who are blessed by Waheguru's Grace attain Mukti (liberation, redemption)

---

[540] Unto
[541] God, Waheguru
[542] To find
[543] Black soot which women put in their eyes
[544] Merchant
[545] Boat

ਜਿਨੀ ਐਸਾ ਹਰਿ ਨਾਮੁ ਨ ਚੇਤਿਓ ਸੇ ਕਾਹੇ ਜਗਿ ਆਏ ਰਾਮ ਰਾਜੇ ॥

ਜਿਨੀ ਐਸਾ ਹਰਿ ਨਾਮੁ ਨ ਚੇਤਿਏ ਸੇ ਕਾਹੇ ਜਗਿ ਆਏ ਰਾਮ ਰਾਜੇ ॥

jinee aisaa har naam na chayti-o say kaahay jag aa-ay raam raajay.

Those who have not kept Waheguru's Name in their consciousness - why did they bother to come into the world, O King of Kings?

ਇਹੁ ਮਾਨਸ ਜਨਮੁ ਦੁਲੰਭੁ ਹੈ ਨਾਮ ਬਿਨਾ ਬਿਰਥਾ ਸਭੁ ਜਾਏ ॥

ਇਹੁ ਮਾਣਸ ਜਨਮੁ ਦੁਲਮ੍ਭੁ ਹੈ ਨਾਮ ਬਿਨਾ ਬਿਰਥਾ ਸਭੁ ਜਾਏ ॥

ih maanas janam dulambh hai naam binaa birthaa sabh jaa-ay.

It is so difficult to obtain this human incarnation, and without the Nam, it is all futile and useless.

ਹੁਣਿ ਵਤੈ ਹਰਿ ਨਾਮੁ ਨ ਬੀਜਿਓ ਅਗੈ ਭੁਖਾ ਕਿਆ ਖਾਏ ॥

ਹੁਣਿ ਵਤੈ ਹਰਿ ਨਾਮੁ ਨ ਬੀਜਿਏ ਅਗੈ ਭੁਖਾ ਕਿਆ ਖਾਏ ॥

hun vatai har naam na beeji-o agai bhukhaa ki-aa khaa-ay.

Now, when in this most fortunate season, he does not plant the seed of the Name of Waheguru; what will the hungry soul eat, in the world hereafter?

ਮਨਮੁਖਾ ਨੋ ਫਿਰਿ ਜਨਮੁ ਹੈ ਨਾਨਕ ਹਰਿ ਭਾਏ ੨॥

ਮਨਮੁਖਾ ਨੋ ਫਿਰਿ ਜਨਮੁ ਹੈ ਨਾਨਕ ਹਰਿ ਭਾਏ ॥ ੨ ॥

manmukhaa no fir janam hai naanak har bhaa-ay. ||2||

The self-willed non-believers are born again and again. Such is the law of Waheguru. ||2||

Pauri 14 with 2 sloaks (Guru Nanak 2)

ਸਲੋਕੁ ਮਃ ੧ ॥

1. ਸਿੰਮਲ੫੪੬ ਰੁਖੁ੫੪੭ ਸਰਾਇਰਾ੫੪੮ ਅਤਿ੫੪੯ ਦੀਰਘ੫੫੦ ਅਤਿ ਮੁਚੁ੫੫੧ ॥

2. ਓਇ ਜਿ ਆਵਹਿ ਆਸ ਕਰਿ ਜਾਹਿ ਨਿਰਾਸੇ ਕਿਤੁ੫੫੨ ॥

3. ਫਲ ਫਿਕੇ ਫੁਲ ਬਕਬਕੇ੫੫੩ ਕੰਮਿ ਨ ਆਵਹਿ ਪਤ੫੫੪ ॥

4. ਮਿਠਤੁ੫੫੫ ਨੀਵੀ੫੫੬ ਨਾਨਕਾ ਗੁਣ ਚੰਗਿਆਈਆ ਤਤੁ੫੫੭ ॥

5. ਸਭੁ ਕੋ ਨਿਵੈ ਆਪ ਕਉ ਪਰ੫੫੮ ਕਉ ਨਿਵੈ ਨ ਕੋਇ ॥

6. ਧਰਿ ਤਾਰਾਜੂ ਤੋਲੀਐ ਨਿਵੈ ਸੁ ਗਉਰਾ੫੫੯ ਹੋਇ ॥

7. ਅਪਰਾਧੀ ਦੂਣਾ ਨਿਵੈ ਜੋ ਹੰਤਾ੫੬੦ ਮਿਰਗਾਹਿ੫੬੧ ॥

8. ਸੀਸਿ ਨਿਵਾਇਐ ਕਿਆ ਥੀਐ ਜਾ ਰਿਦੈ ਕੁਸੁਧੇ੫੬੨ ਜਾਹਿ ॥ ੧ ॥

सलोकु मः १ ॥

1. सिंमल੫੪੬ रुखु੫੪੭ सराइरा੫੪੮ अति੫੪੯ दीरघ੫੫੦ अति मुचु੫੫੧ ॥

2. उइ जि आवहि आस करि जाहि निरासे कितु੫੫੨ ॥

3. फल फिके फुल बकबके੫੫੩ कंमि न आवहि पत੫੫੪ ॥

4. मिठतु੫੫੫ नीवी੫੫੬ नानका गुण चंगिआईआ ततु੫੫੭ ॥

5. सभु को निवै आप कउ पर੫੫੮ कउ निवै न कोइ ॥

6. धरि ताराजू तोलीऐ निवै सु गउरा੫੫੯ होइ ॥

7. अपराधी दूणा निवै जो हंता੫੬੦ मिरगाहि੫੬੧ ॥

8. सीसि निवाइऐ किआ थीऐ जा रिदै कुसुधे੫੬੨ जाहि ॥ १ ॥

Sloak Mehla 1.

1. simmal[546] rukh[547] saraa-iraa[548] at[549] deeragh[550] at much[551].

2. o-ay je aavahi aas kar jaahi niraasay kit[552].

3. fal fikay ful bakbakay[553] kamm na aavahi pat[554].

4. mithat[555] neevee[556] naankaa gun chang-aa-ee-aa tat[557].

5. sabh ko nivai aap ka-o par[558] ka-o nivai na ko-ay.

6. Dhar taaraajoo tolee-ai nivai so ga-uraa[559] ho-ay.

7. apraaDhee doonaa nivai jo hantaa[560] miragaahi[561].

8. sees nivaa-i-ai ki-aa thee-ai jaa ridai kusuDhay[562] jaahi. ||1||

---

[546] A kind of tree, bombax hepta phylum
[547] Tree
[548] Straight like an arrow
[549] Very
[550] Tall
[551] Thick

[552] Many
[553] Without any fragrance
[554] Leaves
[555] Sweetness
[556] Humility
[557] Essence

[558] For others
[559] Heavier
[560] Hunter
[561] Deer
[562] Filthy

ਮਃ ੧ ॥	ਮਃ ੧ ॥	**Mehla 1.**

ਮਃ ੧ ॥

1. ਪੜਿ ਪੁਸਤਕ ਸੰਧਿਆ ਬਾਦੰ ⁵⁶³ ॥
2. ਸਿਲ⁵⁶⁴ ਪੂਜਸਿ ਬਗੁਲ⁵⁶⁵ ਸਮਾਧੰ⁵⁶⁶ ॥
3. ਮੁਖਿ ਝੂਠ ਬਿਭੂਖਣ⁵⁶⁷ ਸਾਰੰ⁵⁶⁸ ॥
4. ਤ੍ਰੈਪਾਲ⁵⁶⁹ ਤਿਹਾਲ⁵⁷⁰ ਬਿਚਾਰੰ⁵⁷¹ ॥
5. ਗਲਿ ਮਾਲਾ ਤਿਲਕੁ ਲਿਲਾਟੰ⁵⁷² ॥
6. ਦੁਇ⁵⁷³ ਧੋਤੀ ਬਸਤ੍ਰ⁵⁷⁴ ਕਪਾਟੰ⁵⁷⁵ ॥
7. ਜੇ ਜਾਣਸਿ ਬ੍ਰਹਮੰ⁵⁷⁶ ਕਰਮੰ ॥
8. ਸਭਿ ਫੋਕਟ⁵⁷⁷ ਨਿਸਚਉ⁵⁷⁸ ਕਰਮੰ ॥
9. ਕਹੁ ਨਾਨਕ ਨਿਹਚਉ⁵⁷⁹ ਧਿਆਵੈ ॥
10. ਵਿਣੁ ਸਤਿਗੁਰ ਵਾਟ⁵⁸⁰ ਨ ਪਾਵੈ ॥ ੨ ॥

मः १ ॥

1. पड़ि पुसतक संधिआ बादं ⁵⁶³ ॥
2. सिल⁵⁶⁴ पूजसि बगुल⁵⁶⁵ समाधं⁵⁶⁶ ॥
3. मुखि झूठ बिभूखण⁵⁶⁷ सारं⁵⁶⁸ ॥
4. त्रैपाल⁵⁶⁹ तिहाल⁵⁷⁰ बिचारं⁵⁷¹ ॥
5. गलि माला तिलकु लिलाटं⁵⁷² ॥
6. दुइ⁵⁷³ धोती बसत्र⁵⁷⁴ कपाटं⁵⁷⁵ ॥
7. जे जाणसि ब्रहमं⁵⁷⁶ करमं ॥
8. सभि फोकट⁵⁷⁷ निसचउ⁵⁷⁸ करमं ॥
9. कहु नानक निहचउ⁵⁷⁹ धिआवै ॥
10. विणु सतिगुर वाट⁵⁸⁰ न पावै ॥ २ ॥

Mehla 1.

1. parh pustak sanDhi-aa baada[N563].
2. sil[564] poojas bagul[565] samaaDha[N566].
3. mukh jhooth bibhookhan[567] saara[N568].
4. taraipaal[569] tihaal[570] bichaara[N571].
5. gal maalaa tilak lilaata[N572].
6. du-ay[573] Dhotee bastar[574] kapaata[N575].
7. jay jaanas barahma[N576] karma[N].
8. sabh fokat[577] nischa-o[578] karma[N].
9. kaho naanak nihcha-o[579] Dhi-aavai.
10. vin satgur vaat[580] na paavai. ||2||

---

[563] Discourse and prayers
[564] Stone, images
[565] Crane
[566] Trance
[567] Ornaments
[568] Precious
[569] Three-legged Gayatri

[570] Three times
[571] Prayers
[572] Forehead
[573] Both
[574] Headgear
[575] Head
[576] Waheguru

[577] Useless, in vain
[578] Belief
[579] Faith
[580] Way to God

Theme	Literal Meaning

Theme

Sloak Mehla 1

Waheguru can be realised by humility and compassion.

Mehla 1

Useless rituals and superstitions are impediments rather than aids to realise God.

Literal Meaning

Sloak Mehla 1

1. The Simmal tree is straight like an arrow, tall and hefty
2. Yet, those who come to it for fruit and shelter, they go back dismayed with their hopes shattered.
3. For its fruit is tasteless, flowers have no fragrance and leaves are also useless.
4. Of all virtues, sweetness and humility are two sterling qualities.
5. Some pretend to be humble for their selfish interests and not to serve others.
6. Still, it is a universal truth that of the two sides of a weighing scale, one that dips lower, is surely heavier than the other.
7. Beware, when you see a sinner bowing twice and a hunter bowing to aim at a deer.
8. So bowing is a bluff; bowing means nothing if the heart is impure and the mind is filled with cunningness.

Mehla 1

1. The pretentious (one who makes false claims) pundit reads books, says prayers and is ever ready for a dialogue.
2. He worships stones and sits before them in a trance, much as a crane would do when it aims at its target.
3. He stores numerous lies in his heart and presents fake ornaments as pure and expensive jewellery.
4. He recites 'Gayatri Mantra' thrice a day.
5. He wears a necklace and applies saffron mark on his forehead.
6. He carries both a cotton sari and a towel as his headgear.
7. If only he knew Waheguru's true instructions,
8. He would not have practised these hollow actions.
9. One is required to pray to Waheguru with purity of mind and heart (and needs no surrounding rituals)
10. For the right path one should follow the instructions of a true Guru-teacher.

ਪਉੜੀ ॥

1. ਕਪੜੁ ਰੂਪੁ ਸੁਹਾਵਣਾ ਛਡਿ ਦੁਨੀਆ ਅੰਦਰਿ ਜਾਵਣਾ ॥

2. ਮੰਦਾ ਚੰਗਾ ਆਪਣਾ ਆਪੇ ਹੀ ਕੀਤਾ ਪਾਵਣਾ ॥

3. ਹੁਕਮ ਕੀਏ ਮਨਿ ਭਾਵਦੇ⁵⁸¹ ਰਾਹਿ ਭੀੜੈ ਅਗੈ ਜਾਵਣਾ ⁵⁸² ॥

4. ਨੰਗਾ ਦੋਜਕਿ ਚਲਿਆ⁵⁸³ ਤਾ ਦਿਸੈ ਖਰਾ ਡਰਾਵਣਾ ⁵⁸⁴ ॥

5. ਕਰਿ ਅਉਗਣ ਪਛੋਤਾਵਣਾ ॥ ੧੪ ॥

ਪਉੜੀ ॥

1. ਕਪੜੁ ਰੂਪੁ ਸੁਹਾਵਣਾ ਛਡਿ ਦੁਨੀਆ ਅੰਦਰਿ ਜਾਵਣਾ ॥

2. ਮੰਦਾ ਚੰਗਾ ਆਪਣਾ ਆਪੇ ਹੀ ਕੀਤਾ ਪਾਵਣਾ ॥

3. ਹੁਕਮ ਕੀਏ ਮਨਿ ਭਾਵਦੇ⁵⁸¹ ਰਾਹਿ ਭੀੜੈ ਅਗੈ ਜਾਵਣਾ ⁵⁸² ॥

4. ਨੰਗਾ ਦੋਜਕਿ ਚਲਿਆ⁵⁸³ ਤਾ ਦਿਸੈ ਖਰਾ ਡਰਾਵਣਾ ⁵⁸⁴ ॥

5. ਕਰਿ ਅਉਗਣ ਪਛੋਤਾਵਣਾ ॥ ੧੪ ॥

Pauri.

1. kaparh roop suhaavanaa chhad dunee-aa andar jaavnaa.

2. mandaa changa aapnaa aapay hee keetaa paavnaa.

3. hukam kee-ay man bhaavday[581] raahi bheerhai agai jaavnaa[582].

4. nangaa dojak chaali-aa[583] taa disai kharaa daraavanaa[584].

5. kar a-ugan pachhotaavanaa. ||14||

Theme

Pauri

Only karmas go with human beings to the next world and not any of their belongings

Literal Meaning

Pauri

1. This beautiful human body, perforce, would be forsaken when one would leave this world.
2. Hereafter, one has to harvest good or bad harvest according to one's action (sowing seed)
3. Even those who had their commands followed here, shall have to traverse (move across) the narrow bridge in the world to go.
4. One who is sent to hell and exposed there, he/she shall have most horrifying and terrible experience.
5. Such a person would certainly repent for his transgression (breaking of ethical and religious laws).

---

581 Orders given according to one's heart/mind
582 Hereafter the passage to cross is very narrow

583 One goes to the hell all naked
584 To look terrible

ਤੂੰ ਹਰਿ ਤੇਰਾ ਸਭੁ ਕੋ ਸਭਿ ਤੁਧੁ ਉਪਾਏ ਰਾਮ ਰਾਜੇ ॥

ਤੂੰ ਹਰਿ ਤੇਰਾ ਸਭੁ ਕੋ ਸਭਿ ਤੁਧੁ ਉਪਾਇਏ ਰਾਮ ਰਾਜੇ ॥

too^N har tayraa sabh ko sabh tuDh upaa-ay raam raajay.

You, O Waheguru, belong to all, and all belong to You.
You created all, O King of the Kings.

ਕਿਛੁ ਹਾਥਿ ਕਿਸੈ ਦੈ ਕਿਛੁ ਨਾਹੀ ਸਭਿ ਚਲਹਿ ਚਲਾਏ ॥

ਕਿਛੁ ਹਾਥਿ ਕਿਸੈ ਦੈ ਕਿਛੁ ਨਾਹੀ ਸਭਿ ਚਲਹਿ ਚਲਾਏ ॥

kichh haath kisai dai kichh naahee sabh chaleh chalaa-ay.

Nothing is in anyone's hands; all walk as Waheguru
causes them to walk.

ਜਿਨ ਤੂੰ ਮੇਲਹਿ ਪਿਆਰੇ ਸੇ ਤੁਧੁ ਮਿਲਹਿ ਜੋ ਹਰਿ ਮਨਿ ਭਾਏ ॥

ਜਿਨੁ ਤੂੰ ਮੇਲਹਿ ਪਿਆਰੇ ਸੇ ਤੁਧੁ ਮਿਲਹਿ ਜੋ ਹਰਿ ਮਨਿ ਭਾਏ ॥

jin^H too^N mayleh pi-aaray say tuDh mileh jo har man bhaa-ay.

They alone are united with You, O beloved,
whom You cause to be so united; they alone are pleasing to Your
mind.

ਜਨ ਨਾਨਕ ਸਤਿਗੁਰੁ ਭੇਟਿਆ ਹਰਿ ਨਾਮਿ ਤਰਾਏ ॥੩॥

ਜਨ ਨਾਨਕ ਸਤਿਗੁਰੁ ਭੇਟਿਆ ਹਰਿ ਨਾਮਿ ਤਰਾਏ ॥ ੩ ॥

jan naanak satgur bhayti-aa har naam taraa-ay. ||3||

Those who find the true Guru, they are carried across
through the raft of his Name ||3||

*Pauri 15 with 4 sloaks
(Guru Nanak 4)*

ਸਲੋਕੁ ਮਃ ੧ ॥

1. ਦਇਆ[585] ਕਪਾਹ[586] ਸੰਤੋਖੁ[587] ਸੂਤੁ[588] ਜਤੁ[589] ਗੰਢੀ[590] ਸਤੁ[591] ਵਟੁ[592] ॥
2. ਏਹੁ ਜਨੇਊ[593] ਜੀਅ ਕਾ ਹਈ ਤ[594] ਪਾਡੇ ਘਤੁ[595] ॥
3. ਨਾ ਏਹੁ ਤੁਟੈ ਨ ਮਲੁ[596] ਲਗੈ ਨਾ ਏਹੁ ਜਲੈ ਨ ਜਾਇ ॥
4. ਧੰਨੁ ਸੁ ਮਾਣਸ ਨਾਨਕਾ ਜੋ ਗਲਿ ਚਲੇ ਪਾਇ[597] ॥
5. ਚਉਕੜਿ[598] ਮੁਲਿ[599] ਅਣਾਇਆ[600] ਬਹਿ ਚਉਕੈ[601] ਪਾਇਆ ॥
6. ਸਿਖਾ ਕੰਨਿ ਚੜਾਈਆ[602] ਗੁਰੁ ਬ੍ਰਾਹਮਣੁ ਥਿਆ[603] ॥
7. ਓਹੁ ਮੁਆ[604] ਓਹੁ ਝੜਿ ਪਇਆ[605] ਵੇਤਗਾ ਗਇਆ [606] ॥ ੧ ॥

ਸਲੋਕੁ ਮਃ ੧ ॥

1. ਦਇਆ[585] ਕਪਾਹ[586] ਸੰਤੋਖੁ[587] ਸੂਤੁ[588] ਜਤੁ[589] ਗੰਢੀ[590] ਸਤੁ[591] ਵਟੁ[592] ॥
2. ਇਹੁ ਜਨੇਤੂ[593] ਜੀਅ ਕਾ ਹਈ ਤ[594] ਪਾਡੇ ਘਤੁ[595] ॥
3. ਨਾ ਇਹੁ ਤੁਟੈ ਨ ਮਲੁ[596] ਲਗੈ ਨਾ ਇਹੁ ਜਲੈ ਨ ਜਾਇ ॥
4. ਧੰਨੁ ਸੁ ਮਾਣਸ ਨਾਨਕਾ ਜੋ ਗਲਿ ਚਲੇ ਪਾਇਆ[597] ॥
5. ਚਉਕੜਿ[598] ਮੁਲਿ[599] ਅਣਾਇਆ[600] ਬਹਿ ਚਉਕੈ[601] ਪਾਇਆ ॥
6. ਸਿਖਾ ਕੰਨਿ ਚੜਾਈਆ[602] ਗੁਰੁ ਬ੍ਰਾਹਮਣੁ ਥਿਆ[603] ॥
7. ਉਹੁ ਮੁਆ[604] ਉਹੁ ਝੜਿ ਪਇਆ[605] ਵੇਤਗਾ ਗਇਆ [606] ॥ ੧ ॥

Sloak Mehla 1.

1. da-i-aa[585] kapaah[586] santokh[587] soot[588] jat[589] gandhee[590] sat[591] vat[592].
2. ayhu janay-oo[593] jee-a kaa ha-ee ta[594] paaday ghat[595].
3. naa ayhu tutai naa mal[596] lagai naa ayhu jalai na jaa-ay.
4. Dhan so maanas naankaa jo gal chalay paa-ay[597].
5. cha-ukarh[598] mul[599] anaa-i-aa[600] bahi cha-ukai[601] paa-i-aa.
6. sikhaa kann charhaa-ee-aa[602] gur baraahman thi-aa[603].
7. oh mu-aa[604] oh jharh pa-i-aa[605] vaytgaa ga-i-aa.[606] ||1||

---

[585] Compassion
[586] Cotton
[587] Contentment
[588] Cotton thread
[589] Continence, to abstain from sex
[590] Knot
[591] Truth
[592] Twist

[593] Hindu sacred thread
[594] If you have such a sacred thread
[595] To bring
[596] To get soiled
[597] Those who wear such a thread
[598] Four coins
[599] Value, price
[600] To buy, to purchase

[601] Enclosure
[602] Instructions are whispered in the ears
[603] Brahmin (Pandit) acts as a teacher
[604] When the man wearing the thread dies
[605] The thread falls
[606] The person goes to the next world without the thread

ਮਃ ੧ ॥

1. ਲਖ ਚੋਰੀਆ ਲਖ ਜਾਰੀਆਂ⁶⁰⁷ ਲਖ ਕੂੜੀਆਂ⁶⁰⁸ ਲਖ ਗਾਲਿ⁶⁰⁹ ॥
2. ਲਖ ਠਗੀਆਂ⁶¹⁰ ਪਹਿਨਾਮੀਆਂ⁶¹¹ ਰਾਤਿ ਦਿਨਸੁ ਜੀਅ ਨਾਲਿ⁶¹² ॥
3. ਤਗੁ ਕਪਾਹਹੁ ਕਤੀਐ ਬਾਮ੍ਣੁ ਵਟੇ ਆਇ ॥
4. ਕੁਹਿ⁶¹³ ਬਕਰਾ⁶¹⁴ ਰਿੰਨਿ ਖਾਇਆ ਸਭ ਕੋ ਆਖੈ ਪਾਇ⁶¹⁵ ॥
5. ਹੋਇ ਪੁਰਾਣਾ ਸੁਟੀਐ ਭੀ ਫਿਰਿ ਪਾਈਐ ਹੋਰੁ ॥
6. ਨਾਨਕ ਤਗੁ ਨ ਤੁਟਈ ਜੇ ਤਗਿ ਹੋਵੈ ਜੋਰੁ⁶¹⁶ ॥ ੨ ॥

ਮਃ ੧ ॥

1. ਨਾਇ ਮੰਨਿਐ⁶¹² ਪਤਿ ਉਪਜੈ⁶¹⁸ ਸਾਲਾਹੀ ਸਚੁ ਸੂਤੁ⁶¹⁹ ॥
2. ਦਰਗਹ ਅੰਦਰਿ ਪਾਈਐ ਤਗੁ ਨ ਤੁਟਸਿ ਪੂਤ⁶²⁰ ॥ ੩ ॥

म: १ ॥

1. लख चोरीआ लख जारीआ⁶⁰⁷ लख कूड़ीआ⁶⁰⁸ लख गालि⁶⁰⁹ ॥
2. लख ठगीआ⁶¹⁰ पहिनामीआ⁶¹¹ राति दिनसु जीअ नालि⁶¹² ॥
3. तगु कपाहहु कतीऐ बामणु वटे आइ ॥
4. कुहि⁶¹³ बकरा⁶¹⁴ रिंनि खाइआ सभु को आखै पाइ⁶¹⁵ ॥
5. होइ पुराणा सुतीऐ भी फिरि पाईऐ होरु ॥
6. नानक तगु न तुटई जे तगि होवै जोरु⁶¹⁶ ॥ २ ॥

म: १ ॥

1. नाइ मंनिऐ⁶¹⁷ पति उपजै⁶¹⁸ सालाही सचु सूतु⁶¹⁹ ॥
2. दरगह अंदरि पाईऐ तगु न तूटसि पूत⁶²⁰ ॥ ३ ॥

Mehla 1.

1. lakh choree-aa lakh jaaree-aa⁶⁰⁷ lakh koorhee-aa⁶⁰⁸ lakh gaal⁶⁰⁹.
2. lakh thagee-aa⁶¹⁰ pahinaamee-aa⁶¹¹ raat dinas jee-a naal⁶¹².
3. tag kapaahahu katee-ai baamᴴan vatay aa-ay.
4. kuhi⁶¹³ bakraa⁶¹⁴ rinniᴴ khaa-i-aa sabh ko aakhai paa-ay⁶¹⁵.
5. ho-ay puraanaa sutee-ai bhee fir paa-ee-ai hor.
6. naanak tag na tut-ee jay tag hovai jor.⁶¹⁶ ||2||

Mehla 1.

1. naa-ay mani-ai⁶¹⁷ pat oopjai⁶¹⁸ saalaahee sach soot⁶¹⁹.
2. dargeh andar paa-ee-ai tag na tootas poot.⁶²⁰ ||3||

---

⁶⁰⁷ Adulteries
⁶⁰⁸ Falsehood
⁶⁰⁹ Abuses
⁶¹⁰ Deceptions
⁶¹¹ Villainous acts

⁶¹² With fellow friends
⁶¹³ Kill
⁶¹⁴ Goat
⁶¹⁵ To put on the thread
⁶¹⁶ Strong

⁶¹⁷ Believing in the name of Waheguru
⁶¹⁸ Receiving honour
⁶¹⁹ The glories of Waheguru is the real thread
⁶²⁰ Sacred

ਮਃ ੧ ॥

1. ਤਗੁ[621] ਨ ਇੰਦ੍ਰੀ[622] ਤਗੁ ਨ ਨਾਰੀ ॥
2. ਭਲਕੇ ਥੁਕ ਪਵੈ ਨਿਤ ਦਾੜੀ [623] ॥
3. ਤਗੁ ਨ ਪੈਰੀ ਤਗੁ ਨ ਹਥੀ ॥
4. ਤਗੁ ਨ ਜਿਹਵਾ ਤਗੁ ਨ ਅਖੀ ॥
5. ਵੇਤਗਾ[624] ਆਪੇ ਵਤੈ[625] ॥
6. ਵਟਿ ਧਾਗੇ ਅਵਰਾ[626] ਘਤੈ[627] ॥
7. ਲੈ ਭਾੜਿ[628] ਕਰੇ ਵੀਆਹੁ ॥
8. ਕਢਿ ਕਾਗਲੁ[629] ਦਸੇ ਰਾਹੁ ॥
9. ਸੁਣਿ ਵੇਖਹੁ ਲੋਕਾ ਇਹੁ ਵਿਡਾਣੁ[630] ॥
10. ਮਨਿ ਅੰਧਾ ਨਾਉ ਸੁਜਾਣੁ[631] ॥ ੪ ॥

Mehla 1.

1. tag[621] na indree[622] tag na naaree.
2. bhalkay thuk pavai nit daarhee[623].
3. tag na pairee tag na hathee.
4. tag na jihvaa tag na akhee.
5. vaytgaa[624] aapay vatai[625].
6. vat Dhaagay avraa[626] ghatai[627].
7. lai bhaarh[628] karay vee-aahu.
8. kadh kaagal[629] dasay raahu.
9. sun vaykhhu lokaa ayhu vidaan[630].
10. man anDhaa naa-o sujaan[631]. ||4||

---

[621] Thread
[622] Private parts, sexual organs
[623] To be insulted
[624] Without the thread
[625] To wander aimlessly
[626] Others
[627] To call
[628] Fees, commission
[629] Calendar
[630] Strange things
[631] One who can see

Theme

Sloak Mehla 1

A real *Janaeo* (Hindu sacred thread) should be made of compassion, contentment, continence and truth rather than of cotton.

Mehla 1

The thread made of cotton is destroyed with time but the thread made of the above four ingredients lasts for ever and even goes into the next world with the deceased.

Literal Meaning

Sloak Mehla 1

1. O! Pundit, alas you had spun your *Janaeo* with **compassion** rather than cotton-fibre, and had used **contentment** as the yarn, **continence** as the knot and **truth** as its twist.
2. Then only, O! Pundit, I would have worn it, but certainly not the one you have offered me.
3. My thread would not break, neither get soiled, nor burn or even be worn out.
4. That person will, indeed, be the most fortunate who will ascend to skies with such a *Janaeo* around his shoulder.
5. The thread you have brought is not worth even a penny, though you are making people to sit in the sanctified square and wear it.
6. Besides, you also whisper your *'mantra'* into their ears and make them believe that you were their Guru.
7. With the passage of time, the wearer would die, and the thread on him will also burn with his corpse.

Mehla 1

1. Wearing your kind of *Janaeo* people commit thefts, indulge in adultery, utter lies and speak foul language.
2. Furthermore they enter into deceptive transactions day and night.
3. In fact it is merely a cotton thread spun by the Pundit,
4. The ceremony which follows involves slaughtering and eating of he-goat, and those attending the ceremony then congratulate and bless the wearer.
5. When the first thread is worn out, it is replaced with a new one.
6. But, O! Pundit my thread is so strong that it will never wear off.

Theme	Literal Meaning

Mehla 1

The real human honour is the one which comes out of the Name of Waheguru rather than from the worldly achievements.

Mehla 1

1. The intrinsic faith in Waheguru brings one real honour; it is his grace, which presents the genuine *Janaeo*.
2. Which never wears off and ascends with the wearer into the next world.

Mehla 1

One can not realise God with useless rituals.

Mehla 1

1. The Pundit himself has no control (thread) on his sexual drive and on flirting with women.
2. Every daybreak exposes him of his ugly designs.
3. Again he has no control (thread) on his feet walking towards evil houses and his hands holding innocent preys.
4. Also he has no control (thread) on his foul language and lusty looks.
5. Thus he himself wanders around without a divine thread which could have controlled all his movements and kept him under restraint.
6. Yet he goes on offering others the useless thread of his brand.
7. The Pundit performs all ceremonies (including marriages) for material gains.
8. He reads the horoscope and guides others.
9. But folks, listen to this truth,
10. That the Pundit is fake for he cannot see the Truth either with his eyes or with his mind.

ਪਉੜੀ ॥

1. ਸਾਹਿਬੁ ਹੋਇ ਦਇਆਲੁ ਕਿਰਪਾ ਕਰੇ ਤਾ ਸਾਈ ਕਾਰ⁶³² ਕਰਾਇਸੀ ॥

2. ਸੋ ਸੇਵਕੁ ਸੇਵਾ ਕਰੇ ਜਿਸ ਨੋ ਹੁਕਮੁ ਮਨਾਇਸੀ ॥

3. ਹੁਕਮਿ ਮੰਨਿਐ ਹੋਵੈ ਪਰਵਾਣੁ ਤਾ ਖਸਮੈ⁶³³ ਕਾ ਮਹਲੁ ਪਾਇਸੀ ॥

4. ਖਸਮੈ ਭਾਵੈ ਸੋ ਕਰੇ ਮਨਹੁ ਚਿੰਦਿਆ ਸੋ ਫਲੁ ਪਾਇਸੀ ॥

5. ਤਾ ਦਰਗਹ ਪੈਧਾ ਜਾਇਸੀ ॥ ੧੫ ॥

पउड़ी ॥

1. साहिबु होइ दइआलु किरपा करे ता साई कार⁶³² कराइसी ॥

2. सो सेवकु सेवा करे जिस नो हुकमु मनाइसी ॥

3. हुकमि मंनिऐ होवै परवाणु ता खसमै⁶³³ का महलु पाइसी ॥

4. खसमै भावै सो करे मनहु चिंदिआ सो फलु पाइसी ॥

5. ता दरगह पैधा जाइसी ॥ १५ ॥

Pauri.

1. saahib ho-ay da-i-aal kirpaa karay taa saa-ee kaar⁶³² karaa-isee.

2. so sayvak sayvaa karay jis no hukam manaa-isee.

3. hukam mani-ai hovai parvaan taa khasmai⁶³³ kaa mahal paa-isee.

4. khasmai bhaavai so karay manhu chindi-aa so fal paa-isee.

5. taa dargeh paiDhaa jaa-isee. ||15||

Theme

Pauri

All our belongings are achieved with the grace of Waheguru.

Literal Meaning

Pauri

1. When Waheguru blesses a person, and showers his grace upon him/her,
2. Then such a person serves him as his will prompts him/her to do.
3. Persons who submit themselves to Waheguru's will they as his will find a place near his abode.
4. Persons who accept his will without sulking get all their desires fulfilled.
5. And Waheguru receives such persons personally at his court.

---

⁶³² The way of mercy

⁶³³ Waheguru

ਕੋਈ ਗਾਵੈ ਰਾਗੀ ਨਾਦੀ ਬੇਦੀ ਬਹੁ ਭਾਂਤਿ ਕਰਿ ਨਹੀ ਹਰਿ ਹਰਿ ਭੀਜੈ ਰਾਮ ਰਾਜੇ ॥

कोई गावै रागी नादी बेदी बहु भाति करि नही हरि हरि भीजै राम राजे ॥

ko-ee gaavai raagee naadee baydee baho bhaat kar nahee har har bheejai raam raajay.

Some sing Shabads in musical ragas. Some hum the sound of Nad by reciting Vedas. But Waheguru is not necessarily pleased by these, O King of Kings.

ਜਿਨਾ ਅੰਤਰਿ ਕਪਟੁ ਵਿਕਾਰੁ ਹੈ ਤਿਨਾ ਰੋਇ ਕਿਆ ਕੀਜੈ ॥

जिना अंतरि कपटु विकारु है तिना रोइ किआ कीजै ॥

jinaa antar kapat vikaar hai tinaa ro-ay ki-aa keejai.

Those who are filled with fraud and corruption within - what good does it do for them to cry out?

ਹਰਿ ਕਰਤਾ ਸਭੁ ਕਿਛੁ ਜਾਣਦਾ ਸਿਰਿ ਰੋਗ ਹਥੁ ਦੀਜੈ ॥

हरि करता सभु किछु जाणदा सिरि रोग हथु दीजै ॥

har kartaa sabh kichh jaandaa sir rog hath deejai.

The Creator knows everything, although they may try to hide their sins and the causes of their diseases.

ਜਿਨਾ ਨਾਨਕ ਗੁਰਮੁਖਿ ਹਿਰਦਾ ਸੁਧੁ ਹੈ ਹਰਿ ਭਗਤਿ ਹਰਿ ਲੀਜੈ ॥੪॥੧੧॥੧੮॥

जिना नानक गुरमुखि हिरदा सुधु है हरि भगति हरि लीजै ॥ ੪ ॥ ੧੧ ॥ ੧੮ ॥

jinaa naanak gurmukh hirdaa suDh hai har bhagat har leejai. ||4||11||18||

Those true devotees whose hearts are pure, obtain Waheguru by their intense devotional worship. ||4||11||18||

Pauri 16 with 2 sloaks
(Guru Nanak 2)

ਸਲੋਕੁ ਮਃ ੧ ॥

1. ਗਊ ਬਿਰਹਮਨ ਕਉ ਕਰੁ[634] ਲਾਵਹੁ ਗੋਬਰਿ[635] ਤਰਣੁ[636] ਨ ਜਾਈ ॥
2. ਧੋਤੀ[637] ਟਿਕਾ[638] ਤੈ ਜਪਮਾਲੀ[639] ਧਾਨੁ[640] ਮਲੇਛਾਂ[641] ਖਾਈ ॥
3. ਅੰਤਰਿ[642] ਪੂਜਾ[643] ਪੜਹਿ[644] ਕਤੇਬਾ ਸੰਜਮੁ[645] ਤੁਰਕਾਂ[646] ਭਾਈ ॥
4. ਛੋਡੀਲੇ[647] ਪਾਖੰਡਾ[648] ॥
5. ਨਾਮਿ ਲਇਐ ਜਾਹਿ ਤਰੰਦਾ[649] ॥ ੧ ॥

ਮਃ ੧ ॥

1. ਮਾਨਸ[650] ਖਾਨੇ ਕਰਹਿ ਨਿਵਾਜ[651] ॥
2. ਛੁਰੀ[652] ਵਗਾਇਨਿ[653] ਤਿਨ ਗਲਿ[654] ਤਾਗ ॥
3. ਤਿਨ ਘਰਿ ਬ੍ਰਹਮਣ ਪੂਰਹਿ[655] ਨਾਦ[656] ॥
4. ਉਨਾ ਭਿ ਆਵਹਿ ਓਈ ਸਾਦ[657] ॥
5. ਕੂੜੀ ਰਾਸਿ ਕੂੜਾ ਵਾਪਾਰੁ[658] ॥
6. ਕੂੜੁ ਬੋਲਿ ਕਰਹਿ ਆਹਾਰੁ[659] ॥

सलोकु मः १ ॥

1. गउ बिराहमण कउ करु[634] लावहु गोबरि[635] तरणु[636] न जाई ॥
2. धोती[637] टिका[638] तै जपमाली[639] धानु[640] मलेछाँ[641] खाई ॥
3. अंतरि[642] पूजा[643] पड़हि[644] कतेबा संजमु[645] तुरका[646] भाई ॥
4. छोडीले[647] पाखंडा[648] ॥
5. नामि लइऐ जाहि तरंदा[649] ॥ १ ॥

मः १ ॥

1. माणस[650] खाणे करहि निवाज[651] ॥
2. छुरी[652] वगाइनि[653] तिन गलि[654] ताग ॥
3. तिन घरि ब्रहमण पूरहि[655] नाद[656] ॥
4. तुना भि आवहि एई साद[657] ॥
5. कूड़ी रासि कूड़ा वापारु[658] ॥
6. कूड़ु बोलि करहि आहारु[659] ॥

Sloak Mehla 1.

1. ga-oo biraahman ka-o kar[634] laavhu gobar[635] taran[636] na jaa-ee.
2. Dhotee[637] tikaa[638] tai japmaalee[639] Dhaan[640] malaychhaa[N641] khaa-ee.
3. antar[642] poojaa[643] parheh[644] kataybaa sanjam[645] turkaa[646] bhaa-ee.
4. chhodeelay[647] paakhandaa[648].
5. naam la-i-ai jaahi tarandaa.[649] ||1||

Mehla 1.

1. maanas[650] khaanay karahi nivaaj[651].
2. chhuree[652] vagaa-in[653] tin gal[654] taag.
3. tin ghar barahman pooreh[655] naad[656].
4. un_Haa bhe aavahi o-ee saad[657].
5. koorhee raas koorhaa vaapaar[658].
6. koorh bol karahi aahaar[659].

---

[634] Tax
[635] Cow-dung
[636] Save
[637] Loin-cloth
[638] A mark
[639] Carries a rosary
[640] Provisions
[641] Muslims
[642] Within

[643] Worship
[644] Outside they read
[645] Way of life
[646] Muhammadans or Muslims
[647] Lay aside
[648] The hypocrisy
[649] Swim across
[650] The man-eaters
[651] Say the prayer

[652] The scalpel (knife)
[653] Who wields
[654] Wear thread around their neck
[655] Brahmans sound
[656] The conch
[657] Taste
[658] False their trade
[659] Food

ੴ ਸਰਮ^{੬੬੦} ਧਰਮ ਕਾ ਡੇਰਾ^{੬੬੧} ਦੂਰਿ ॥
ੲ ਨਾਨਕ ਕੂੜੁ ਰਹਿਆ ਭਰਪੂਰਿ^{੬੬੨} ॥
ੳ ਮਥੈ^{੬੬੩} ਟਿਕਾ ਤੇੜਿ ਧੋਤੀ ਕਖਾਈ^{੬੬੪} ॥
੧੦ ਹਥਿ ਛੁਰੀ ਜਗਤ ਕਾਸਾਈ^{੬੬੫} ॥
੧੧ ਨੀਲ ਵਸਤੁ ਪਹਿਰਿ^{੬੬੬} ਹੋਵਹਿ ਪਰਵਾਣੁ^{੬੬੭} ॥
੧੨ ਮਲੇਛ ਧਾਨੁ^{੬੬੮} ਲੇ ਪੂਜਹਿ ਪੁਰਾਣ ॥
੧੩ ਅਭਾਖਿਆ ਕਾ ਕੁਠਾ^{੬੬੯} ਬਕਰਾ ਖਾਣਾ ॥
੧੪ ਚਉਕੇ^{੬੭੦} ਉਪਰਿ ਕਿਸੈ ਨ ਜਾਣਾ^{੬੭੧} ॥
੧੫ ਦੇ ਕੈ ਚਉਕਾ^{੬੭੨} ਕਢੀ^{੬੭੩} ਕਾਰ^{੬੭੪} ॥
੧੬ ਉਪਰਿ ਆਇ ਬੈਠੇ ਕੂੜਿਆਰ ॥
੧੭ ਮਤੁ ਭਿਟੈ ਵੇ ਮਤੁ ਭਿਟੈ ॥
੧੮ ਇਹੁ ਅੰਨੁ ਅਸਾਡਾ ਫਿਟੈ^{੬੭੫} ॥
੧੯ ਤਨਿ ਫਿਟੈ ਫੇੜ ਕਰੇਨਿ^{੬੭੬} ॥
੨੦ ਮਨਿ ਜੂਠੈ^{੬੭੭} ਚੁਲੀ ਭਰੇਨਿ ॥
੨੧ ਕਹ ਨਾਨਕ ਸਚੁ ਧਿਆਈਐ ॥
੨੨ ਸੁਚਿ ਹੋਵੈ ਤਾ ਸਚੁ ਪਾਈਐ ॥ ੨ ॥

੭ ਸਰਮ^{੬੬੦} ਧਰਮ ਕਾ ਡੇਰਾ^{੬੬੧} ਦੂਰਿ ॥
੮ ਨਾਨਕ ਕੂੜੁ ਰਹਿਆ ਭਰਪੂਰਿ^{੬੬੨} ॥
੯ ਮਥੈ^{੬੬੩} ਟਿਕਾ ਤੇੜਿ ਧੋਤੀ ਕਖਾਈ^{੬੬੪} ॥
੧੦ ਹਥਿ ਛੁਰੀ ਜਗਤ ਕਾਸਾਈ^{੬੬੫} ॥
੧੧ ਨੀਲ ਵਸਤ੍ਰ ਪਹਿਰਿ^{੬੬੬} ਹੋਵਹਿ ਪਰਵਾਣੁ^{੬੬੭} ॥
੧੨ ਮਲੇਛ ਧਾਨੁ^{੬੬੮} ਲੇ ਪੂਜਹਿ ਪੁਰਾਣੁ ॥
੧੩ ਅਭਾਖਿਆ ਕਾ ਕੁਠਾ^{੬੬੯} ਬਕਰਾ ਖਾਣਾ ॥
੧੪ ਚਉਕੇ^{੬੭੦} ਉਪਰਿ ਕਿਸੈ ਨ ਜਾਣਾ^{੬੭੧} ॥
੧੫ ਦੇ ਕੈ ਚਉਕਾ^{੬੭੨} ਕਢੀ^{੬੭੩} ਕਾਰ^{੬੭੪} ॥
੧੬ ਉਪਰਿ ਆਇ ਬੈਠੇ ਕੂੜਿਆਰ ॥
੧੭ ਮਤੁ ਭਿਟੈ ਵੇ ਮਤੁ ਭਿਟੈ ॥
੧੮ ਇਹੁ ਅੰਨੁ ਅਸਾਡਾ ਫਿਟੈ^{੬੭੫} ॥
੧੯ ਤਨਿ ਫਿਟੈ ਫੇੜ ਕਰੇਨਿ^{੬੭੬} ॥
੨੦ ਮਨਿ ਜੂਠੈ^{੬੭੭} ਚੁਲੀ ਭਰੇਨਿ ॥
੨੧ ਕਹ ਨਾਨਕ ਸਚੁ ਧਿਆਈਐ ॥
੨੨ ਸੁਚਿ ਹੋਵੈ ਤਾ ਸਚੁ ਪਾਈਐ ॥ ੨ ॥

7. saram[660] Dharam kaa dayraa[661] door.
8. naanak koorh rahi-aa bharpoor[662].
9. mathai[663] tikaa tayrh Dhotee kakhaa-ee[664].
10. hath chhuree jagat kaasaa-ee[665].
11. neel vastar pahir[666] hoveh parvaan[667].
12. malaychh Dhaan[668] lay poojeh puraan.
13. abhaakhi-aa kaa kuthaa[669] bakraa khaanaa.
14. cha-ukay[670] upar kisai na jaanaa[671].
15. day kai cha-ukaa[672] kadhee[673] kaar[674].
16. upar aa-ay baithay koorhi-aar.
17. mat bhitai vay mat bhitai.
18. ih ann asaadaa fitai[675].
19. tan fitai fayrh karayn[676].
20. man joothai[677] chulee bharayn.
21. kaho naanak sach Dhi-aa-ee-ai.
22. such hovai taa sach paa-ee-ai. ||2||

---

[660] Modesty
[661] Abode
[662] Falsehood is fully filling
[663] On the brow
[664] The ochre-coloured
[665] Butcher
[666] Wearing

[667] Becomes acceptable (in the eyes of Muslims)
[668] Bread
[669] He eats the he-goat killed
[670] His cooking enclosure
[671] He allows none to enter
[672] Plastering
[673] He draws

[674] Lines
[675] Will be polluted
[676] They commit
[677] With the impure

Theme

Sloak Mehla 1

Both Brahmins and Mullas are hypocrites

Mehla 1

Both Muslim rulers and their Hindu administrators are fraud.

Literal Meaning

Sloak Mehla 1

1. O! (Hindu) revenue official (in the Mughal administration) you levy tax on both cow and Brahmin; you use the cow-dung to purify your kitchen, but do remember that plastering of this in your cooking-square, will not help you ferry across the ocean of life.
2. Nor will the cotton sari (*dhoti*), the saffron mark (on your forehead) and the rosary (in your hand) guarantee you a safe passage beyond. Despite posing as a practising Hindu you still buy your food from Muslims (*malechhs*).
3. At home you worship images; while outside you read *Qoran* and follow the Code of Muslims.
4. Why you have to pretend of what you are not, why do you lower your self (in your own eyes)?
5. You can get liberation only if you plant the name of Waheguru in your heart; all other actions and rituals are just useless.

Mehla 1

1. The rulers (they were Muslims at that time) suck blood of their subjects and then offer prayers five times a day.
2. Their officials (they were mostly Hindus) persecute innocent people and wear the sacred thread.
3. The Brahmins visit houses of highly placed officials, blow conches, and then beg for alms.
4. They enjoy food, which they preach as forbidden.
5. They enter into transactions and earn profit by deceit.
6. They utter lies and maintain themselves by fraud.

7. They have no sense of shame or morality.
8. Falsehood has taken complete control over their souls.
9. They apply saffron marks on their foreheads, tie dhotis, in their own Brahmanic style, around their loins.
10. They hold knives in their hands and act like butchers.
11. They wear blue robes and seek favours from their Muslim superiors.
12. They live by fraudulent means and recite aloud the story of Puranas.
13. They eat meat, cut the Muslim way.
14. They boast of the sanctity of their kitchens and bar others to enter therein.
15. They draw lines around the cooking squares and highlight them as no entry areas for others.
16. And within these boundaries the so-called hypocrites sit to cook their food.
17. And cry aloud, "Do not enter this area.."
18. Lest the food will get defiled.
19. In fact, they themselves are unholy and act in a most offensive and arrogant way.
20. Their minds are impure and they feign impurity by repeatedly rinsing their mouths.
21. The truth is that everyone should worship one Almighty God, and
22. You will get his vision if you are pure at heart.

ਪਉੜੀ ॥

1. ਚਿਤੈ ਅੰਦਰਿ ਸਭੁ ਕੋ ਵੇਖਿ ਨਦਰੀ ਹੇਠਿ[678] ਚਲਾਇਦਾ ॥
2. ਆਪੇ ਦੇ ਵਡਿਆਈਆ ਆਪੇ ਹੀ ਕਰਮ[679] ਕਰਾਇਦਾ ॥
3. ਵਡਹੁ ਵਡਾ ਵਡ ਮੇਦਨੀ ਸਿਰੇ ਸਿਰਿ ਧੰਧੈ ਲਾਇਦਾ ॥
4. ਨਦਰਿ ਉਪਠੀ ਜੇ ਕਰੇ ਸੁਲਤਾਨਾ[680] ਘਾਹੁ ਕਰਾਇਦਾ ॥
5. ਦਰਿ ਮੰਗਨਿ ਭਿਖ ਨ[681] ਪਾਇਦਾ ॥ ੧੬ ॥

ਪਉੜੀ ॥

1. ਚਿਤੈ ਅੰਦਰਿ ਸਭੁ ਕੋ ਵੇਖਿ ਨਦਰੀ ਹੇਠਿ[678] ਚਲਾਇਦਾ ॥
2. ਆਪੇ ਦੇ ਵਡਿਆਈਆ ਆਪੇ ਹੀ ਕਰਮ[679] ਕਰਾਇਦਾ ॥
3. ਵਡਹੁ ਵਡਾ ਵਡ ਮੇਦਨੀ ਸਿਰੇ ਸਿਰਿ ਧੰਧੈ ਲਾਇਦਾ ॥
4. ਨਦਰਿ ਉਪਠੀ ਜੇ ਕਰੇ ਸੁਲਤਾਨਾ[680] ਘਾਹੁ ਕਰਾਇਦਾ ॥
5. ਦਰਿ ਮੰਗਨਿ ਭਿਖ ਨ[681] ਪਾਇਦਾ ॥ ੧੬ ॥

Pauri.

1. chitai andar sabh ko vaykh nadree hayth[678] chalaa-idaa.
2. aapay day vadi-aa-ee-aa aapay hee karam[679] karaa-idaa.
3. vadahu vadaa vad maydnee siray sir DhanDhai laa-idaa.
4. nadar upthee jay karay sultaanaa[680] ghaahu karaa-idaa.
5. dar mangan bhikh na[681] paa-idaa. ||16||

Theme

Pauri

Beware! Waheguru, the omnipotent, can convert rulers into beggars and beggars into rulers

Literal Meaning

Pauri

1. Waheguru is the ombudsman, he watches and tends everyone.
2. He himself bestows honour and controls our actions.
3. He is the King of Kings and his domain is very vast.
4. His one look can make rulers as beggars.

---

[678] Beneath
[679] Men to do deeds

[680] Monarchs
[681] No alms

ਆਸਾ ਮਹਲਾ ੪ ॥

आसा महला ४ ॥

Asa Mehla 4.

Asa Mehla 4.

ਜਿਨ ਅੰਤਰਿ ਹਰਿ ਹਰਿ ਪ੍ਰੀਤਿ ਹੈ ਤੇ ਜਨ ਸੁਘੜ ਸਿਆਣੇ ਰਾਮ ਰਾਜੇ ॥

जिन अंतरि हरि हरि प्रीति है ते जन सुघड़ सिआणे राम राजे ॥

jin antar har har pareet hai tay jan sugharh si-aanay raam raajay.

Those whose hearts are filled with the love of Waheguru,
they are the wisest and most clever people, O King of Kings.

ਜੇ ਬਾਹਰਹੁ ਭੁਲਿ ਚੁਕਿ ਬੋਲਦੇ ਭੀ ਖਰੇ ਹਰਿ ਭਾਣੇ ॥

जे बाहरहु भुलि चुकि बोलदे भी खरे हरि भाणे ॥

jay baahrahu bhul chuk bolday bhee kharay har bhaanay.

Even if they mis-speak outwardly, they are still very
pleasing to the Master.

ਹਰਿ ਸੰਤਾ ਨੋ ਹੋਰੁ ਥਾਉ ਨਾਹੀ ਹਰਿ ਮਾਣੁ ਨਿਮਾਣੇ ॥

हरि संता नो होरु थाउ नाही हरि माणु निमाणे ॥

har santaa no hor thaa-o naahee har maan nimaanay.

Waheguru's saints have no other place. Waheguru showers
honour even on the dishonoured.

ਜਨ ਨਾਨਕ ਨਾਮੁ ਦੀਬਾਣੁ ਹੈ ਹਰਿ ਤਾਣੁ ਸਤਾਣੇ ॥੧॥

जन नानक नामु दीबाणु है हरि ताणु सताणे ॥ १ ॥

jan naanak naam deebaan hai har taan sataanay. ||1||

We all are bound in the Royal Court of Waheguru;
His power is the ultimate power. ||1||

*Pauri 17 with 2 sloaks
(Guru Nanak 2)*

1. ਜੇ ਮੋਹਾਕਾ[682] ਘਰੁ ਮੁਹੈ[683] ਘਰੁ ਮੁਹਿ[684] ਪਿਤਰੀ[685] ਦੇਇ[686] ॥

2. ਅਗੈ[687] ਵਸਤੁ ਸਿਞਾਣੀਐ[688] ਪਿਤਰੀ ਚੋਰ ਕਰੇਇ[689] ॥

3. ਵਢੀਅਹਿ[690] ਹਥ ਦਲਾਲ[691] ਕੇ ਮੁਸਫੀ ਏਹ ਕਰੇਇ[692] ॥

4. ਨਾਨਕ ਅਗੈ ਸੋ ਮਿਲੈ[693] ਜਿ ਖਟੇ ਘਾਲੇ ਦੇਇ[694] ॥ ੧ ॥

ਮਃ ੧ ॥

1. ਜਿਉ ਜੋਰੂ[695] ਸਿਰਨਾਵਣੀ[696] ਆਵੈ ਵਾਰੋ ਵਾਰ ॥

2. ਜੂਠੇ ਜੂਠਾ ਮੁਖਿ ਵਸੈ[697] ਨਿਤ ਨਿਤ ਹੋਇ ਖੁਆਰੁ ॥

3. ਸੂਚੇ ਏਹਿ ਨ ਆਖੀਅਹਿ ਬਹਨਿ ਜਿ ਪਿੰਡਾ ਧੋਇ[698] ॥

4. ਸੂਚੇ ਸੇਈ ਨਾਨਕਾ ਜਿਨ ਮਨਿ ਵਸਿਆ ਸੋਇ[699] ॥ ੨ ॥

---

1. जे मोहाका[682] घरु मुहै[683] घरु मुहि[684] पितरी[685] देइ[686] ॥

2. अगै[687] वसतु सिञाणीऐ[688] पितरी चोर करेइ[689] ॥

3. वढीअहि[690] हथ दलाल[691] के मुसफी इेह करेइ[692] ॥

4. नानक अगै सो मिलै[693] जि खटे घाले देइ[694] ॥ १ ॥

मः १ ॥

1. जितु जोरू[695] सिरनावणी[696] आवै वारो वार ॥

2. जूठे जूठा मुखि वसै[697] नित नित होइ खुआरु ॥

3. सूचे इेहि न आखीअहि बहनि जि पिंडा धोइ[698] ॥

4. सूचे सेई नानका जिन मनि वसिआ सोइ[699] ॥ २ ॥

Sloak Mehla 1.

1. jay mohaakaa[682] ghar muhai[683] ghar muhi[684] pitree[685] day-ay[686].

2. agai[687] vasat sinjaanee-ai[688] pitree chor karay-i[689].

3. vadhee-ah[690] hath dalaal[691] kay musfee ayh karay-i[692].

4. naanak agai so milai[693] je khatay ghaalay day-ay.[694] ||1||

Mehla 1.

1. ji-o joroo[695] sirnaavanee[696] aavai vaaro vaar.

2. joothay joothaa mukh vasai[697] nit nit ho-ay khu-aar.

3. soochay ayhi na aakhee-ahi bahan je pindaa Dho-ay[698].

4. soochay say-ee naankaa jin man vasi-aa so-ay.[699] ||2||

---

[682] Thief
[683] To rob
[684] The loot
[685] His/her elders
[686] Distribute (the loot)
[687] Next world
[688] To recognise

[689] Ancestors are declared thieves
[690] To cut off
[691] Agent, intermediary
[692] This is the verdict of the Justice (Judge)
[693] Honour which one receives in the next world
[694] That income which is given to the needy
[695] Woman, wife

[696] Monthly menses
[697] Lies dwell in the mouth of a liar
[698] Washing one's body, taking bath
[699] Waheguru

Theme

Sloak Mehla 1

It is one's noble deeds, which are counted hereafter.

Mehla 1

Those are truthful persons who have kept Waheguru's name in their heart.

Literal Meaning

Sloak Mehla 1

1. If a thief breaks into a house and then offers the stolen stuff to appease his/her ancestors.
2. The stolen goods, on identification, can implicate even ancestors as thieves or accomplices in the crime.
3. The judge may then order chopping off their hands as abetter of the unlawful act.
4. Whatever one shares with the needy from his own honest earnings, only that part one receives in the life hereafter.

Mehla 1

1. A woman during her regular menstrual period is called impure.
2. A similar impurity endures in the mouth of a regular liar, for which he ever suffers disgrace.
3. Purity does not come with daily cleaning of one's body.
4. Purity rather comes, by abiding Waheguru's love in one's heart.

ਪਉੜੀ ॥

1. ਤੁਰੇ^{੭੦੦} ਪਲਾਣੇ^{੭੦੧} ਪਉਣ ਵੇਗ^{੭੦੨} ਹਰ ਰੰਗੀ^{੭੦੩} ਹਰਮ^{੭੦੪} ਸਵਾਰਿਆ ॥
2. ਕੋਠੇ ਮੰਡਪ ਮਾੜੀਆ^{੭੦੫} ਲਾਇ ਬੈਠੇ ਕਰਿ ਪਾਸਾਰਿਆ^{੭੦੬} ॥
3. ਚੀਜ ਕਰਨਿ ਮਨਿ ਭਾਵਦੇ^{੭੦੭} ਹਰਿ ਬੁਝਨਿ ਨਾਹੀ^{੭੦੮} ਹਾਰਿਆ^{੭੦੯} ॥
4. ਕਰਿ ਫੁਰਮਾਇਸਿ ਖਾਇਆ^{੭੧੦} ਵੇਖਿ ਮਹਲਤਿ^{੭੧੧} ਮਰਣੁ ਵਿਸਾਰਿਆ ॥
5. ਜਰੁ^{੭੧੨} ਆਈ ਜੋਬਨਿ^{੭੧੩} ਹਾਰਿਆ ॥ ੧੭ ॥

पउड़ी ॥

1. तुरे^{७००} पलाणे^{७०१} पउण वेग^{७०२} हर रंगी^{७०३} हरम^{७०४} सवारिआ ॥
2. कोठे मंडप माड़ीआ^{७०५} लाइ बैठे करि पासारिआ^{७०६} ॥
3. चीज करनि मनि भावदे^{७०९} हरि बुझनि नाही^{७०८} हारिआ^{७०९} ॥
4. करि फुरमाइसि खाइआ^{७१०} वेखि महलति^{७११} मरणु विसारिआ ॥
5. जरु^{७१२} आई जोबनि^{७१३} हारिआ ॥ १७ ॥

Pauri.

1. turay⁷⁰⁰ palaanay⁷⁰¹ pa-un vayg⁷⁰² har rangee⁷⁰³ haram⁷⁰⁴ savaari-aa.
2. kothay mandap maarhee-aa⁷⁰⁵ laa-ay baithay kar paasaari-aa⁷⁰⁶.
3. cheej karan man bhaavday⁷⁰⁷ har bujhan naahee⁷⁰⁸ haari-aa⁷⁰⁹.
4. kar furmaa-is khaa-i-aa⁷¹⁰ vaykh mahlat⁷¹¹ maran visaari-aa.
5. jar⁷¹² aa-ee joban⁷¹³ haari-aa. ||17||

Theme

Pauri

The age catches up with all of us and when end comes all worldly possessions are left behind.

Literal Meaning

Pauri

1. There are people who possess fleet of selected horses swift as strong-wind; and have beautiful dames in their lady-chambers (harems);
2. They may own large palaces, mansions and pavilions displaying their wealth and might, and
3. Indeed, may have all the pleasures of life, yet if they have not abided Waheguru's name in their hearts, they are losers at the end.
4. People in authority may get obsessed with their position and status; and become indifferent of the ghost of death.
5. Yet when they pass the peak of their young age and enter the threshold of old age they realise the everlasting truth of ravages of age.

---

[700] Horses
[701] Saddled
[702] Strong wind
[703] Well adorned, well dressed
[704] Women, a group of women kept by debauched elders for their sexual thirst

[705] Mansions, palaces
[706] Display on a grand scale
[707] Doing things according to one's wishes
[708] Unable to find Waheguru
[709] To suffer defeat
[710] To eat according to one's choice

[711] Mansions (wealth)
[712] Old age
[713] Young age

ਜਿਥੈ ਜਾਇ ਬਹੈ ਮੇਰਾ ਸਤਿਗੁਰੂ ਸੋ ਥਾਨ ਸੁਹਾਵਾ ਰਾਮ ਰਾਜੇ ॥

ਜਿਥੈ ਜਾਇ ਬਹੈ ਮੇਰਾ ਸਤਿਗੁਰੂ ਸੋ ਥਾਨੁ ਸੁਹਾਵਾ ਰਾਮ ਰਾਜੇ ॥

jithai jaa-ay bahai mayraa satguroo so thaan suhaavaa raam raajay.

Wherever my True Guru goes and sits,
that place is beautiful, O King of Kings.

ਗੁਰਸਿਖੀ ਜੋ ਥਾਨ ਭਾਲਿਆ ਲੈ ਧੂਰਿ ਮੁਖਿ ਲਾਵਾ॥

ਗੁਰਸਿਖੀ ਸੋ ਥਾਨੁ ਭਾਲਿਆ ਲੈ ਧੂਰਿ ਮੁਖਿ ਲਾਵਾ ॥

gursikhee^N so thaan bhaali-aa lai Dhoor mukh laavaa.

The true devotees seek out that place;
they take the dust and apply it to their faces.

ਗੁਰਸਿਖਾ ਕੀ ਘਾਲ ਥਾਇ ਪਈ ਜਿਨ ਹਰਿ ਨਾਮੁ ਧਿਆਵਾ॥

ਗੁਰਸਿਖਾ ਕੀ ਘਾਲ ਥਾਇ ਪਈ ਜਿਨ ਹਰਿ ਨਾਮੁ ਧਿਆਵਾ ॥

gursikhaa kee ghaal thaa-ay pa-ee jin har naam Dhi-aavaa.

The works of the devotees, who meditate on the
Waheguru's Name, are approved.

ਜਿਨ ਨਾਨਕੁ ਸਤਿਗੁਰੁ ਪੂਜਿਆ ਤਿਨ ਹਰਿ ਪੂਜ ਕਰਾਵਾ ॥੨॥

ਜਿਨ ਨਾਨਕੁ ਸਤਿਗੁਰੁ ਪੂਜਿਆ ਤਿਨ ਹਰਿ ਪੂਜ ਕਰਾਵਾ ॥ ੨ ॥

jin^H naanak satgur pooji-aa tin har pooj karaavaa. ||2||

Those who worship the True Guru, Waheguru Himself
causes them to be worshipped in turn. ||2||

*Pauri 18 with 3 sloaks
(Guru Nanak 3)*

ਸਲੋਕੁ ਮਃ ੧ ॥

1. ਜੇ ਕਰਿ ਸੂਤਕੁ[714] ਮੰਨੀਐ ਸਭ ਤੈ ਸੂਤਕੁ ਹੋਇ[715] ॥
2. ਗੋਹੇ ਅਤੈ ਲਕੜੀ ਅੰਦਰਿ ਕੀੜਾ ਹੋਇ ॥
3. ਜੇਤੇ ਦਾਨੇ ਅੰਨ ਕੇ ਜੀਆ ਬਾਝ ਨ ਕੋਇ[716] ॥
4. ਪਹਿਲਾ ਪਾਣੀ ਜੀਉ ਹੈ[717] ਜਿਤੁ ਹਰਿਆ ਸਭੁ ਕੋਇ[718] ॥
5. ਸੂਤਕੁ ਕਿਉ ਕਰਿ ਰਖੀਐ[719] ਸੂਤਕੁ ਪਵੈ ਰਸੋਇ[720] ॥
6. ਨਾਨਕ ਸੂਤਕੁ ਏਵ ਨ ਉਤਰੈ ਗਿਆਨੁ ਉਤਾਰੇ ਧੋਇ[721] ॥ ੧ ॥

सलोकु मः १ ॥

1. जे करि सूतकु[714] मंनीऐ सभ तै सूतकु होइ[715] ॥
2. गोहे अतै लकड़ी अंदरि कीड़ा होइ ॥
3. जेते दाणे अंन के जीआ बाझु न कोइ[716] ॥
4. पहिला पाणी जीउ है[717] जितु हरिआ सभु कोइ[718] ॥
5. सूतकु किउ करि रखीऐ[719] सूतकु पवै रसोइ[720] ॥
6. नानक सूतकु एव न उतरै गिआनु उतारे धोइ[721] ॥ १ ॥

Sloak Mehla 1.

1. jay kar sootak[714] mannee-ai sabh tai sootak ho-ay[715].
2. gohay atai lakrhee andar keerhaa ho-ay.
3. jaytay daanay ann kay jee-aa baajh na ko-ay[716].
4. pahilaa paanee jee-o hai[717] jit hari-aa sabh ko-ay[718].
5. sootak ki-o kar rakhee-ai[719] sootak pavai raso-ay[720].
6. naanak sootak ayv na utrai gi-aan utaaray Dho-ay.[721] ||1||

---

[714] Impure, profaned
[715] Impurity is everywhere
[716] There is life in every grain of food
[717] Firstly, there is life in water
[718] Which gives life to all others
[719] How can we escape impurity?
[720] Impurity starts from our kitchen
[721] Only wisdom can wash off impurity

ਮਃ ੧ ॥

1. ਮਨ ਕਾ ਸੂਤਕੁ ਲੋਭੁ ਹੈ ਜਿਹਵਾ ਸੂਤਕ ਕੂੜੁ ॥
2. ਅਖੀ ਸੂਤਕੁ ਵੇਖਣਾ ਪਰ ਤ੍ਰਿਅ[722] ਪਰ ਧਨ[723] ਰੂਪੁ[724] ॥
3. ਕੰਨੀ ਸੂਤਕੁ ਕੰਨਿ ਪੈ ਲਾਇਤਬਾਰੀ ਖਾਹਿ[725] ॥
4. ਨਾਨਕ ਹੰਸਾ[726] ਆਦਮੀ ਬਧੇ[727] ਜਮ[728] ਪੁਰਿ[729] ਜਾਹਿ ॥ ੨ ॥

ਮਃ ੧ ॥

1. ਸਭੋ[730] ਸੂਤਕੁ ਭਰਮੁ[731] ਹੈ ਦੂਜੈ ਲਗੈ ਜਾਇ[732] ॥
2. ਜੰਮਣੁ ਮਰਣਾ ਹੁਕਮੁ ਹੈ ਭਾਣੈ ਆਵੈ ਜਾਇ ॥
3. ਖਾਣਾ ਪੀਣਾ ਪਵਿਤੁ ਹੈ ਦਿਤੋਨੁ ਰਿਜਕੁ ਸੰਬਾਹਿ[733] ॥
4. ਨਾਨਕ ਜਿਨੀ ਗੁਰਮੁਖਿ ਬੁਝਿਆ ਤਿਨਾ ਸੂਤਕੁ ਨਾਹਿ ॥ ੩ ॥

मः १ ॥

1. मन का सूतकु लोभु है जिहवा सूतकु कूड़ु ॥
2. अखी सूतकु वेखणा पर त्रिअ[722] पर धन[723] रूपु[724] ॥
3. कंनी सूतकु कंनि पै लाइतबारी खाहि[725] ॥
4. नानक हंसा[726] आदमी बधे[727] जम[728] पुरि[729] जाहि ॥ २ ॥

मः १ ॥

1. सभो[730] सूतकु भरमु[731] है दूजै लगे जाइ[732] ॥
2. जंमणु मरणा हुकमु है भाणै आवै जाइ ॥
3. खाणा पीणा पवितु है दितोनु रिजकु संबाहि[733] ॥
4. नानक जिनी गुरमुखि बुझिआ तिना सूतकु नाहि ॥ ३ ॥

Mehla 1.

1. man kaa sootak lobh hai jihvaa sootak koorh.
2. akhee sootak vaykh-naa par tari-a[722] par Dhan[723] roop[724].
3. kannee sootak kann pai laa-itbaaree khaahi[725].
4. naanak hansaa[726] aadmee baDhay[727] jam[728] pur[729] jaahi. ||2||

Mehla 1.

1. sabho[730] sootak bharam[731] hai doojai lagai jaa-ay[732].
2. jaman marnaa hukam hai bhaanai aavai jaa-ay.
3. khaanaa peenaa pavitar hai diton rijak sambaahi[733].
4. naanak jin[H]ee gurmukh bujhi-aa tin[H]aa sootak naahi. ||3||

---

[722] Other person's wife
[723] Other person's wealth
[724] Beauty
[725] Backbiting, bitching, listening and talking about others
[726] Soul
[727] According to written law
[728] Death
[729] City of death
[730] To all
[731] Doubts
[732] Attachment to duality
[733] Provisions have been given to all of us

Theme	Literal Meaning

Sloak Mehla 1

Impurity is washed off with the wisdom of Shabad and not with useless rituals.

Sloak Mehla 1

1. If the concept of impurity be linked with killing lives, then every living being would be found impure.
2. The cow-dung and wood harbour varied forms of life (when we use them as fuel we burn the lives which live in there).
3. Every piece of grain has life in it (we kill the living beings residing in there when we crush or cook the grain).
4. Water that sustains the living, also has many forms of life in it (we swallow or kill the lives in it when we drink it, boil it or use it for other purposes).
5. Then how can this impurity (killing lives) be kept out, for it begins from our kitchen.
6. The notion of this type of impurity is held in vain. The divine wisdom can surely expel such a notion.

Mehla 1

Impurity is all around us. The mortar organs of our body are creating impurities every moment of time.

Mehla 1

1. The real impurity of mind lies in our greed, or the lies we speak, or
2. The lustful look we put at other people's wife and wealth, or
3. Hearing and relishing slander.
4. The people guilty of above are sent to hell tied in chains.

Mehla 1

Those who follow the path of *Gurmukhs* (the holy), impurity does not stick to them

Mehla 1

1. Impurity in every form is superstition, belief in which amounts to duality.
2. Both birth and death are according to Waheguru's will, people come and go from this world according to his plans.
3. Food and drinks given to us by Waheguru are all pure.
4. *Gurmukhs*, God-fearing people, have found the divine secrets and are free from all impurities.

ਪਉੜੀ ॥

1. ਸਤਿਗੁਰ ਵਡਾ ਕਰਿ ਸਾਲਾਹੀਐ ਜਿਸੁ ਵਿਚਿ ਵਡੀਆ
   ਵਡਿਆਈਆ ॥
2. ਸਹਿ ਮੇਲੇ²³⁴ ਤਾ ਨਦਰੀ ਆਈਆ ॥
3. ਜਾ ਤਿਸ ਭਾਣਾ²³⁵ ਤਾ ਮਨ ਵਸਾਈਆਂ ॥
4. ਕਰਿ ਹੁਕਮੁ ਮਸਤਕਿ ਹਥੁ ਧਰਿ ਵਿਚਹੁ ਮਾਰਿ
   ਕਢੀਆ²³⁶ ਬੁਰਿਆਈਆਂ²³⁷ ॥
5. ਸਹਿ ਤੁਠੈ ਨਉ ਨਿਧਿ²³⁸ ਪਾਈਆ ॥ ੧੮ ॥

पउड़ी ॥

1. सतिगुरु वडा करि सालाहिऐ जिसु विचि वडीआ
   वडिआईआ ॥
2. सहि मेले⁹³⁴ ता नदरी आईआ ॥
3. जा तिसु भाणा⁹³⁵ तां मन वसाईआ ॥
4. करि हुकमु मसतकि हथु धरि विचहु मारि
   कढीआ⁹³⁶ बुरिआईआ⁹³⁷ ॥
5. सहि तुठै नउ निधि⁹³⁸ पाईआ ॥ १८ ॥

Pauri.

1. satgur vadaa kar salaahee-ai jis vich vadee-aa vadi-aa-ee-aa.
2. seh maylay[734] taa nadree aa-ee-aa.
3. jaa tis bhaanaa[735] taa man vasaa-ee-aa.
4. kar hukam mastak hath Dhar vichahu maar kadhee-aa[736] buri-aa-ee-aa[737].
5. seh tuthai na-o niDh[738] paa-ee-aa. ||18||

Theme

Pauri
If and when Waheguru pleases, one gets all worldly treasures.

Literal Meaning

Pauri
1. Teacher-Guru is the embodiment of truth and all praise be to him.
2. He manifests his qualities into his devotees and lead them to have a union with God.
3. The devotees then develop those qualities in them.
4. When the teacher-Guru blesses his followers he eradicates all evil from their minds.
5. The devotees' souls are then enlightened with virtues showered by Waheguru.

---

[734] If one has the vision of Waheguru
[735] Will
[736] To beat off
[737] Wickedness

[738] Nine treasures – Padam (Valuable metals), Mahan Padam (Gems), Sankh (delicious food), Makar (training in arms), Kachhap (clothing), Kund (dealings in gold), Neel (trading in Gems), Mukand (master in fine arts), Kharub (riches of all kinds)

ਗੁਰਸਿਖਾ ਮਨਿ ਹਰਿ ਪ੍ਰੀਤਿ ਹੈ ਹਰਿ ਨਾਮ ਹਰਿ ਤੇਰੀ ਰਾਮ ਰਾਜੇ ॥

गुरसिखा मनि हरि प्रीति है हरि नाम हरि तेरी राम राजे ॥

gursikhaa man har pareet hai har naam har tayree raam raajay.

The devotees keep the love of Waheguru and
His Name in their mind, O King of Kings.

ਕਰਿ ਸੇਵਹਿ ਪੂਰਾ ਸਤਿਗੁਰੂ ਭੁਖ ਜਾਇ ਲਹਿ ਮੇਰੀ ॥

करि सेवहि पूरा सतिगुरू भुख जाइ लहि मेरी ॥

kar sayveh pooraa satguroo bhukh jaa-ay leh mayree.

One who serves the Perfect True Guru,
his hunger and self-conceit are eliminated.

ਗੁਰਸਿਖਾ ਕੀ ਭੁਖ ਸਭ ਗਈ ਤਿਨ ਪਿਛੈ ਹੋਰ ਖਾਇ ਘਨੇਰੀ ॥

गुरसिखा की भुख सभ गई तिन पिछै होर खाइ घनेरी ॥

gursikhaa kee bhukh sabh ga-ee tin pichhai hor khaa-ay ghanayree.

The hunger of the devotee is totally eliminated;
indeed, many others are also blessed with him.

ਜਨ ਨਾਨਕ ਹਰਿ ਪੁੰਨੁ ਬੀਜਿਆ ਫਿਰਿ ਤੋਟਿ ਨ ਆਵੈ ਹਰਿ ਪੁੰਨ ਕੇਰੀ ॥੩॥

जन नानक हरि पुंनु बीजिआ फिरि तोटि न आवै हरि पुंन केरी ॥ ३ ॥

jan naanak har punn beeji-aa fir tot na aavai har punn kayree. ||3||

One in whose heart is planted the seed of the Goodness;
this righteousness shall never be exhausted. ||3||

*Pauri 19 with 2 sloaks
(Guru Nanak 2)*

ਸਲੋਕੁ ਮਃ ੧ ॥

1. ਪਹਿਲਾ ਸੁਚਾ²³⁹ ਆਪਿ ਹੋਇ ਸੁਚੈ ਬੈਠਾ ਆਇ²⁴⁰ ॥
2. ਸੁਚੇ²⁴¹ ਅਗੈ ਰਖਿਓਨੁ ਕੋਇ ਨ ਭਿਟਿਓ ਜਾਇ²⁴² ॥
3. ਸੁਚਾ ਹੋਇ ਕੈ ਜੇਵਿਆ²⁴³ ਲਗਾ ਪੜਨਿ ਸਲੋਕੁ²⁴⁴ ॥
4. ਕੁਹਥੀ ਜਾਈ ਸਟਿਆ²⁴⁵ ਕਿਸੁ ਏਹੁ ਲਗਾ ਦੋਖੁ²⁴⁶ ॥
5. ਅੰਨੁ ਦੇਵਤਾ ਪਾਣੀ ਦੇਵਤਾ ਬੈਸੰਤਰੁ²⁴⁷ ਦੇਵਤਾ ਲੂਣ ਪੰਜਵਾ ਪਾਇਆ ਘਿਰਤੁ²⁴⁸ ॥
6. ਤਾ ਹੋਆ ਪਾਕੁ²⁴⁹ ਪਵਿਤੁ ॥
7. ਪਾਪੀ ਸਿਉ²⁵⁰ ਤਨੁ ਗਡਿਆ²⁵¹ ਥੁਕਾ ਪਈਆ ਤਿਤੁ ॥
8. ਜਿਤੁ ਮੁਖਿ ਨਾਮੁ ਨ ਊਚਰਹਿ ਬਿਨੁ ਨਾਵੈ ਰਸ ਖਾਹਿ²⁵² ॥
9. ਨਾਨਕ ਏਵੈ ਜਾਣੀਐ ਤਿਤੁ ਮੁਖਿ ਥੁਕਾ ਪਾਹਿ ॥ ੧ ॥

सलोकु मः १ ॥

1. पहिला सुचा⁹३९ आपि होइ सुचै बैठा आइ⁹४० ॥
2. सुचे⁹४१ अगै रखिएनु कोइ न भिटिए जाइ⁹४² ॥
3. सुचा होइ कै जेविआ⁹४³ लगा पड़नि सलोकु⁹४४ ॥
4. कुहथी जाई सटिआ⁹४५ किसु इेहु लगा दोखु⁹४६ ॥
5. अंनु देवता पाणी देवता बैसंतरु⁹४७ देवता लूण पंजवा पाइआ घिरतु⁹४८ ॥
6. ता होआ पाकु⁹४९ पवितु ॥
7. पापी सिउ⁹५० तनु गडिआ⁹५¹ थुका पईआ तितु ॥
8. जितु मुखि नामु न ऊचरहि बिनु नावै रस खाहि⁹५² ॥
9. नानक इेवै जाणीअै तितु मुखि थुका पाहि ॥ १ ॥

Sloak Mehla 1.

1. pahilaa suchaa[739] aap ho-ay suchai baithaa aa-ay[740].
2. suchay[741] agai rakhi-on ko-ay na bhiti-o jaa-ay[742].
3. suchaa ho-ay kai jayvi-aa[743] lagaa parhan salok[744].
4. kuhthee jaa-ee sati-aa[745] kis ayhu lagaa dokh[746].
5. ann dayvtaa paanee dayvtaa baisantar[747] dayvtaa loon panjvaa paa-i-aa ghirat[748].
6. taa ho-aa paak[749] pavit.
7. paapee si-o[750] tan gadi-aa[751] thukaa pa-ee-aa tit.
8. jit mukh naam na oochrahi bin naavai ras khaahi[752].
9. naanak ayvai jaanee-ai tit mukh thukaa paahi. ||1||

---

[739] Clean
[740] Brahmin comes and sits in the cleansed enclosure
[741] The purified food
[742] Which no one has touched
[743] He then starts eating the sanctified food

[744] To read religious hymns
[745] Then thrown in a filthy place
[746] Whose fault is this?
[747] Fire
[748] Ghee, butter

[749] Pure
[750] With
[751] To come into contact with
[752] To eat delicacies

111

ਮਃ ੧ ॥

1. ਭੰਡਿ[753] ਜੰਮੀਐ ਭੰਡਿ[754] ਨਿੰਮੀਐ[75਼] ਭੰਡਿ ਮੰਗਣੁ[755] ਵੀਆਹੁ ॥
2. ਭੰਡਹੁ ਹੋਵੈ ਦੋਸਤੀ ਭੰਡਹੁ ਚਲੈ ਰਾਹੁ [75੬] ॥
3. ਭੰਡੁ ਮੂਆ[75੭] ਭੰਡੁ ਭਾਲੀਐ ਭੰਡਿ ਹੋਵੈ ਬੰਧਾਨੁ[75੮] ॥
4. ਸੋ ਕਿਉ ਮੰਦਾ ਆਖੀਐ ਜਿਤੁ ਜੰਮਹਿ ਰਾਜਾਨ ॥
5. ਭੰਡਹੁ ਹੀ ਭੰਡੁ ਊਪਜੈ ਭੰਡੈ ਬਾਝੁ ਨ ਕੋਇ[75੯] ॥
6. ਨਾਨਕ ਭੰਡੈ ਬਾਹਰਾ[7੬0] ਏਕੋ ਸਚਾ ਸੋਇ ॥
7. ਜਿਤੁ ਮੁਖਿ ਸਦਾ ਸਾਲਾਹੀਐ ਭਾਗਾ[7੬1] ਰਤੀ[7੬2] ਚਾਰਿ[7੬3] ॥
8. ਨਾਨਕ ਤੇ ਮੁਖ ਉਜਲੇ ਤਿਤੁ ਸਚੈ ਦਰਬਾਰਿ [7੬4] ॥ ੨ ॥

मः १ ॥

1. भंडि[753] जंमीऐ भंडि निंमीऐ[754] भंडि मंगणु[755] वीआहु ॥
2. भंडहु होवै दोसती भंडहु चलै राहु [756] ॥
3. भंडु मुआ[757] भंडु भालीऐ भंडि होवै बंधानु[758] ॥
4. सो किउ मंदा आखीऐ जितु जंमहि राजान ॥
5. भंडहु ही भंडु ऊपजै भंडै बाझु न कोइ[759] ॥
6. नानक भंडै बाहरा[760] एको सचा सोइ ॥
7. जितु मुखि सदा सालाहीऐ भागा[761] रती[762] चारि[763] ॥
8. नानक ते मुख ऊजले तितु सचै दरबारि [764] ॥ २ ॥

Mehla 1.

1. bhand[753] jammee-ai bhand[754] nimmee-ai bhand mangan[755] vee-aahu.
2. bhandahu hovai dostee bhandahu chalai raahu[756].
3. bhand mu-aa[757] bhand bhaalee-ai bhand hovai banDhaan[758].
4. so ki-o mandaa aakhee-ai jit jameh raajaan.
5. bhandahu hee bhand oopjai bhandai baajh na ko-ay[759].
6. naanak bhandai baahraa[760] ayko sachaa so-ay.
7. jit mukh sadaa salaahee-ai bhaagaa[761] ratee[762] chaar[763].
8. naanak tay mukh oojlay tit sachai darbaar[764]. ||2||

---

[753] Woman
[754] To conceive
[755] Engagement
[756] The system of births

[757] When first wife dies
[758] To satisfy sexual desires
[759] Without a woman there will be no children
[760] Born without a woman

[761] Fortunate
[762] Rosy
[763] Beautiful
[764] In the court of Waheguru

Theme

Sloak Mehla 1

A sinner can pollute the purity

Mehla 2

How dare you call woman inferior, when she has given birth to kings and prophets.

Literal Meaning

Sloak Mehla 1

1. The Pundit first bathes himself, then enters the ritually sanctified cooking-square.
2. Therein he is served food untouched by other hands.
3. He eats the food while hymns from scriptures are read out.
4. Later, he discharges the food as excreta. Whom to blame for this defilement?
5. The corn is considered to be a *devta* (holy), so is water, fire and salt. These ingredients are often mixed with a fifth *devta* – butter.
6. The mixture of the above churns out wholesome nourishing food.
7. Yet, if these holy inputs come into contact with a sinful person the output becomes repugnant to sight.
8. The mouth that fails to utter the Name of Waheguru, and enjoys the delicacies,
9. Such a person is accursed and is to be frowned at.

Mehla 2

1. It is the woman who conceives and gives birth to a man; it is the woman who nourishes the foetus in her womb and later tends the new-born baby; it is the woman whom one gets engaged to and then marries.
2. It is the woman who makes the best friend and holds the promise of future progeny.
3. When one's wife dies he seeks another woman. The woman gives everlasting bond of love and sexual satisfaction.
4. How dare then men call her inferior when she has given birth to kings and emperors.
5. It is again woman that gives birth to another woman. The cycle of human life is not possible without her.
6. Only Waheguru himself is not born of woman.
7. Blessed and gracious is the tongue which utters his name.
8. Such people are always welcome in the court of Waheguru.

ਪਉੜੀ ॥

1. ਸਭੁ ਕੋ ਆਖੈ ਆਪਣਾ ਜਿਸੁ ਨਾਹੀ ਸੋ ਚੁਣਿ ਕਢੀਐ²⁶⁵ ॥

2. ਕੀਤਾ ਆਪੋ ਆਪਣਾ ਆਪੇ ਹੀ ਲੇਖਾ ਸੰਢੀਐ²⁶⁶ ॥

3. ਜਾ ਰਹਣਾ ਨਾਹੀ ਐਤੁ ਜਗਿ ਤਾ ਕਾਇਤੁ²⁶⁷ ਗਾਰਬਿ²⁶⁸ ਹੰਢੀਐ²⁶⁹ ॥

4. ਮੰਦਾ ਕਿਸੈ ਨ ਆਖੀਐ ਪੜਿ ਅਖਰੁ²⁷⁰ ਏਹੋ ਬੁਝੀਐ²⁷¹ ॥

5. ਮੂਰਖੈ ਨਾਲਿ ਨ ਲੁਝੀਐ²⁷² ॥ ੧੯ ॥

ਪਉੜੀ ॥

1 ਸਭੁ ਕੋ ਆਖੈ ਆਪਣਾ ਜਿਸੁ ਨਾਹੀ ਸੋ ਚੁਣਿ ਕਢੀਐ²⁶⁵ ॥

2. ਕੀਤਾ ਆਪੋ ਆਪਣਾ ਆਪੇ ਹੀ ਲੇਖਾ ਸੰਢੀਐ²⁶⁶ ॥

3. ਜਾ ਰਹਣਾ ਨਾਹੀ ਐਤੁ ਜਗਿ ਤਾ ਕਾਇਤੁ²⁶⁷ ਗਾਰਬਿ²⁶⁸ ਹੰਢੀਐ²⁶⁹ ॥

4. ਮੰਦਾ ਕਿਸੈ ਨ ਆਖੀਐ ਪੜਿ ਅਖਰੁ²⁷⁰ ਏਹੋ ਬੁਝੀਐ²⁷¹ ॥

5. ਮੂਰਖੈ ਨਾਲਿ ਨ ਲੁਝੀਐ²⁷² ॥ ੧੬ ॥

Pauri.

1. sa<u>bh</u> ko aa<u>kh</u>ai aap<u>n</u>aa jis naahee so chu<u>n</u> ka<u>dh</u>ee-ai[765].

2. kee<u>t</u>aa aapo aap<u>n</u>aa aapay hee lay<u>kh</u>aa san<u>dh</u>ee-ai[766].

3. jaa rah<u>n</u>aa naahee ai<u>t</u> jag <u>t</u>aa kaa-i<u>t</u>[767] gaarab[768] han<u>dh</u>ee-ai[769].

4. man<u>d</u>aa kisai na aa<u>kh</u>ee-ai[770] par<u>h</u> a<u>kh</u>ar ayho bu<u>jh</u>ee-ai[771].

5. moor<u>kh</u>ai naal na lu<u>jh</u>ee-ai[772]. ||19||

Pauri

Why practise pride when nothing belongs to you

Pauri

1. Everyone is obsessed with accursed notion of ego; there is hardly any one who is free from this enigma.
2. Everyone must harvest whatever one has sown.
3. Since human beings are not destined to be here forever, why need they be obsessed with the notion of ego.
4. Let also not speak ill or foul language for others. This virtue of restraint has to be nourished in every mind.
5. Besides do not indulge in an argument with a stupid fool.

---

[765] Thrown out
[766] Settle, to pay for, to adjust
[767] Why

[768] Ego
[769] To practise
[770] Teachings of the scriptures

[771] The teaching
[772] To argue

ਗੁਰਸਿਖਾ ਮਨਿ ਵਾਧਾਈਆ ਜਿਨ ਮੇਰਾ ਸਤਿਗੁਰੁ ਡਿਠਾ ਰਾਮ ਰਾਜੇ ॥

ਗੁਰਸਿਖਾ ਮਨਿ ਵਾਧਾਈਆ ਜਿਨ ਮੇਰਾ ਸਤਿਗੁਰੂ ਡਿਠਾ ਰਾਮ ਰਾਜੇ ॥

gursikhaa man vaaDhaa-ee-aa jin mayraa satguroo dithaa raam raajay.

The minds of devotees rejoice, because they have seen my
True-Guru, O King of Kings.

ਕੋਈ ਕਰਿ ਗਲ ਸੁਣਾਵੈ ਹਰਿ ਨਾਮ ਕੀ ਸੋ ਲਗੈ ਗੁਰਸਿਖਾ ਮਨਿ ਮਿਠਾ ॥

ਕੋਈ ਕਰਿ ਗਲ ਸੁਣਾਵੈ ਹਰਿ ਨਾਮ ਕੀ ਸੋ ਲਗੇ ਗੁਰਸਿਖਾ ਮਨਿ ਮਿਠਾ ॥

ko-ee kar gal sunaavai har naam kee so lagai gursikhaa man mithaa.

If someone recites to them the story of Waheguru's Name,
it seems so sweet to the mind of those devotees.

ਹਰਿ ਦਰਗਹ ਗੁਰਸਿਖ ਪੈਨਾਈਅਹਿ ਜਿਨਾ ਮੇਰਾ ਸਤਿਗੁਰੁ ਤੁਠਾ ॥

ਹਰਿ ਦਰਗਹ ਗੁਰਸਿਖ ਪੈਨਾਈਅਹਿ ਜਿਨਾ ਮੇਰਾ ਸਤਿਗੁਰੁ ਤੁਠਾ ॥

har dargeh gursikh painaa-ee-ah jin^haa mayraa satgur tuthaa.

The devotees are robed in honour in the Court of Waheguru;
my True-Guru is very pleased with them.

ਜਨ ਨਾਨਕੁ ਹਰਿ ਹਰਿ ਹੋਇਆ ਹਰਿ ਹਰਿ ਮਨਿ ਵੁਠਾ ॥੪॥੧੨॥੧੯॥

ਜਨ ਨਾਨਕੁ ਹਰਿ ਹਰਿ ਹੋਇਆ ਹਰਿ ਹਰਿ ਮਨਿ ਵੁਠਾ ॥ ੪ ॥ ੧੨ ॥ ੧੯ ॥

jan naanak har har ho-i-aa har har man vuthaa. ||4||12||19||

Devotee then becomes pure and
Waheguru abides within his mind. ||4||12||19||

*Pauri 20 with 2 sloaks
(Guru Nanak 2)*

ਸਲੋਕੁ ਮਃ ੧ ॥

1. ਨਾਨਕ ਫਿਕੈ[773] ਬੋਲਿਐ ਤਨੁ ਮਨੁ ਫਿਕਾ ਹੋਇ ॥
2. ਫਿਕੋ ਫਿਕਾ ਸਦੀਐ ਫਿਕੇ ਫਿਕੀ ਸੋਇ[774] ॥
3. ਫਿਕਾ ਦਰਗਹ ਸਟੀਐ[775] ਮੁਹਿ ਥੁਕਾ ਫਿਕੇ ਪਾਇ ॥
4. ਫਿਕਾ ਮੂਰਖੁ[776] ਆਖੀਐ ਪਾਣਾ[777] ਲਹੈ ਸਜਾਇ ॥ ੧ ॥

सलोकु मः १ ॥

1. नानक फिकै[773] बोलिऐ तनु मनु फिका होइ ॥
2. फिको फिका सदीऐ फिके फिकी सोइ[774] ॥
3. फिका दरगह सटीऐ[775] मुहि थुका फिके पाइ ॥
4. फिका मूरखु[776] आखीऐ पाणा[777] लहै सजाइ ॥ १ ॥

Sloak Mehla 1.

1. naanak fikai[773] boli-ai ṯan man fikaa ho-ay.
2. fiko fikaa saḏee-ai fikay fikee so-ay[774].
3. fikaa ḏargeh satee-ai[775] muhi thukaa fikay paa-ay.
4. fikaa moorakẖ[776] aakẖee-ai paaṇaa[777] lahai sajaa-ay. ‖1‖

---

[773] Colourless, dry, boring
[774] Reputation
[775] Discarded
[776] Stupid
[777] Ignominy

ਸਃ ੧ ॥

1. ਅੰਦਰਹੁ ਝੂਠੇ ਪੈਜ[778] ਬਾਹਰਿ ਦੁਨੀਆ ਅੰਦਰਿ ਫੈਲੁ[779] ॥
2. ਅਠਸਠਿ ਤੀਰਥ ਜੇ ਨਾਵਹਿ ਉਤਰੈ ਨਾਹੀ ਮੈਲੁ ॥
3. ਜਿਨ ਪਟੁ[780] ਅੰਦਰਿ ਬਾਹਰਿ ਗੁਦੜੁ[781] ਤੇ[782] ਭਲੇ[783] ਸੰਸਾਰਿ ॥
4. ਤਿਨ ਨੇਹੁ ਲਗਾ ਰਬ ਸੇਤੀ ਦੇਖਨੇ[784] ਵੀਚਾਰਿ[785] ॥
5. ਰੰਗਿ[786] ਹਸਹਿ ਰੰਗਿ ਰੋਵਹਿ ਚੁਪ ਭੀ ਕਰਿ ਜਾਹਿ ॥
6. ਪਰਵਾਹ ਨਾਹੀ ਕਿਸੈ ਕੇਰੀ ਬਾਝੁ[787] ਸਚੇ ਨਾਹ ॥
7. ਦਰਿ[788] ਵਾਟ[789] ਉਪਰਿ ਖਰਚੁ[790] ਮੰਗਾ ਜਬੈ[791] ਦੇਇ ਤ ਖਾਹਿ ॥
8. ਦੀਬਾਨੁ ਏਕੋ ਕਲਮ ਏਕਾ ਹਮਾ ਤੁਮਾ ਮੇਲੁ ॥
9. ਦਰਿ ਲਏ ਲੇਖਾ ਪੀੜਿ ਛੁਟੈ[792] ਨਾਨਕਾ ਜਿਉ ਤੇਲੁ ॥ ੨ ॥

Mehla 1.

1. andrahu jhoothay paij[778] baahar dunee-aa andar fail[779].
2. athsath tirath jay naaveh utrai naahee mail.
3. jin[H] pat[780] andar baahar gudarh[781] tay[782] bhalay[783] sansaar.
4. tin[H] nayhu lagaa rab saytee daykhn[H]ay[784] veechaar[785].
5. rang[786] haseh rang roveh chup bhee kar jaahi.
6. parvaah naahee kisai kayree baajh[787] sachay naah.
7. dar[788] vaat[789] upar kharach[790] mangaa jabai [791]day-ay ta khaahi.
8. deebaan ayko kalam aykaa hamaa tum[H]aa mayl.
9. dar la-ay laykhaa peerh chhutai[792] naankaa ji-o tayl. ||2||

---

[778] Posing honourable
[779] Abundant
[780] Silk, goodness, riches
[781] Humility, poverty
[782] They are
[783] Good, respectable
[784] Beholding
[785] To contemplate, to remember
[786] Being coloured with the name of Waheguru
[787] Except
[788] Door
[789] Road that leads to Waheguru's abode
[790] Everything
[791] When
[792] Crushed

Theme	Literal Meaning

Sloak Mehla 1

An arrogant person gets severe punishment hereafter for his harsh and hurting speech

Literal Meaning — Sloak Mehla 1

1. Talking foul about others pollutes one's own thoughts and soul.
2. A person who regularly speaks slanderous words is called a 'stupid idiot' and his bad reputation spreads all over.
3. He is not welcomed in the court of Waheguru and is spurned by everyone.
4. Such a person is branded as a 'dope' (thick headed), and is hated by all.

Mehla 1

To realise Waheguru a person must wash both his body and inner thoughts

Literal Meaning — Mehla 1

1. Those who are sinners inside and pose to be virtuous outside, and have spread there false fame far and wide.
2. They will not be able to wash off their grime even if they go and wash themselves at all (counted as 68) Hindu holy places.
3. Those who are virtuous inside and humble outside, they are perfect human beings.
4. They are drenched with the love of Waheguru and long for a vision of him.
5. In deep trance and imbued in His thoughts they sometimes laugh and sometimes weep and sometimes even turn dumb.
6. They have a lot of everything around them except the sweet memories of Waheguru.
7. They wait at the doorway of Waheguru and accept, with grace, whatever is given to them.
8. There is only one Divine Court for all humanity, his judgements are final and in his presence every one is equal.
9. In his court of judgement, all will receive a just verdict; the sinners will be doomed to be crushed like seeds and will wail for forgiveness.

ਪਉੜੀ ॥

1. ਆਪੇ ਹੀ ਕਰਣਾ ਕੀਓ[793] ਕਲ[794] ਆਪੇ ਹੀ ਤੈ ਧਾਰੀਐ[795] ॥

2. ਦੇਖਹਿ ਕੀਤਾ ਆਪਣਾ ਧਰਿ[796] ਕਚੀ ਪਕੀ ਸਾਰੀਐ॥

3. ਜੋ ਆਇਆ ਸੋ ਚਲਸੀ ਸਭੁ ਕੋਈ ਆਈ ਵਾਰੀਐ ॥

4. ਜਿਸ ਕੇ ਜੀਅ ਪਰਾਣ[797] ਹਹਿ ਕਿਉ ਸਾਹਿਬੁ ਮਨਹੁ ਵਿਸਾਰੀਐ ॥

5. ਆਪਣ ਹਥੀ ਆਪਣਾ ਆਪੇ ਹੀ ਕਾਜੁ ਸਵਾਰੀਐ ॥ ੨੦ ॥

ਪਉੜੀ ॥

1. ਆਪੇ ਹੀ ਕਰਣਾ ਕੀਏ[793] ਕਲ[794] ਆਪੇ ਹੀ ਤੈ ਧਾਰੀਐ[795] ॥

2. ਦੇਖਹਿ ਕੀਤਾ ਆਪਣਾ ਧਰਿ[796] ਕਚੀ ਪਕੀ ਸਾਰੀਐ ॥

3. ਜੋ ਆਇਆ ਸੋ ਚਲਸੀ ਸਭੁ ਕੋਈ ਆਈ ਵਾਰੀਐ ॥

4. ਜਿਸ ਕੇ ਜੀਅ ਪਰਾਣ[797] ਹਹਿ ਕਿਉ ਸਾਹਿਬੁ ਮਨਹੁ ਵਿਸਾਰੀਐ ॥

5. ਆਪਣ ਹਥੀ ਆਪਣਾ ਆਪੇ ਹੀ ਕਾਜੁ ਸਵਾਰੀਐ ॥ ੨੦ ॥

Pauri.

1. aapay hee karnaa kee-o[793] kal[794] aapay hee ṯai Dhaaree-ai[795].

2. ḏaykheh keeṯaa aapnaa Dhar[796] kachee pakee saaree-ai.

3. jo aa-i-aa so chalsee sabh ko-ee aa-ee vaaree-ai.

4. jis kay jee-a paraan[797] heh ki-o saahib manhu visaaree-ai.

5. aapan hathee aapnaa aapay hee kaaj savaaree-ai. ||20||

Pauri

Breaths given to us to live in this world are counted, let us make the best of them.

Pauri

1. Waheguru himself has created the universe and is the sole sustainer of it.
2. He watches his play with curiosity and notices every moment of chess pawns moving on the wider chessboard of life.
3. Every one of us has been given a role to play in the worldly drama. When this role ends we have to go back to skies (to report back to the director of the big drama).
4. Every breath is given to us by Waheguru, then why should we be oblivious of him?
5. We must do our best to perform our role with honesty and loyalty.

---

[793] You created the world
[794] Power

[795] To infuse
[796] Land (*dharti*)

[797] Breath

ਆਸਾ ਮਹਲਾ ੪ ॥

आसा महला ੪ ॥

Asa mehla 4.

Asa Mehla 4.

ਜਿਨਾ ਭੇਟਿਆ ਮੇਰਾ ਪੂਰਾ ਸਤਿਗੁਰੂ ਤਿਨ ਹਰਿ ਨਾਮੁ ਦ੍ਰਿੜਾਵੈ ਰਾਮ ਰਾਜੇ ॥

जिना भेटिआ मेरा पूरा सतिगुरू तिन हरि नामु द्रिड़ावै राम राजे ॥

jinHaa bhayti-aa mayraa pooraa satguroo tin har naam
darirh-aavai raam raajay.

Those who meet my perfect teacher-Guru - He implants
within them the Name of Waheguru, the King of Kings.

ਤਿਸ ਕੀ ਤ੍ਰਿਸਨਾ ਭੁਖ ਸਭ ਉਤਰੈ ਜੋ ਹਰਿ ਨਾਮੁ ਧਿਆਵੈ ॥

तिस की त्रिसना भुख सभ तुतरै जो हरि नामु धिआवै ॥

tis kee tarisnaa bhukh sabh utrai jo har naam Dhi-aavai.

Those who meditate on His Name have all of their desire and hunger
removed.

ਜੋ ਹਰਿ ਹਰਿ ਨਾਮੁ ਧਿਆਇਦੇ ਤਿਨੁ ਜਮੁ ਨੇੜਿ ਨ ਆਵੈ ॥

जो हरि हरि नामु धिआइदे तिनु जमु नेड़ि न आवै ॥

jo har har naam Dhi-aa-iday tinH jam nayrh na aavai.

Those who meditate on His Name - the Messenger of
Death cannot even approach them.

ਜਨ ਨਾਨਕ ਕਉ ਹਰਿ ਕ੍ਰਿਪਾ ਕਰਿ ਨਿਤ ਜਪੈ ਹਰਿ ਨਾਮੁ ਹਰਿ ਨਾਮਿ ਤਰਾਵੈ ॥੧॥

जन नानक कउ हरि क्रिपा करि नित जपै हरि नामु हरि नामि तरावै ॥ ੧ ॥

jan naanak ka-o har kirpaa kar nit japai har naam har
naam taraavai. ||1||

O! Waheguru shower Your Mercy upon us, that we may
ever chant your Name; through your Name, we all saved. ||1||

*Pauri 21 with 2 sloaks
(Guru Angad 2)*

ਸਲੋਕੁ ਮਹਲਾ ੨ ॥

1. ਏਹ ਕਿਨੇਹੀ[798] ਆਸਕੀ[799] ਦੂਜੈ ਲਗੈ ਜਾਇ[800] ॥
2. ਨਾਨਕ ਆਸਕੁ ਕਾਂਢੀਐ[801] ਸਦ[802] ਹੀ ਰਹੈ ਸਮਾਇ ॥
3. ਚੰਗੈ ਚੰਗਾ ਕਰਿ ਮੰਨੇ[803] ਮੰਦੈ ਮੰਦਾ ਹੋਇ[804] ॥
4. ਆਸਕੁ ਏਹੁ ਨ ਆਖੀਐ ਜਿ ਲੇਖੈ ਵਰਤੈ ਸੋਇ[805] ॥ ੧ ॥

ਮਹਲਾ ੨ ॥

1. ਸਲਾਮੁ[806] ਜਬਾਬੁ[807] ਦੋਵੈ ਕਰੇ ਮੁੰਢਹੁ[808] ਘੁਥਾ[809] ਜਾਇ ॥
2. ਨਾਨਕ ਦੋਵੈ ਕੂੜੀਆ[810] ਥਾਇ ਨ ਕਾਈ ਪਾਇ[811] ॥ ੨ ॥

सलोकु महला २ ॥

1. ऐह किनेही[798] आसकी[799] दूजै लगै जाइ[800] ॥
2. नानक आसकु काँढीऐ[801] सद[802] ही रहै समाइ ॥
3. चंगै चंगा करि मंने[803] मंदै मंदा होइ[804] ॥
4. आसकु ऐहु न आखीऐ जि लेखै वरतै सोइ[805] ॥ १ ॥

महला २ ॥

1. सलामु[806] जबाबु[807] दोवै करे मुंढहु[808] घुथा[809] जाइ ॥
2. नानक दोवै कूड़ीआ[810] थाइ न काई पाइ[811] ॥ २ ॥

Sloak Mehla 2.

1. ayh kinayhee[798] aaskee[799] doojai lagai jaa-ay[800].
2. naanak aasak kaaNdhee-ai[801] sad[802] hee rahai samaa-ay.
3. changai changa kar mannay[803] mandai mandaa ho-ay[804].
4. aasak ayhu na aakhee-ai je laykhai vartai so-ay[805]. ||1||

Mehla 2.

1. salaam[806] jabaab[807] dovai karay mundhhu[808] ghuthaa[809] jaa-ay.
2. naanak dovai koorhee-aa[810] thaa-ay na kaa-ee paa-ay[811]. ||2||

---

[798] What kind of ?
[799] Love
[800] When you have someone else in mind
[801] Called
[802] Always

[803] When good happens to you (then you believe)
[804] But fail to believe in adversity
[805] One who only trades in
[806] To believe in (salutation)
[807] No belief

[808] From the beginning
[809] To go wrong
[810] Both actions are false
[811] He finds no place near Waheguru

Theme	Literal Meaning

Sloak Mehla 1

In true love you remain engrossed in the love of your beloved.

Sloak Mehla 1

1. What kind of love is this when one forsakes the true lover (Waheguru) and runs after others.
2. The true lovers always remain absorbed in the sweet symphony of their beloveds.
3. Should the adversity befall, still welcome it as a boon of Waheguru.
4. One is surely not a true lover, if one was to calculate cost-benefit of the relationship.

Mehla 2

A person who divides his/her love between many is not a true lover.

Mehla 2

1. It does not suit a person to bow to his Master and at the same time argue with him.
2. The two attitudes contradict each other. The Master will not approve of such a dubious behaviour.

ਪਉੜੀ ॥

1. ਜਿਤੁ ਸੇਵਿਐ ਸੁਖੁ ਪਾਈਐ ਸੋ ਸਾਹਿਬ ਸਦਾ ਸਮਾਲੀਐ^{੧੨} ॥

2. ਜਿਤੁ ਕੀਤਾ ਪਾਈਐ ਆਪਣਾ^{੧੩} ਸਾ ਘਾਲ ਬੁਰੀ ਕਿਉ ਘਾਲੀਐ^{੧੪} ॥

3. ਮੰਦਾ ਮੂਲਿ ਨ ਕੀਚਈ ਦੇ ਲੰਮੀ ਨਦਰਿ^{੧੫} ਨਿਹਾਲੀਐ^{੧੬} ॥

4. ਜਿਉ ਸਾਹਿਬ ਨਾਲਿ ਨ ਹਾਰੀਐ ਤੇਵੇਹਾ ਪਾਸਾ ਢਾਲੀਐ^{੧੭} ॥

5. ਕਿਛੁ ਲਾਹੇ^{੧੮} ਉਪਰਿ ਘਾਲੀਐ^{੧੯} ॥ ੨੧ ॥

ਪਉੜੀ ॥

1. ਜਿਤੁ ਸੇਵਿਐ ਸੁਖੁ ਪਾਈਐ ਸੋ ਸਾਹਿਬੁ ਸਦਾ ਸਮਾਲੀਐ^{੧੨} ॥

2. ਜਿਤੁ ਕੀਤਾ ਪਾਈਐ ਆਪਣਾ^{੧੩} ਸਾ ਘਾਲ ਬੁਰੀ ਕਿਉ ਘਾਲੀਐ^{੧੪} ॥

3. ਮੰਦਾ ਮੂਲਿ ਨ ਕੀਚਈ ਦੇ ਲੰਮੀ ਨਦਰਿ^{੧੫} ਨਿਹਾਲੀਐ^{੧੬} ॥

4. ਜਿਤੁ ਸਾਹਿਬ ਨਾਲਿ ਨ ਹਾਰੀਐ ਤੇਵੇਹਾ ਪਾਸਾ ਢਾਲੀਐ^{੧੭} ॥

5. ਕਿਛੁ ਲਾਹੇ^{੧੮} ਉਪਰਿ ਘਾਲੀਐ^{੧੬} ॥ ੨੧ ॥

Pauri.

1. jit sayvi-ai sukh paa-ee-ai so saahib sadaa sam^Haalee-ai[812].

2. jit keetaa paa-ee-ai aapnaa[813] saa ghaal buree ki-o ghaalee-ai[814].

3. mandaa mool na keech-ee day lammee nadar[815] nihaalee-ai[816].

4. ji-o saahib naal na haaree-ai tavayhaa paasaa dhaalee-ai[817].

5. kichh laahay[818] upar ghaalee-ai[819]. ||21||

Theme

Pauri

Always remember and meditate on the name of Waheguru who has given you all the comforts in life.

Literal Meaning

Pauri

1. Waheguru, whose service brings us everlasting joy, why not always remember him and not forget him, even for a moment.
2. Why, in the first place, one has to indulge in an evil act for which one has to regret later.
3. One must not indulge in wrongdoing, rather act with due discretion.
4. One must not do the act, which does not carry approval of the Master.
5. Look for heavenly instructions to guide you in all your pursuits.

---

[812] To meditate upon
[813] Actions for which one is to suffer
[814] Why to commit such an evil act

[815] Far-sightedness
[816] To look ahead
[817] Throw that side of the dice that you do not loose the faith in Waheguru

[818] Some benefit
[819] Render such a service

ਜਿਨੀ ਗੁਰਮੁਖਿ ਨਾਮੁ ਧਿਆਇਆ ਤਿਨਾ ਫਿਰਿ ਬਿਘਨੁ ਨ ਹੋਈ ਰਾਮ ਰਾਜੇ ॥

ਜਿਨੀ ਗੁਰਮੁਖਿ ਨਾਮੁ ਧਿਆਇਆ ਤਿਨਾ ਫਿਰਿ ਬਿਘਨੁ ਨ ਹੋਈ ਰਾਮ ਰਾਜੇ ॥

jinee gurmukh naam Dhi-aa-i-aa tinaa fir bighan na ho-ee raam raajay.

Those who, as true devotees, meditate on the Nam,
meet no obstacles in their path, O King of Kings.

ਜਿਨੀ ਸਤਿਗੁਰ ਪੁਰਖੁ ਮਨਾਇਆ ਤਿਨ ਪੂਜੇ ਸਭੁ ਕੋਈ ॥

ਜਿਨੀ ਸਤਿਗੁਰ ਪੁਰਖੁ ਮਨਾਇਆ ਤਿਨ ਪੂਜੇ ਸਭੁ ਕੋਈ ॥

jinee satgur purakh manaa-i-aa tin poojay sabh ko-ee.

Those who are pleasing to the Almighty Waheguru,
they are respected by everyone.

ਜਿਨੀ ਸਤਿਗੁਰ ਪਿਆਰਾ ਸੇਵਿਆ ਤਿਨਾ ਸੁਖੁ ਸਦ ਹੋਈ ॥

ਜਿਨੀ ਸਤਿਗੁਰ ਪਿਆਰਾ ਸੇਵਿਆ ਤਿਨਾ ਸੁਖੁ ਸਦ ਹੋਈ ॥

jinᴴee satgur pi-aaraa sayvi-aa tinᴴaa sukh sad ho-ee.

Those who serve their Beloved True Guru obtain eternal peace.

ਜਿਨਾ ਨਾਨਕੁ ਸਤਿਗੁਰ ਭੇਟਿਆ ਤਿਨਾ ਮਿਲਿਆ ਹਰਿ ਸੋਈ ॥੨॥

ਜਿਨਾ ਨਾਨਕੁ ਸਤਿਗੁਰ ਭੇਟਿਆ ਤਿਨਾ ਮਿਲਿਆ ਹਰਿ ਸੋਈ ॥ ੨ ॥

jinᴴaa naanak satgur bhayti-aa tinᴴaa mili-aa har so-ee. ||2||

Those who long to meet the True-Guru,
He Himself comes forward to meet them. ||2||

*Pauri 22 with 5 sloaks
(Guru Angad 5)*

ਸਲੋਕੁ ਮਹਲਾ ੨ ॥

1. ਚਾਕਰੁ[820] ਲਗੈ ਚਾਕਰੀ[821] ਨਾਲੇ ਗਾਰਬੁ[822] ਵਾਦੁ[823] ॥
2. ਗਲਾ ਕਰੇ ਘਨੇਰੀਆ[824] ਖਸਮ ਨ ਪਾਏ ਸਾਦੁ[825] ॥
3. ਆਪੁ ਗਵਾਇ[826] ਸੇਵਾ ਕਰੇ ਤਾ ਕਿਛੁ ਪਾਏ ਮਾਨੁ ॥
4. ਨਾਨਕ ਜਿਸ ਨੋ ਲਗਾ[827] ਤਿਸੁ ਮਿਲੈ ਲਗਾ ਸੋ ਪਰਵਾਣੁ ॥ ੧ ॥

ਮਹਲਾ ੨ ॥

1. ਜੋ[828] ਜੀਇ[829] ਹੋਇ ਸੁ ਉਗਵੈ[830] ਮੁਹ ਕਾ ਕਹਿਆ ਵਾਉ[831] ॥
2. ਬੀਜੇ ਬਿਖੁ[832] ਮੰਗੈ ਅੰਮ੍ਰਿਤੁ ਵੇਖਹੁ ਏਹੁ ਨਿਆਉ ॥ ੨ ॥

सलोकु महला २ ॥

1. चाकरु[820] लगै चाकरी[821] नाले गारबु[822] वादु[823] ॥
2. गला करे घनेरीआ[824] खसम न पाइ सादु[825] ॥
3. आपु गवाइ[826] सेवा करे ता किछु पाइ मानु ॥
4. नानक जिस नो लगा[827] तिसु मिलै लगा सो परवानु ॥ १ ॥

महला २ ॥

1. जो[828] जीइ[829] होइ सु उगवै[830] मुह का कहिआ वाउ[831] ॥
2. बीजे बिखु[832] मंगै अंम्रितु वेखहु इेहु निआउ ॥ २ ॥

Sloak Mehla 2.

1. chaakar[820] lagai chaakree[821] naalay gaarab[822] vaad[823].
2. galaa karay ghanayree-aa[824] khasam na paa-ay saad[825].
3. aap gavaa-ay[826] sayvaa karay taa kichh paa-ay maan.
4. naanak jis no lagaa[827] tis milai lagaa so parvaan. ||1||

Mehla 2.

1. jo[828] jee-ay[829] ho-ay so ugvai[830] muh kaa kahi-aa vaa-o[831].
2. beejay bikh[832] mangai amrit vaykhhu ayhu ni-aa-o. ||2||

---

[820] Servant
[821] Service
[822] Vain, futile
[823] Annoying arguments
[824] Talkative

[825] Not acceptable
[826] To lose one's ego
[827] Who are in love with Waheguru
[828] Whatever
[829] Is in the mind

[830] That comes forth
[831] Of no use
[832] Poison

ਮਹਲਾ ੨ ॥

1. ਨਾਲਿ ਇਆਨੇ ਦੋਸਤੀ ਕਦੇ ਨ ਆਵੈ ਰਾਸਿ ॥
2. ਜੇਹਾ ਜਾਣੈ ਤੇਹੋ ਵਰਤੈ^{੮੩੩} ਵੇਖਹੁ ਕੋ ਨਿਰਜਾਸਿ^{੮੩੪} ॥
3. ਵਸਤੁ ਅੰਦਰਿ ਵਸਤੁ ਸਮਾਵੈ ਦੂਜੀ ਹੋਵੈ ਪਾਸਿ^{੮੩੫} ॥
4. ਸਾਹਿਬ ਸੇਤੀ ਹੁਕਮੁ ਨ ਚਲੈ ਕਹੀ ਬਣੈ ਅਰਦਾਸਿ^{੮੩੬} ॥
5. ਕੂੜਿ ਕਮਾਣੈ ਕੂੜੋ ਹੋਵੈ ਨਾਨਕ ਸਿਫਤਿ ਵਿਗਾਸਿ^{੮੩੭} ॥ ੩ ॥

ਮਹਲਾ ੨ ॥

1. ਨਾਲਿ ਇਆਨੇ^{੮੩੮} ਦੋਸਤੀ ਵਡਾਰੂ^{੮੩੯} ਸਿਉ ਨੇਹੁ ॥
2. ਪਾਣੀ ਅੰਦਰਿ ਲੀਕ ਜਿਉ ਤਿਸ ਦਾ ਥਾਉ ਨ ਥੇਹੁ ॥ ੪ ॥

ਮਹਲਾ ੨ ॥

1. ਹੋਇ ਇਆਣਾ ਕਰੇ ਕੰਮੁ ਆਣਿ ਨ ਸਕੈ ਰਾਸਿ ॥
2. ਜੇ ਇਕ ਅਧ ਚੰਗੀ ਕਰੇ ਦੂਜੀ ਭੀ ਵੇਰਾਸਿ^{੮੪੦} ॥ ੫ ॥

महला २ ॥

1. नालि इआणे दोसती कदे न आवै रासि ॥
2. जेहा जाणै तेहो वरतै^{੮੩੩} वेखहु को निरजासि^{੮੩੪} ॥
3. वसतू अंदरि वसतु समावै दूजी होवै पासि^{੮੩੫} ॥
4. साहिब सेती हुकमु न चलै कही बणै अरदासि^{੮੩੬} ॥
5. कूड़ि कमाणै कूड़ो होवै नानक सिफति विगासि^{੮੩੭} ॥ ३ ॥

महला २ ॥

1. नालि इआणे^{੮੩੮} दोसती वडारू^{੮੩੯} सिउ नेहु ॥
2. पाणी अंदरि लीक जिउ तिस दा थाउ न थेहु॥ ੪ ॥

महला २ ॥

1. होइ इआणा करे कंमु आणि न सकै रासि ॥
2. जे इक अध चंगी करे दूजी भी वेरासि^{੮੪੦} ॥ ੫ ॥

Mehla 2.

1. naal i-aanay dostee kaday na aavai raas.
2. jayhaa jaanai tayho vartai[833] vaykhhu ko nirjaas[834].
3. vastoo andar vasat samaavai doojee hovai paas[835].
4. saahib saytee hukam na chalai kahee banai ardaas[836].
5. koorh kamaanai koorho hovai naanak sifat vigaas[837]. ||3||

Mehla 2.

1. naal i-aanay[838] dostee vadaaroo[839] si-o nayhu.
2. paanee andar leek ji-o tis daa thaa-o na thayhu. ||4||

Mehla 2.

1. ho-ay i-aanaa karay kamm aan na sakai raas.
2. jay ik aDh changee karay doojee bhee vayraas[840]. ||5||

---

[833] He does whatever he knows
[834] To ascertain
[835] If the other one is taken out
[836] There only supplication is accepted
[837] Praise begets praise
[838] Stupid, fool
[839] A man of higher status
[840] Another goes wrong

Theme	Literal Meaning
Sloak Mehla 2 Those who have imbibed in Waheguru's name they have been accepted by Him.	**Sloak Mehla 2** 1. If a servant, while performing his duty, acts arrogantly or behaves in a quarrelsome way, 2. And chatters nonsense, that servant will not get master's approval. 3. On the other hand, if a servant acts meekly and serves his master well, he will surely get his master's approval. 4. They surely get approved who remain absorbed in the love of the master.
Mehla 2 How can one harvest nectar when one sows poison.	**Mehla 2** 1. Whatever thoughts boil in one's mind, they do ultimately come out, though one's outward mask may be completely different. 2. How funny it is that a person sows seeds of poison and yet longs for nectar.
Mehla 2 Friendship with a stupid fool is never successful.	**Mehla 2** 1. A friendship with a stupid fool does never pay. 2. The fool would surely be responding in a dubious way, though one may try talking to him, if one so wishes. 3. Similar things do merge into each other, but non-similar things stand ever apart. 4. No one dare to utter an egoistic word in the court of the Master. There, only gentle request is acceptable. 5. Falsehood begets falsehood. True loving adoration of Waheguru brings everlasting joy.

Theme	Literal Meaning

Mehla 2

Friendship with both a fool and a big man does not last long.

Mehla 2

1. Friendship with a fool and friendship with one of higher stature;
2. Both are as fragile as a line drawn on water. These leave no trace behind.

Mehla 2

A stupid-fool's actions always fail.

Mehla 2

1. If an amateur undertakes a responsibility, he may spoil it.
2. If, by chance, he does succeed in doing one thing right, in the next he may go absolutely wrong.

ਪਉੜੀ ॥

1. ਚਾਕਰੁ ਲਗੈ ਚਾਕਰੀ ਜੇ ਚਲੈ ਖਸਮੈ ਭਾਇ ॥
2. ਹੁਰਮਤਿ[841] ਤਿਸ ਨੋ ਅਗਲੀ[842] ਓਹੁ ਵਜਹੁ[843] ਭਿ ਦੂਣਾ ਖਾਇ ॥
3. ਖਸਮੈ ਕਰੇ ਬਰਾਬਰੀ ਫਿਰਿ ਗੈਰਤਿ ਅੰਦਰਿ ਪਾਇ[844] ॥
4. ਵਜਹੁ ਗਵਾਏ ਅਗਲਾ ਮੁਹੇ ਮੁਹਿ ਪਾਣਾ[845] ਖਾਇ ॥
5. ਜਿਸ ਦਾ ਦਿਤਾ ਖਾਵਣਾ ਤਿਸੁ ਕਹੀਐ ਸਾਬਾਸਿ ॥
6. ਨਾਨਕ ਹੁਕਮੁ ਨ ਚਲਈ ਨਾਲਿ ਖਸਮ ਚਲੈ ਅਰਦਾਸਿ ॥ ੨੨ ॥

ਪਉੜੀ ॥

1. ਚਾਕਰੁ ਲਗੈ ਚਾਕਰੀ ਜੇ ਚਲੈ ਖਸਮੈ ਭਾਇ ॥
2. ਹੁਰਮਤਿ[841] ਤਿਸ ਨੋ ਅਗਲੀ[842] ਏਹੁ ਵਜਹੁ[843] ਭਿ ਦੂਣਾ ਖਾਇ ॥
3. ਖਸਮੈ ਕਰੇ ਬਰਾਬਰੀ ਫਿਰਿ ਗੈਰਤਿ ਅੰਦਰਿ ਪਾਇ[844] ॥
4. ਵਜਹੁ ਗਵਾਏ ਅਗਲਾ ਮੁਹੇ ਮੁਹਿ ਪਾਣਾ[845] ਖਾਇ ॥
5. ਜਿਸ ਦਾ ਦਿਤਾ ਖਾਵਣਾ ਤਿਸੁ ਕਹੀਐ ਸਾਬਾਸਿ ॥
6. ਨਾਨਕ ਹੁਕਮੁ ਨ ਚਲਈ ਨਾਲਿ ਖਸਮ ਚਲੈ ਅਰਦਾਸਿ ॥ ੨੨ ॥

Pauri.

1. chaakar lagai chaakree jay chalai <u>kh</u>asmai bhaa-ay.
2. hurma<u>t</u>[841] <u>t</u>is no aglee[842] oh vajahu[843] <u>bh</u>e doonaa <u>kh</u>aa-ay.
3. <u>kh</u>asmai karay baraabaree fir gairat an<u>d</u>ar paa-ay[844].
4. vajahu gavaa-ay aglaa muhay muhi paanaa[845] <u>kh</u>aa-ay.
5. jis <u>d</u>aa <u>d</u>i<u>t</u>aa <u>kh</u>aavnaa <u>t</u>is kahee-ai saabaas.
6. naanak hukam na chal-ee naal <u>kh</u>asam chalai ar<u>d</u>aas. ||22||

Theme

Pauri

In the court of God only supplications of human beings are accepted, there is certainly no room for their orders.

Literal Meaning

Pauri

1. If one, in the service of a master, acts according to his will.
2. His creditworthiness will be high and he may receive good wages as well.
3. But if he disobeys his master, he would earn only his annoyance.
4. He may loose his due wages and suffer humiliating disgrace.
5. The Master of the masters, who sustains the whole universe, He must always be held in very high esteem.
6. In His court defiance does not pay, instead prayers are doubly rewarded.

---

[841] Honour
[842] To get magnified
[843] Wages
[844] The displeasure of Waheguru
[845] Ignominy

ਜਿਨਾ ਅੰਤਰਿ ਗੁਰਮੁਖਿ ਪ੍ਰੀਤਿ ਹੈ ਤਿਨੁ ਹਰਿ ਰਖਣਹਾਰਾ ਰਾਮ ਰਾਜੇ ॥

ਜਿਨ੍ਹਾ ਅੰਤਰਿ ਗੁਰਮੁਖਿ ਪ੍ਰੀਤਿ ਹੈ ਤਿਨੁ ਹਰਿ ਰਖਣਹਾਰਾ ਰਾਮ ਰਾਜੇ ॥

jin^Haa antar gurmukh pareet hai tin^H har rakhanhaaraa raam raajay.

Those true devotees, who are filled with His love,
have Waheguru as their saving Grace, O King of Kings.

ਤਿਨ ਕੀ ਨਿੰਦਾ ਕੋਈ ਕਿਆ ਕਰੇ ਜਿਨ ਹਰਿ ਨਾਮੁ ਪਿਆਰਾ ॥

ਤਿਨੁ ਕੀ ਨਿੰਦਾ ਕੋਈ ਕਿਆ ਕਰੇ ਜਿਨੁ ਹਰਿ ਨਾਮੁ ਪਿਆਰਾ ॥

tin^H kee nindaa ko-ee ki-aa karay jin^H har naam pi-aaraa.

How can anyone slander them? Waheguru's Name is dear to them.

ਜਿਨ ਹਰਿ ਸੇਤੀ ਮਨੁ ਮਾਨਿਆ ਸਭ ਦੁਸਟ ਝਖ ਮਾਰਾ ॥

ਜਿਨ ਹਰਿ ਸੇਤੀ ਮਨੁ ਮਾਨਿਆ ਸਭ ਦੁਸਟ ਝਖ ਮਾਰਾ ॥

jin har saytee man maani-aa sabh dusat jhakh maaraa.

Those whose minds are in harmony with Waheguru - all
their enemies attack them in vain.

ਜਨ ਨਾਨਕ ਨਾਮੁ ਧਿਆਇਆ ਹਰਿ ਰਖਣਹਾਰਾ ॥੩॥

ਜਨ ਨਾਨਕ ਨਾਮੁ ਧਿਆਇਆ ਹਰਿ ਰਖਣਹਾਰਾ ॥ ੩ ॥

jan naanak naam Dhi-aa-i-aa har rakhanhaaraa. ||3||

Those who meditate on the Nam, Waheguru,
always protects them. ||3||

*Pauri 23 with 2 sloaks
(Guru Angad 2)*

ਸਲੋਕੁ ਮਹਲਾ ੨ ॥

1. ਏਹ ਕਿਨੇਹੀ ਦਾਤਿ੮੪੬ ਆਪਸ ਤੇ ਜੋ ਪਾਈਐ੮੭ ॥
2. ਨਾਨਕ ਸਾ ਕਰਮਾਤਿ੮੮ ਸਾਹਿਬ ਤੁਠੈ ਜੋ ਮਿਲੈ ॥ ੧ ॥

ਮਹਲਾ ੨ ॥

1. ਏਹ ਕਿਨੇਹੀ ਚਾਕਰੀ੮੪੬ ਜਿਤੁ ਭਉ ਖਸਮ ਨ ਜਾਇ ॥
2. ਨਾਨਕ ਸੇਵਕੁ ਕਾਢੀਐ੮੫੦ ਜਿ ਸੇਤੀ ਖਸਮ ਸਮਾਇ ॥ ੨ ॥

सलोकु महला २ ॥

1. इेह किनेही दाति੮੪੬ आपस ते जो पाइीऐ੮੭ ॥
2. नानक सा करमाति੮੮ साहिब तुठै जो मिलै ॥ १ ॥

महला २ ॥

1. इेह किनेही चाकरी੮੪੬ जितु भउ खसम न जाइ ॥
2. नानक सेवकु काढीऐ੮੫੦ जि सेती खसम समाइ ॥ २ ॥

Sloak Mehla 2.

1. ayh kinayhee daat[846] aapas tay jo paa-ee-ai[847].
2. naanak saa karmaat[848] saahib tuthai jo milai. ||1||

Mehla 2.

1. ayh kinayhee chaakree[849] jit bha-o khasam na jaa-ay.
2. naanak sayvak kaadhee-ai[850] je saytee khasam samaa-ay. ||2||

Theme

Sloak Mehla 1
The real gift is that which God himself bestows upon us.

Mehla 2
The true servant is that who merges in his master.

Literal Meaning

Sloak Mehla 1
1. A real gift is not that which one gets with worldly efforts.
2. The real gift is that which one receives with the Grace of Waheguru.

Mehla 2
1. That service is not true which fails to shed Waheguru's fear from heart.
2. The true devotion absorbs the devotee in the meditation of Waheguru.

---

[846] What type of gift is this?
[847] Which we ourselves ask for

[848] Gift
[849] Service

[850] Called

ਪਉੜੀ ॥

1. ਨਾਨਕ ਅੰਤ ਨ ਜਾਪਨੀ ਹਰਿ ਤਾ ਕੇ ਪਾਰਾਵਾਰ ॥
2. ਆਪਿ ਕਰਾਏ ਸਾਖਤੀ^{੮੫੧} ਫਿਰਿ ਆਪਿ ਕਰਾਏ ਮਾਰ^{੮੫੨} ॥
3. ਇਕਨਾ ਗਲੀ ਜੰਜੀਰੀਆ ਇਕਿ ਤੁਰੀ ਚੜਹਿ ਬਿਸੀਆਰ^{੮੫੩} ॥
4. ਆਪਿ ਕਰਾਏ ਕਰੇ ਆਪਿ ਹਉ ਕੈ ਸਿਉ ਕਰੀ ਪੁਕਾਰ^{੮੫੪} ॥
5. ਨਾਨਕ ਕਰਣਾ ਜਿਨਿ ਕੀਆ ਫਿਰਿ ਤਿਸੁ ਹੀ ਕਰਣੀ ਸਾਰ ॥ ੨੩ ॥

पउुड़ी ॥

1. नानक अंत न जापनी हरि ता के पारावार ॥
2. आपि कराइ साखती^{८५१} फिरि आपि कराइ मार^{८५२} ॥
3. इकना गली जंजीरीआ इकि तुरी चड़हि बिसीआर^{८५३} ॥
4. आपि कराइ करे आपि हउ कै सिउ करी पुकार^{८५४} ॥
5. नानक करणा जिनि कीआ फिरि तिस ही करणी सार ॥ २३ ॥

Pauri.

1. naanak ant na jaapn^Hee har taa kay paaraavaar.
2. aap karaa-ay saa<u>kh</u>-tee⁸⁵¹ fir aap karaa-ay maar⁸⁵².
3. ikn^Haa galee janjeeree-aa ik <u>t</u>uree char<u>h</u>eh bisee-aar⁸⁵³.
4. aap karaa-ay karay aap ha-o kai si-o karee pukaar⁸⁵⁴.
5. naanak kar<u>n</u>aa jin kee-aa fir <u>t</u>is hee kar<u>n</u>ee saar. ||23||

Theme

Pauri

Waheguru, who has created the universe, Himself looks after it.

Literal Meaning

Pauri

1. Waheguru's limits are beyond our apprehension.
2. He is the creator and he is the destroyer.
3. Some of us are made slaves and remain chained (due to our bad karmas). Others are made masters and enjoy freedom.
4. He himself is the sole controller of all operations; no one else is authorised to listen to our complains.
5. He, who has created the Cosmos, sustains it too.

---

⁸⁵¹ To create
⁸⁵² To destroy

⁸⁵³ Some ride many horses, are free
⁸⁵⁴ To whom should I lodge a complaint

ਹਰਿ ਜੁਗੁ ਜੁਗੁ ਭਗਤ ਉਪਾਇਆ ਪੈਜ ਰਖਦਾ ਆਇਆ ਰਾਮ ਰਾਜੇ ॥

हरि जुगु जुगु भगत उपाइआ पैन रखदा आइआ राम रनि ॥

har jug jug bhagat upaa-i-aa paij rakh-daa aa-i-aa raam raajay.

In each and every age, Waheguru creates His devotees
and preserves their honour, O King of Kings.

ਹਰਣਾਖਸ ਦੁਸਟੁ ਹਰਿ ਮਾਰਿਆ ਪ੍ਰਹਲਾਦੁ ਤਰਾਇਆ ॥

हरणारवसु दुसटु हरि मारिआ पहलादु तराइआ ॥

harnaakhas dusat har maari-aa parahlaad taraa-i-aa.

Waheguru killed the wicked Harnaakhash, and saved Prahlaad.

ਅਹੰਕਾਰੀਆ ਨਿੰਦਕਾ ਪਿਠਿ ਦੇਇ ਨਾਮਦੇਉ ਮੁਖਿ ਲਾਇਆ ॥

अहंकारिआ निंदका पिठि देइ नादेउ मुखि लाइआ ॥

aha^Nkaaree-aa nindkaa pith day-ay naamday-o mukh laa-i-aa.

He turned his back on the egoists and slanderers,
and showed His face to Nam Dev (Bhagat).

ਜਨ ਨਾਨਕ ਐਸਾ ਹਰਿ ਸੇਵਿਆ ਅੰਤਿ ਲਏ ਛਡਾਇਆ ॥੪॥੧੩॥੨੦॥

जन नानक ऐसा हरि सेविआ अंति लए छडाइआ ॥

jan naanak aisaa har sayvi-aa ant la-ay chhadaa-i-aa. ||4||13||20||

We have sincerely served our Waheguru and He will surely release us
from the painful cycle of transmigration. ||4||13||20||

Pauri 24 with 2 sloaks

(Guru Nanak 1, Guru Angad 1)

ਸਲੋਕੁ ਮਃ ੧ ॥

1. ਆਪੇ ਭਾਂਡੇ⁸⁵⁵ ਸਾਜਿਅਨੁ ਆਪੇ ਪੂਰਣੁ ਦੇਇ⁸⁵⁶ ॥
2. ਇਕਨੀ ਦੁਧੁ ਸਮਾਈਐ⁸⁵⁷ ਇਕਿ ਚੁਲੈ ਰਹਨਿ ਚੜੇ⁸⁵⁸ ॥
3. ਇਕਿ ਨਿਹਾਲੀ⁸⁵⁹ ਪੈ ਸਵਨਿ ਇਕਿ ਉਪਰਿ ਰਹਨਿ ਖੜੇ⁸⁶⁰ ॥
4. ਤਿਨਾ ਸਵਾਰੇ ਨਾਨਕਾ ਜਿਨ੍ ਕਉ ਨਦਰਿ ਕਰੇ ॥ ੧ ॥

ਮਹਲਾ ੨ ॥

1. ਆਪੇ ਸਾਜੇ ਕਰੇ ਆਪਿ ਜਾਈ ਭਿ ਰਖੈ⁸⁶¹ ਆਪਿ ॥
2. ਤਿਸੁ ਵਿਚਿ ਜੰਤ ਉਪਾਇ ਕੈ ਦੇਖੈ ਥਾਪਿ⁸⁶² ਉਥਾਪਿ⁸⁶³ ॥
3. ਕਿਸ ਨੋ ਕਹੀਐ ਨਾਨਕਾ ਸਭੁ ਕਿਛੁ ਆਪੇ ਆਪਿ ॥ ੨ ॥

सलोकु मः १ ॥

1. आपे भाँडे⁸⁵⁵ साजिअनु आपे पूरणु देइ⁸⁵⁶ ॥
2. इकनी दुधु समाईऐ⁸⁵⁷ इकि चुलै रहनि चड़े⁸⁵⁸ ॥
3. इकि निहाली⁸⁵⁹ पै सवनि इकि उुपरि रहनि खड़े⁸⁶⁰ ॥
4. तिना सवारे नानका जिनु कउ नदरि करे ॥ १ ॥

महला २ ॥

1. आपे साजे करे आपि जाई भि रखै⁸⁶¹ आपि ॥
2. तिसु विचि जंत उुपाइ कै देखै थापि⁸⁶² उथापि⁸⁶³ ॥
3. किस नो कहीऐ नानका सभु किछु आपे आपि ॥ २ ॥

Sloak Mehla 1.

1. aapay bha^Nday⁸⁵⁵ saaji-an aapay pooran day-ay⁸⁵⁶.
2. ikn^Hee duDh samaa-ee-ai⁸⁵⁷ ik chul^Hai rehni^H charhay⁸⁵⁸.
3. ik nihaalee⁸⁵⁹ pai savni^H ik upar rahan kharhay⁸⁶⁰.
4. tin^Haa savaaray naankaa jin^H ka-o nadar karay. ||1||

Mehla 2.

1. aapay saajay karay aap jaa-ee bhe rakhai⁸⁶¹ aap.
2. tis vich jant upaa-ay kai daykhai thaap⁸⁶² uthaap⁸⁶³.
3. kis no kahee-ai naankaa sabh kichh aapay aap. ||2||

---

855 Vessels, cooking pots – human beings
856 Fills them up – puts soul in them
857 Contain milk (good qualities)

858 Remains on oven (bad qualities)
859 Warm sheets, wadded covers
860 To give the duty of watchmen

861 To keep in place
862 Birth
863 Death

Theme	Literal Meaning

Theme

Sloak Mehla 1

Waheguru decorates those whom he chooses

Mehla 2

He is omnipotent and has no parallel to Him

Literal Meaning

Sloak Mehla 1

1. Waheguru creates his vessels – the human beings; and himself fills them up – puts soul into them.
2. Some people are gifted and have the best in life (good karmas), while others suffer in pain (bad karmas).
3. There are some who sleep in warm and cosy beds, yet others act as their caretakers and give a stand-by duty.
4. Those people are truly privileged on whom Waheguru showers his blessings.

Mehla 2

1. Waheguru, the creator, has himself shaped the whole world.
2. He then created life, and kept the power of birth and death with himself.
3. He himself is the absolute Master of everything

ਪਉੜੀ ॥

1. ਵਡੇ ਕੀਆ ਵਡਿਆਈਆ ਕਿਛੁ ਕਹਣਾ ਕਹਣੁ ਨਾ ਜਾਇ ॥
2. ਸੋ ਕਰਤਾ ਕਾਦਰੁ⁸⁶⁴ ਕਰੀਮੁ⁸⁶⁵ ਦੇ ਜੀਆ ਰਿਜਕੁ ਸੰਬਾਹਿ⁸⁶⁶ ॥
3. ਸਾਈ ਕਾਰ ਕਮਾਵਣੀ ਧੁਰਿ⁸⁶⁷ ਛੋਡੀ ਤਿੰਨੈ ਪਾਇ ॥
4. ਨਾਨਕ ਏਕੀ ਬਾਹਰੀੀ ਹੋਰ ਦੂਜੀ ਨਾਹੀ ਜਾਇ ॥
5. ਸੋ ਕਰੇ ਜਿ ਤਿਸੈ ਰਜਾਇ ॥ ੨੪ ॥ ੧ ॥

पउड़ी ॥

1. वडे कीआ वडिआईआ किछु कहणा कहणु ना जाइ ॥
2. सो करता कादर⁸⁶⁴ करीमु⁸⁶⁵ दे जीआ रिजकु संबाहि⁸⁶⁶ ॥
3. साई कार कमावणी धुरि⁸⁶⁷ छोडी तिंनै पाइ ॥
4. नानक एकी बाहरी होर दूजी नाही जाइ ॥
5. सो करे जि तिसै रजाइ ॥ २४ ॥ १ ॥

Pauri.

1. vaday kee-aa vadi-aa-ee-aa kichh kahnaa kahan na jaa-ay.
2. so kartaa kaadar⁸⁶⁴ kareem⁸⁶⁵ day jee-aa rijak sambaahi⁸⁶⁶.
3. saa-ee kaar kamaavnee Dhur⁸⁶⁷ chhodee tinnai paa-ay.
4. naanak aykee baahree hor doojee naahee jaa-ay.
5. so karay je tisai rajaa-ay. ||24||1||

Theme

Pauri
Waheguru does everything according to His own will

Literal Meaning

Pauri
1. Waheguru is the greatest of all, and it is beyond human pen and tongue to describe him.
2. He is Omnipotent and Bounteous. He sustains the whole universe.
3. The judgement of our deeds is according to his eternal laws.
4. There is no other refuge for us, except for his shelter.
5. Everything around us happens according to his will.

---

⁸⁶⁴ Omnipotent
⁸⁶⁵ Bounteous

⁸⁶⁶ He provides sustenance to all
⁸⁶⁷ From the beginning